Humanitarian Borders

Humanitarian Borders

Unequal Mobility and Saving Lives

Polly Pallister-Wilkins

VERSO
London • New York

First published by Verso 2022
© Polly Pallister-Wilkins 2022

All rights reserved

The moral rights of the author have been asserted

1 3 5 7 9 10 8 6 4 2

Verso
UK: 6 Meard Street, London W1F 0EG
US: 388 Atlantic Avenue, Brooklyn NY 11217
versobooks.com

Verso is the imprint of New Left Books

ISBN-13: 978-1-83976-599-5
ISBN-13: 978-1-83976-601-5 (US EBK)
ISBN-13: 978-1-83976-600-8 (UK EBK)

British Library Cataloguing in Publication Data
A catalogue record for this book is available from the British Library

Library of Congress Cataloging-in-Publication Data
A catalog record for this book is available from the Library of Congress

Typeset in Minion by Hewer Text UK Ltd, Edinburgh
Printed and bound by CPI Group (UK) Ltd, Croydon, CR0 4YY

For my father, Bric
1935–2020

Contents

Acknowledgments ix

1 Introduction 1
2 Unequal Mobility and Humanitarian Borderwork 19
    The Global Colour Line 21
    The Tools of the Global Colour Line:
        Passports, Visas and Border Controls 26
    The Politics of Saving Lives: from Colonial Amelioration
        to Structuring Violence 38
    Humanitarian Borderwork 48
3 Care and (Border) Control 53
    The Good, the Bad and the Invisible 54
    Extending the Line 62
    Deepening the Line 70
    Blurring the Line 76
    Pre-emptive Rescue 84
4 Médecins Avec Frontières 91
    Mobile Humanitarians 92
    Pop-Up Humanitarianism 95
    Humanitarianism on the Move 102
    Viscose Velocity in Humanitarian Medical Care 107
    Search and Rescue, Visibility, and the Making of Publics 114

Feasibility, and the Political Possibilities of Humanitarian Intervention	122
Humanitarian Solutions to Political Problems?	127
5 Grassroots™ Humanitarianism	133
The Privileges of the Ordinary	136
The Entrepreneurial Lightness of Being	141
The Frontiers of Fame	148
A Bag of Chocolate Milk and a Shoe . . .	154
No White Saviour Bullshit Here	158
Mapping Border Spaces, Making Mobility	163
Criminalising Humanitarianism	166
No Borders?	171
6 Decolonising Mobility and Humanitarianism?	179
Humanitarian Borderwork and the Debilitation of Movement	181
Developmental Borderwork	184
Autonomy of Migration and Mobility Justice	187
Decolonising Mobility	190
Post-humanist Possibilities	193
Decolonising Humanitarianism	197
Humanitarian Futures	200
Index	205

Acknowledgments

This book is the culmination of many years of research that has benefitted from the input of so many who have shaped and encouraged my thinking along the way.

Firstly, Beste İşleyen for reading early drafts and encouraging my progress. To Mara Malagodi for always being there since the beginning. Special mention to those friends who have proved invaluable sounding boards, offered unconditional solidarity and the odd bottle or two of whiskey include Anja Franck and Darshan Vigneswaran. Thanks also go to Julien Jeandesboz for the friendship and collaboration.

Along with the guidance of Sebastian Budgen at Verso, special thanks go to Elisa Pascucci and Katerina Rozakou for their close and collaborative reading, to Sharri Plonski for her invaluable comments that pushed me in the direction I knew I needed to go. Thanks also to Afsoun Afsahi for her encouragement, and to James Smith and Tammam Aloudat for their long-running interest in the project. As always thanks to Laleh Khalili for being my continued champion. Thanks also to Reece Jones for all his support and for sharing his book proposal with me.

At the University of Amsterdam, I am indebted to the support of (in no particular order): Rocco Bellanova, Luiza Bialasiewicz, Saskia Bonjour, Dimitris Bouris, Sarah Bracke, Ursula Daxecker, Jeroen Doomernik, Marlies Glasius, Marieke de Goede, John Grin, Imke Harbers, Anja van Heelsum, Barak Kalir, David Laws, Virginie

Mamadouh, Hanna Mühlenhoff, Eric Schliesser, Abbey Steele, Nel Vandekerckhove and Floris Vermeulen.

Aspects of this work have been presented to, workshopped with and received feedback from so many over the years, including many of those already mentioned, as well as: Chris Agius, Anthony Amicelle, Louise Amoore, Natasha Anastasiadou, Joseph Trawicki Anderson, Ruben Andersson, Tasniem Anwar, Claudia Aradau, Silvia Aru, Monique Jo Beerli, Alexandra Bousiou, Hanno Brankamp, Karine Côté-Boucher, Paolo Cuttitta, Anne-Marie D'Aoust, Flavia Dzodan, Shoshana Fine, Christiane Fröhlich, Philippe Frowd, Emily Gilbert, David Grondin, Cengiz Günay, Sophia Hoffmann, Marijn Hoijtink, Ali Howell, Heather Johnson, Maria Gabrielsen Jumbert, Sibel Karadağ, Pafsanias Karathanasis, Tina Kempin Reuter, Xymena Kurowska, Martin Lemberg-Pedersen, Debbie Lisle, Vivienne Matthies-Boon, Claudio Minca, Katharyne Mitchell, Corinna Mullin, Can Mutlu, Evie Papada, Evthymios Papataxiarchis, Michelle Pace, Nina Perkowski, Alexandra Rijke, Saskia Stachowitsch, Mark B Salter, Kristin Bergtora Sandvik, Tom Scott-Smith, Damien Simonneau, Vicki Squire, Samid Suliman, Ben Tallis, Martina Tazzioli, Ayşen Üstübici, Cecilia Vergnano, Antonis Vradis, William Walters, Natalie Welfens and Chenchen Zhang. Thanks also to my students who have heard many of the arguments made in this book and who have pushed me to refine them.

Much of this book would not have been possible without the support and help of Hernan del Valle, Unni Karunakara, Linn Biorklund, Apostolos Veizis, Aurélie Ponthieu and Marietta Provopoulou. Ilias Papagiannopoulos-Mialousis has been a source of hospitality and help over the years, as has Antonis Vradis. An extra special mention is needed here for Philippa and Eric Kempson. Financial support for some of the fieldwork has come from the Institute for Migration and Ethnic Studies, the Amsterdam Centre for European Studies and the European Research Council.

Finally, thanks go to my family. To my mum Penny for always believing in me, encouraging my curiosity, for listening to my ideas and for being my adventure travel companion. To my father Bric who died of Coronavirus during the final stages of writing this book, thank you for giving me a love of geography and the absurd, for your righteous anger and unwavering sense of justice that continue to fuel me. To my aunt Gilli, who like my father did not get to see this book come into the world

Acknowledgments

in material form, thank you for the love, food and sense of humour. To my family in Aotearoa-New Zealand, hopefully I can deliver copies of this in person soon! Thanks to the Lawy-Thrift family for all their support over the years and last, but definitely not least, thanks to Richard, my rock, shopper, vintner, cat feeder, close reader, comrade-in-struggle, love and partner for life.

1
Introduction

It is a September morning in 2012 and the Greek police commander offers a wry smile. I have spent the morning sitting in his smoky office watching grainy video footage documenting the Greek police's daily work rescuing migrants from the nearby river that marks the border with Turkey. Rescue after rescue has been recorded and catalogued by the surveillance cameras strung along the border. For hours, I have watched images of the Greek police and their colleagues from other EU countries, in Greece as part of Joint Operation Poseidon Land, rescue migrants from the river in response to my standard opening question – 'can you tell me about your daily work?' – intended as an icebreaker. I am sitting in this office in Orestiada in Evros, north-eastern Greece, with its dark wooden furniture and oversized Greek and EU flags, to learn more about how the EU and its member states are controlling their external borders.

Evros, it is argued, is on the frontline, sharing, as it does, a land border with Turkey. I have yet to ask any of my prepared questions about surveillance technologies, the fence being built, operational decisions and working relationships. The Greek police commander's wry smile comes in response to the question: 'Will these rescues ever stop?' I get no more than the wry smile. It is gone midday now, and over the course of the morning, I have been introduced to an aspect of border control I had only recently started hearing about: the humanitarian side.

This book's journey begins here in this smoke-filled office in Orestiada lying just 5km west of the border with Turkey. This border, marked, for nearly its whole length, by the fast-flowing Evros river, is dangerous. Between 2000 and 2017 it is known to have claimed 352 victims, only 105 of whom have been identified.[1] The inability to identify the dead is not only caused by the often severe decomposition of the bodies. In many instances, the dead were not carrying identity documents or had become separated from their families, choosing to travel in smaller, less detectable groups or divided into smaller groups by the smugglers that are used to cross the border. In Evros, this inability to identify victims because of a lack of documents, the attempts to cross the border undetected and the use of smugglers are intimately related to a border that starkly differentiates between European citizens and non-European citizens. Migrants, if they have identity documents at all, may choose to travel without documents to make it harder to be deported. They aim to travel undetected because they are not allowed through the two official border crossings, and, in many instances, Europe will not let them stay, or, at least, does not want them to. Smugglers are on hand to assist in these clandestine journeys, responding to a market created by people's desire to seek lives in Europe and a system that aims to prevent them from doing so. It is impossible to know how many people have crossed the river in little boats or by clinging to ropes. Numbers collected by European authorities only count those detected by border control.[2] Often, these detections occur when migrants find themselves in need of rescue by people like the aforementioned police commander and his colleagues.

The day after my encounter with the police commander in Orestiada, I spent the day at Kastanies, one of the official border crossings between Greece and Turkey. Here, I watched Greeks travel backwards and forwards to go shopping in the nearby Turkish city of Edirne. Cars and buses passed freely through the border post adorned with a 'Welcome to Evros' sign and a collection of flags from various European countries.

---

1   ICRC, 'Tragedy at Evros: A Perilous River Crossing to Greece', 2017, icrc.org. See also Laurence Lee, 'Evros River: Tales of Death and Despair at the Edge of the EU', Al Jazeera, 16 December 2017, aljazeera.com.

2   For example, see the figures produced by the European Border and Coast Guard Agency, Frontex. These are made available in a range of reports from quarterly reports to yearly reviews to reports on specific border issues, frontex.europa.eu/publications.

Here, some people chose to stop and pick up last-minute purchases at the 'Hellenic Duty Free Shop' with its sign of bright blue and white lettering and a large orange smile. Cartons of cigarettes, bottles of whisky and large humanoid M&M figures emerged from under the orange smile, contrasting sharply with the previous day's footage of migrants being pulled out of the treacherous waters of the Evros river, running only a few hundred metres away. This contrast, like the 352 people known to have lost their lives in this region, is the result of unequal mobility. That is differentiation in who is allowed to move and how they are allowed to move. Put simply, it is who gets to buy M&Ms in duty free shops, and who, at best, gets rescued from drowning or, at worst, becomes an unidentified corpse.

The 352 people who are known to have died in Evros between 2000 and 2017 are only a small fraction of those who have lost their lives at borders. During the same period, over 46,000 people are known to have died at the world's borders,[3] and there are, no doubt, many more unaccounted for. As well as drowning, these deaths have been caused by: gunshot wounds; dehydration; starvation; suffocation; hypothermia; lack of access to medicine/medical care; physical abuse, including sexual violence; accidents involving unsafe transportation such as being hit by or falling from trains, electrocution on rail lines or road-related accidents involving vehicles; and even one recorded death by hippopotamus.

Within this tragic catalogue, a geographical pattern emerges that hints at unequal mobility and how that unequal mobility shapes what type of border people encounter and how they are put at risk. For instance, drowning causes the majority of deaths in Europe and the Mediterranean; other deaths are caused by fuel burns from unsafe boats, being hit by vehicles, suffocation in sealed containers and electrocution on rail tracks. This tells us about the geographies of Europe's borders and how unequal mobility shapes how people move, in unseaworthy vessels across the Mediterranean, in the backs of lorries, through hiding on trains or walking along roads and train tracks. In Central America, the most common causes of death are falling from trains – the usual form of transportation – murder and sexual violence, most often

---

3 Data is compiled by the International Organisation for Migration (IOM)'s Missing Migrants Project which is run in conjunction with UKAid, missingmigrants.iom.int/latest-global-figures.

gang-related. Here, people denied access to the luxuries of air travel journey north on the roofs of the long, slow goods trains, known as Tren de la Muerte, La Bestia or El Tren de los Descondidos. Their precarious status makes them easy targets for sexual predators and the various criminal gangs in Central America that facilitate their journeys. On the US–Mexico border, dehydration and hypothermia caused by exposure to the harsh elements of the desert landscape are the most common causes of death. In South and South East Asia, alongside murder by criminal smuggling networks, border guards regularly shoot and kill, especially on the India–Bangladesh border.[4] Even the death by hippopotamus on the Zimbabwean–South African border speaks of people having to traverse rivers in risky ways rather than use official crossings.

These deaths speak to the need to save lives at borders. These deaths are what mobilise rescues on land and sea. Since my time in Evros with the Greek police, rescues in border spaces have increased, responding to the risks of death and suffering. There have been Italian naval search and rescue (SAR) operations, such as Mare Nostrum, in the central southern Mediterranean and humanitarian organisations have also engaged in SAR. At various times since the Migrant Offshore Aid Station (MOAS) began operations based on the apparently simple claim that 'no one deserves to die at sea',[5] well-known humanitarian organisations such as Médecins Sans Frontières, Save the Children and Médecins du Monde as well as other newer and smaller organisations such as Proactiva Open Arms and Sea-Watch have launched one or more search and rescue vessels in the Mediterranean. Meanwhile, when, in 2015, increasing numbers of people arrived in Greece seeking futures free from war, human rights abuses and economic precarity, thousands of volunteers mobilised in solidarity to provide basic needs including: clean, dry clothes; warm meals and bottled water; small tents; practical information; and basic medical care. Similar volunteer actions extended through

---

4 R Jones, *Violent Borders: Refugees and the Right to Move*, London: Verso, 2016.

5 R Young Pelton, 'No One Deserves to Die at Sea', *Refugees Deeply*, 16 March 2016, newsdeeply.com; see also the Migrant Offshore Aid Station's Homepage moas.eu; and their Facebook page where they have specifically articulated this plea that 'no one deserves to die at sea', facebook.com/migrantoffshoreaidstation/posts/427406920781329. For discussion on the limits of this approach, see P Pallister-Wilkins, 'Humanitarian Rescue/Sovereign Capture and the Policing of Possible Responses to Violent Borders', *Global Policy* 8(S1), 2017, 19–24.

the Western Balkans and into Hungary, Austria, Germany and elsewhere, following the refugees and migrants as they moved, waited and stayed.

In Calais, long a place of migrant encampment for those trying to reach the UK, activists and volunteers from across Europe (including the UK) have assisted the migrants who have created informal migrant camps known as the 'Jungles'. Attention towards the Jungles reached a peak in 2015–16, during the height of the 'refugee crisis', and among worsening conditions and threats by the French authorities to clear the Calais Jungle once and for all. Celebrities from the UK, including Lily Allen and Jude Law, crossed the Channel to raise awareness and pressure Westminster to do more to assist asylum seekers, especially children. Meanwhile, Médecins Sans Frontières built a refugee camp along the coast in Dunkirk.

All of these actions to save lives and reduce suffering rely on the ability to identify with and feel empathy for the physical and psychological suffering of strangers alongside a cataloguing of suffering by, for example, counting and publicising the dead to mobilise compassion.[6] However, this compassion and cataloguing does not highlight the causes of such suffering. In the case of borders, the need to save lives is caused by unequal regimes of mobility.[7] These unequal regimes underpinned the wry smile of the Greek police commander in answer to my question about whether the rescues would ever stop. His smile told of a reality of hardened borders, or what political geographer Reece Jones has recently called 'violent borders'.[8] The wry smile told of a global structure of inequality underpinning the daily work of the Greek police that was much larger than them and their small, everyday acts of intervention. It told of a politics in which the haves of the world increasingly secure themselves and their privileges from the have-nots through mobility controls because it is thought unchecked mobility threatens privileged

---

6   M Barnett, *Empire of Humanity: A History of Humanitarianism*, Ithaca, NY: Cornell University Press, 2011.

7   P Pallister-Wilkins, 'The Humanitarian Politics of European Border Policing: Frontex and Border Police in Evros', *International Political Sociology* 9(1), 2015, 53–69; P Pallister-Wilkins, 'Médecins Avec Frontières and the Making of a Humanitarian Borderscape', *Environment and Planning D: Society and Space* 36(1), 2018, 114–38; Pallister-Wilkins, 'Humanitarian Rescue/Sovereign Capture'.

8   Jones, *Violent Borders*.

ways of life.⁹ This politics, in turn, structures the very possibility of needing to spend your working days on the Greek-Turkish border rescuing the have-nots from the river. However, unequal mobility is not caused by inequality in and of itself. Unequal mobility is not the natural outcome of the disparities between rich and poor, but, instead, is the outcome of particular histories, political decisions, and the everyday work of border guards, local government officials, transport officials, landlords, healthcare workers, teachers and a host of other people who help to make borders an everyday, material reality.¹⁰ Unequal mobility is why people take unsafe boats across the Mediterranean, hide in sealed containers to cross the Channel, brave the elements of the Sonoran Desert, or stow themselves away in the landing gear of airplanes, freezing and suffocating to death and sometimes falling out of the sky.

José Matada, the man believed to have fallen from the landing gear of a Heathrow-bound plane onto the leafy and affluent streets of East Sheen in West London in 2013,¹¹ and many others like him, are not able to travel by plane. This is unequal mobility. It is not known whether José Matada could have afforded the ticket for flight BA76 from Luanda, Angola. However, even if he could, to be allowed to board the flight by ground staff in Luanda if he was not a UK citizen, an EU citizen or a citizen of a country covered by the UK visa-waiver scheme, he would have had to show proof of a valid UK visa. A tourist visa would have cost José Matada £89, and he would also have had to provide the following information/documentation in order to obtain a UK tourist visa: a current passport; his current home address and length of residency; his parents' names and dates of birth; proof of a return ticket; details of where he would stay in the UK; proof of being able to support himself during the duration of his stay, including bank statements and pay slips for the previous 6 months; evidence of how much his trip would cost; and details outlining how much he earned in a year. He might also have

---

9   Ibid.
10 C Rumford, 'Introduction: Citizens and Borderwork in Europe', *Space and Polity* 12(1), 2008, 1–12; N Vaughan-Williams, 'Borderwork Beyond Inside/Outside?: Frontex, the Citizen-Detective and the War on Terror', *Space and Polity* 2(1), 2008, 63–79; C Zhang, 'Mobile Borders and Turbulent Mobilities: Mapping the Geopolitics of the Channel Tunnel', *Geopolitics* 24(3), 2019, 728–755.
11 P Walker, 'Man Found Dead on London Street Was Probably Stowaway Who Fell from Plane', the *Guardian*, 25 April 2013, theguardian.com.

needed to show: details of his travel history for the past ten years (as shown in his passport); his employer's address and telephone number; his partner's name, date of birth, and passport number; the name and address of anyone paying for his trip; the name, address and passport number of any family members he had in the UK; and details of any criminal, civil or immigration offences he had committed. All of this documentation, if not in English or Welsh, would have had to have been translated and certified.[12] He would have had to have filled the information in online and then have his fingerprints and photograph taken at a visa application centre. In Angola, there is only one centre in Luanda.

It is not known whether José Matada could have obtained a visa. Little is known about him, in fact. According to a report in the *Guardian* newspaper, he died on his twenty-sixth birthday, on 9 September 2013. It is thought he was originally from Mozambique, though authorities have been unable to trace his family for official confirmation. José Matada was only identified as José Matada, also known as Youssoup, after analysis of an Angolan SIM card found in his pocket, along with a single pound coin and some money from Botswana. On this SIM card were old messages between him and his former employer, an Anglo-Swiss woman for whom he had worked as a housekeeper and gardener in South Africa. One of the messages on the SIM card included a conversation in which he talked about wanting to 'travel to Europe for a better life'. Interestingly, the report in the *Guardian* concludes with discussions not about the security of 'stowaways' like José Matada but about security concerns for aircraft.[13]

As much as the need to save lives in border spaces is the product of unequal mobility, saving lives is not an inherent response to this crisis. The concern for the security of aircraft over concern for and questions about why a man would climb inside the landing gear of said aircraft to get to the UK attest to this. Instead, the need to save lives is the product of particular rationalities about life and our role in relation to each other and our societies. This need to save lives is perhaps best known as humanitarianism. Humanitarianism is most widely understood as saving lives, relieving suffering and upholding human dignity through

---

12   Standard Visitor Visa information for the United Kingdom, gov.uk.
13   Walker, 'Man Found Dead on London Street Was Probably Stowaway Who Fell from Plane'.

the provision of life's basic needs in emergency situations by NGOs.[14] The motivation to save lives, relieve suffering and uphold human dignity is based on compassion for those who suffer, beyond the bonds of kinship, friendship or community. Put simply, this motivation grows from attempts to catalogue and articulate suffering combining 'as a moral imperative to undertake ameliorative action'.[15] Such compassion for distant strangers that grows from the cataloguing of suffering – how can you care if you are not aware? – and undertaking ameliorative actions are intimately related to the growth of a distinctly European, modern liberalism over the previous 500 years. It has had an impact on everything from fighting wars to governing colonies.[16] In conjunction with this growth of compassion and the cataloguing of suffering, European liberal modernity has been concerned with processes of rationality and efficiency that would aid the growth of capitalist markets and alleviate inequality created by such markets, thus protecting profits, societies and states from upheaval and revolution in the process.[17] It is, according to historian James Vernon, at the heart of how, for example, Britain came to be modern and achieve imperial domination.[18] Therefore, humanitarianism should be understood as occurring within particular Eurocentric, colonial and white supremacist contexts and histories. The appearance of rescues and humanitarianism at borders as a response to global inequality generally and unequal mobility in particular is a continuation of these processes or what anthropologist

14   Barnett, *Empire of Humanity*; E Bornstein and P Redfield eds, *Forces of Compassion: Humanitarianism between Ethics and Politics*, Santa Fe, NM: School for Advanced Research, 2011; D Fassin, *Humanitarian Reason: A Moral History of the Present*, Berkeley: University of California Press, 2012; I Feldman and M Ticktin eds, *In the Name of Humanity: The Government of Threat and Care*, Durham, NC: Duke University Press, 2012; J Hyndman, *Managing Displacement: Refugees and the Politics of Humanitarianism*, Minneapolis, MN: University of Minnesota Press, 2000; P Redfield, *Life in Crisis: The Ethical Journey of Doctors Without Borders*, Berkeley: University of California Press, 2013.

15   TW Lacquer, 'Bodies, Details, and the Humanitarian Narrative', in L Hunt ed., *The New Cultural History*, Berkeley: University of California Press, 1989, 176.

16   Ibid.

17   SM Reid-Henry, 'Humanitarianism as Liberal Diagnostic: Humanitarian Reason and the Political Rationalities of the Liberal Will-to-Care', *Transactions of the Institute of British Geographers* 39(3), 2014, 418–31.

18   J Vernon, *Distant Strangers: How Britain Became Modern*, Berkeley: University of California Press, 2014.

Didier Fassin has called 'humanitarian reason'[19] – a particular way of seeing and acting in the world.

In the popular imagination and in the fundraising calls of humanitarian organisations, humanitarianism remains something linked to moments of emergency or crisis. Humanitarian, life-saving missions are mobilised in moments, such as natural disasters and wars, that overwhelm existing systems, infrastructures and modes of governing. Humanitarianism responds to the effects of such disasters and conflicts on displaced populations or refugees. There is a long history of providing life-saving facilities to refugee populations within humanitarianism, and displaced populations are a common feature in complex emergencies. As an emergency undertaking, humanitarianism is meant to end when the crisis is over and the safety of affected populations guaranteed. However, as the United Nations High Commission for Refugees (UNHCR) estimates that most refugees are displaced for an average twenty-six years,[20] this suggests anything but a temporary emergency or crisis situation. So, for all the shiny fundraising brochures with their emergency imagery, humanitarianism has a more complex relationship with moments of crisis. When Médecins Sans Frontières (MSF) won the Nobel Peace Prize in 1999 they explained that 'humanitarianism occurs where the political has failed or is in crisis'.[21] Such a contextualisation is important, suggesting that emergencies and crises are less than accidental. Instead, it points to the central role of the political in the existence of emergencies and crises and subsequent human suffering.

The events and actions that have become popularly known as the 'Mediterranean Migration Crisis', 'Migration Crisis' or 'Refugee Crisis' are not limited to the past few years. In the Mediterranean and European context, humanitarian concerns for the well-being of refugees and migrants from Albania were a regular feature of the 1990s and early 2000s.[22] Meanwhile, the contentious politics of humanitarian rescues at sea came to the fore in July 2004 when the captain and first officer of the *Cap Anamur*, along with the head of the organisation of the same name, were arrested and faced charges of aiding and abetting illegal immigration

---

19 Fassin, *Humanitarian Reason*.
20 UNHCR, 'Global Trends: Forced Displacement in 2015', unhcr.org., 20.
21 J Orbinkski, 'MSF Nobel Peace Prize Lecture', 1999, nobelprize.org.
22 M Albahari, *Crimes of Peace: Mediterranean Migrations at the World's Deadliest Border*, Philadelphia, PA: University of Pennsylvania Press, 2015.

after rescuing 37 migrants in the Strait of Sicily and disembarking them at an Italian port. This led to the beginnings of a Europe-wide debate about boat migration to Europe, with the German government (Cap Anamur was a German organisation) arguing that camps should be set up for asylum seekers in North Africa in order to save lives at sea.[23] These arguments are reminiscent of present-day discussions about outsourcing migration control to Libya and paying Turkey to prevent refugees from getting to Greece. Such actions are not limited to Europe or the Mediterranean. Since the early 2000s, activists in the United States have been trying to alleviate the dangers of the US-Mexico border crossing by, for example, leaving water in the desert.[24]

However, as the Greek police commander with the wry smile suggests, these life-saving activities at borders are not only undertaken by traditional humanitarian organisations or activist-volunteers. Border control efforts are being increasingly reshaped around the need to save lives as they simultaneously uphold unequal mobility by enforcing increasingly violent borders that costs lives. Saving lives while taking lives is the perverse logic of global borders today. It is the perverse logic that underpins Australia's 'Pacific Solution' and the Operation Sovereign Borders approach to asylum seekers[25] that used camp-prisons on the islands of Nauru (Federated States of Micronesia) and Manus (Papua New Guinea) to detain asylum seekers in appalling conditions that have been condemned by the UN High Commissioner for Human Rights and the UNHCR.[26] Manus lies to the north of Papua New Guinea and Nauru lies over 2,000km from Australia, deep into the Pacific Ocean, where its nearest neighbour is the Kiribati archipelago some 300km away.[27] The

---

23 P Cuttitta, 'Delocalization, Humanitarianism and Human Rights: The Mediterranean Border Between Exclusion and Inclusion', *Antipode* 50(3), 2017, 783–803.

24 RL Doty, 'Fronteras Compasivas and the Ethics of Unconditional Hospitality', *Millennium: Journal of International Studies* 35(1), 2006, 53–74.

25 A Little and N Vaughan-Williams, 'Stopping Boats, Saving Lives, Securing Subjects: Humanitarian Borders in Europe and Australia', *European Journal of International Relations* 23(2), 2016, 533–56.

26 L Murdoch, 'UN Human Rights Chief Tells Turnbull Government to Restore Services to Manus Immediately', *Sydney Morning Herald*, 4 November 2017, smh.com; B Doherty, 'Australia Should Bring Manus and Nauru Refugees to Immediate Safety, UN Says', the *Guardian*, 9 November 2017, theguardian.com.

27 B Doherty, 'A Short History of Nauru, Australia's Dumping Ground for Refugees', the *Guardian*, 9 August 2016, theguardian.com.

logic of the Australian government, desperate to stop unauthorised boat arrivals at any price and cost, is that such 'off-shoring' saves lives by preventing dangerous boat journeys across the Arafura and Timor Seas or Torres Strait through deterrence. The use of and location of these island prisons is deliberately meant to deter future refugees and migrants from making the journey to Australia and is perversely politically justified through its supposed ability to save lives by preventing journeys.[28] And it is what led the former Australian prime minister Tony Abbott to declare in 2015: 'The only way you can stop the deaths is in fact to stop the boats.'[29] This is the politics of the crisis of death and human suffering at borders. This logic is what leads MSF to identify the deaths of people in the Mediterranean as a 'failure of politics'.[30] But it also suggests that saving lives in response to unequal mobility is not simply compassion for distant strangers, but, instead, something more complicated. Something that exists not only in the emergency imaginary of humanitarian agencies' glossy fundraising brochures or the Facebook groups of volunteer-organising efforts, something more integral to the way we are governed; in short, something far more political.

This is a book about humanitarianism in response to unequal mobility. It is not, principally, a book about refugees or migrants, the differences between them or the politics of such labels, which, themselves, are a symptom and a cause of unequal mobility through the different rights attached to each category. Nor is it a book about why people choose to seek life elsewhere. Instead, this book is intended as both a recognition of the life-saving efforts that occur in response to violent borders and unequal mobility, and a contribution to the call by various humanitarian organisations and activist groups for safe and legal routes (or #safepassage as it became known on Twitter). It is a book about what critical

---

28   A Little and N Vaughan-Williams, 'Stopping Boats, Saving Lives, Securing Subjects'; A McNevin, A Missbach and D Mulyana, 'The Rationalities of Migration Management: Control and Subversion in an Indonesia-Based Counter-Smuggling Campaign', *International Political Sociology* 10(3), 2016, 223–40.
29   R Ackland, 'If Europe Listens to Tony Abbott, the Future for Refugees Will Be Cruel', the *Guardian*, 21 April 2015, theguardian.com.
30   Personal correspondence with author.

security studies scholar William Walters has termed 'humanitarian borders',[31] their politics and effects.

The following chapters are a cataloguing of my research journey since 2012 and my visit to the smoky office of the police commander where I first encountered the 'humanitarian border'. As events in the real world unfolded and my once-niche research subject became a feature on the nightly news, this work on the caring side of border control led me to widen my focus to the work of humanitarian organisations who began SAR operations in the Mediterranean in 2014. This new, growing field of action and expanding research agenda led me one morning in late April 2015 to the Amsterdam offices of Médecins Sans Frontières. My initial interest in MSF's decision to offer medical assistance on board MOAS' ship, the *MY Phoenix*, quickly snowballed, as the crisis picked up pace, into an extensive research engagement with the organisation as they ramped up their SAR efforts by launching two more boats in quick succession. They also expanded their operations on land in response to increasing numbers of refugees and migrants arriving in Greece. As a result, I was one of many thousands of people who found themselves in Greece in the late summer and autumn of 2015 as the 'migration crisis' was in full swing. Here, I followed not only the life-saving efforts of the Greek border police, who I had begun following back in 2012, and the many activities of MSF across the Greek islands, the Greek mainland and up into the Western Balkans; I also encountered the work of thousands of volunteers and activists who had been mobilised into action by the images of seemingly desperate people arriving in small rubber dinghies on what were once better known as tourist beaches.

As I made the most of a period of research leave and headed to Greece, I found myself in the middle of what can only be described as a humanitarianesque carnival. Waiting to board the short flight from Athens to Lesvos, I was surrounded by the different coloured vests of various humanitarian organisations and news camera crews from across Europe and North America, and even one from Australia, with equipment and clothing that looked more suited to covering a war zone. Hardened journalists caught up with old friends, while younger

---

31 W Walters, 'Foucault and Frontiers: Notes on the Birth of the Humanitarian Border', in U Bröckling, S Krassman and T Lemke eds, *Governmentality: Current Issues and Future Challenges*, London: Routledge, 2011, 138–64.

prototypes hoped to cut their teeth on this crisis that had arrived at their shores with their digital SLR cameras, shiny MacBooks, unlimited data roaming, and Twitter accounts at the ready. Among this scene that seemed surreal in a European airport, with its trendy coffee stalls and perfume counters, were small groups of volunteers belonging to quickly assembled grassroots organisations. There were also people travelling alone, hoping to find a use for their compassion upon arrival in Lesvos.

I continue to follow and research the work of border police, humanitarian organisations such as MSF, and volunteer-activists in saving lives through ethnographic work in Europe, located in a range of places, from boats at sea, to beaches, 'hotspots',[32] transit camps and offices in various cities. These spaces will all be visited over the course of this book as well as places and spaces I have not been able to visit in person, such as Australia's offshore prisons on Manus and Nauru. When ethnographic work has not been possible I rely on the secondary sources of other scholars, humanitarian actors, journalists, the testimonies and reflections of present and former border guards and immigration employees, and the documented experiences of refugees and migrants themselves.

Building on and making sense of these research experiences, this book is structured around three in-depth case studies into the main actors involved in providing humanitarian assistance in border spaces: the border police acting on behalf of the state and transnational institutions such as the European Union; Médecins Sans Frontières, as a traditional large-scale humanitarian organisation; and the volunteer-activists of the grassroots. Through focusing on these three cases, I show the intimate relationship between violent borders and unequal mobility and the life-saving rescue efforts that occur in response. Furthermore, by

---

32   The hotspots are poorly defined by the European Union itself, yet are presented as the Union's technical answer to how to manage refugees and migrants found within its ever-hardening external borders. The EU is unclear about what a hotspot actually *is* and *does* in policy documents and public pronouncements, preferring to refer to a 'hotspot approach' that is intended to 'provide a platform for the agencies to intervene, rapidly and in an integrated manner, in frontline Member States when there is a crisis due to specific and disproportionate migratory pressure at their external borders', Statewatch, 'Explanatory Note on the "Hotspot" Approach', 2015, statewatch.org. See also European Commission, 'Fact Sheet: The Hotspot Approach to Managing Exceptional Migratory Flows', 8 September 2015, europarl.europa.eu; and D Neville, S Sy and A Rigon, 'On the Frontline: The Hotspot Approach to Managing Migration', European Parliament, Brussels, May 2016, europarl.europa.eu.

focusing on these three main actors, I show the differences between them: differences in motivation; differences in how they exercise compassion; different ideas about action in times of crisis; how different border spaces impact the types of risks faced by refugees and migrants and subsequent forms of rescue; the different resources at rescuers' disposal; divergent standpoints on the violence of borders and unequal mobility; and the complex politics that these differences suggest. As such, these three cases – while all responding to the reality of borders and mobility today and all contributing to saving lives – highlight the diversity of such efforts and the contentious politics around them, not just in relation to those who advocate that lives should not be saved and that borders should become even more exclusionary and dangerous, but also within the humanitarian border community itself.

However, as all these different efforts rest on the intertwining of unequal mobility regimes and humanitarian action, it is necessary to explore how and why humanitarian action is practised in border settings. This is done to provide the reader with both the structural and normative foundations of such action. Therefore, in chapter two, I detail the development of unequal regimes of mobility dictating how people move around the world and across and within state borders. I historically ground exclusive and dangerous borders within the creation of a global colour line through transatlantic slavery, plantation capitalism, subsequent abolition and emancipation, and settler colonialism that has consolidated and linked whiteness to free mobility and subjected Blackness and Indigeneity to a range of mobility controls. I focus on how overtly racialised regimes of immobility have been replaced by controls on nationalities and levels of development and the tools – passports and visas – that work to maintain such differential regimes or mobility. Alongside this, I link early humanitarian attempts to relieve suffering to concerns about the excessive mobility of Black and Indigenous populations in plantation economies and white settler colonies, highlighting how humanitarianism is a modernist liberal tool facilitating and upholding white supremacy. Finally, I introduce my concept of humanitarian borderwork in which humanitarian practices that not only limit but also structure violence come into effect in border spaces, (re)producing unequal mobility in the present.

I turn my attention to state actors in chapter three, which explores how tensions between guarding borders and saving lives structure the daily work of the likes of the Greek police in Evros. But I also explore this tension in the approach taken by the European Union through their European Border and Coast Guard Agency, more commonly known as Frontex. Here, I situate life-saving by state actors within much longer histories of state action, arguing that we should not be surprised to find what appear at first glance to be contradictory actions of care and control in processes of state security and that such actions might not in fact be contradictory at all.

In chapter four I follow the humanitarian borderwork of MSF in detail. Doing this enables me to illustrate how the particular geographies of border spaces structure humanitarian assistance, limiting it in some instances and creating new opportunities in others, reshaping humanitarian care provision around transport infrastructures and mobile solutions. I show how the visibility of search and rescue at sea, perhaps MSF's most well-known border intervention, has resulted in the mobilisation of divergent publics with opposing attitudes to border deaths and restrictive borders. Meanwhile, I stress the contingent nature of much humanitarian work by focusing on how the rescue work of MSF depends on the permission of states, which results in MSF becoming unintentionally, though unavoidably, part of the border apparatus whose effects it seeks to alleviate. In addition, I demonstrate how humanitarian work in border spaces reconfigures mobility access around hierarchies of vulnerability rather than universal rights to mobility, reaffirming inequality in the process. Unsurprisingly this all creates challenges for traditional ways of working in static, fixed settings and with fixed populations, raising ethical questions for medical professionals and other humanitarians alike.

Chapter five focuses on grassroots volunteer-activist responses to violent borders and unequal mobility. Often responding much faster to those in need than the cumbersome machineries of states and large international organisations, this grassroots humanitarianism highlights the politics and problems of both state and more traditional NGO responses, including speed, presence and top-down standardised models of intervention. At the same time, I explore how grassroots humanitarianism highlights the very reasons why humanitarian action comes to be institutionalised in large international organisations with management oversight, hierarchies of responsibility, ethical codes of conduct and access to vast resources. Focused principally on the work of grassroots humanitarians in Lesvos, Greece but with insights from Calais and elsewhere, this chapter discusses the possibilities for a more radical politics of mobility within such grassroots action. Chapter five also highlights the limits of action based on responding to crises and providing care, rather than demands for the right to move, the reform of current border policies or the call for an end to state borders all together.

In chapter six, the final chapter, these various threads come together and I discuss in more detail the limits of humanitarianism to address violent borders and unequal mobility. In doing so, I answer the following: What is humanitarianism, and who is it for? I probe the limits of humanitarianism as a form of debilitation and the subsequent shift to developmental solutions alongside questioning the political ethics of an autonomous approach to mobility that privileges the right to move above all else, including the right to stay. I explore alternative ways of living with both mobility and staying in place through a turn to how Indigenous, post-humanist and decolonial approaches have the potential to reorient humanitarianism's relationship with mobility and humanity in the future.

Much of the research that forms the foundation of this book has been compiled in close collaboration and concert with the research subjects themselves. At times, I have found my role of researcher become more one of activist-researcher or humanitarian-researcher. I have, for example, been involved in training EU policymakers in responding to the risks faced by refugees and migrants at borders. I have (co-)organised events in collaboration with MSF and spoken at and offered my research expertise at others. All of this work has helped in part to structure my own research field in conversation with those I study. In other instances, I have become friends with some of my research respondents, underlining the deeply human aspect of much of this work, whether as rescuer or researcher, and our shared politics and commitment to humanity. I am not therefore a dispassionate, disconnected researcher. I cannot be one, nor do I wish to be. As such, this book is written in celebration of a shared stand against unequal mobility and the dangers inflicted by borders today. Alongside other scholars, students and socially engaged citizens, this book is written for those I stand in solidarity with in their attempts to lessen the risks of unequal mobility and reaffirm the human dignity of refugees and migrants.

But this book is also intended as a caution against seeing humanitarian life-saving efforts at borders as a panacea or as a sustainable or just 'solution' to the violence and harm caused by unequal mobility. There are many who demand kinder responses to refugees on the basis of a claim that Europe, with its current violent approach, is undermining its cosmopolitanism and culture of hospitality. I argue this claim is a myth exceptionalising Europe and hiding a deeply racist, white supremacist and exclusionary history. And, with this book, I argue for constraint in the self-congratulation of Europeans and others for their good deeds in 'helping' refugees and migrants in distress. Humanitarian solutions are not political solutions. The emergence of humanitarian solutions to the fundamentally political issues of global inequality and unequal mobility hide the structural causes of such inequalities and ultimately depoliticise them, presenting them as natural rather than a product of human decisions and actions. As the chapters will show, the politics of such 'good deeds' are more complex than they first appear. 'Good deeds' and the humanitarian ideal of 'do no harm' often have perverse effects that work to strengthen existing inequalities rather than offer a substantive change. As such, the humanitarian border is a symptom and not a cure.

2

Unequal Mobility and Humanitarian Borderwork

Migration should not be a humanitarian issue; it is the policies and practices of states that makes it so.[1]

This statement by a displacement specialist working for Médecins Sans Frontières gets to the heart of the relationship between unequal mobility and the need to save lives in the present. But how did we get to this point? How did migration become such a threat to life that it has become an issue in which humanitarians intervene? This is important exactly because the movement of people to new lands and lives is nothing new. But who can move, and how, has been, and is, determined by a range of political, social and economic factors including, but not limited to, nationality, gender, race and class.[2] As changes in transport have made travel easier for some, others have been met with ever-greater restrictions. These interferences and preventions have not stopped people's desire to exercise mobility, but have led those excluded from the privileges of safe and legal travel to take riskier, life-threatening journeys. As such, organised life-saving at borders is a relatively recent practice, intimately tied to changes in the way mobility is controlled and unequal

---

1 Humanitarian specialist on displacement, Médecins Sans Frontières, Amsterdam, 12 September 2015.
2 M Sheller, *Mobility Justice: The Politics of Movement in an Age of Extremes*, London: Verso, 2018.

mobility entrenched. Safe and legal travel has become a privilege of the few, while being denied to the many, not only in the currently well-known Mediterranean/European context but also in North and Central America, Africa, the Middle East, South and South East Asia and Oceania. The increasing exclusivity of borders designed to entrench and protect the wealth of the haves from the have-nots and to, in the words of the EU Commission, 'Protect Our European Way of Life', is a growing, worldwide phenomenon.[3] As the case of José Matada highlights, risk, harm and death to those excluded from privileged mobility are the increasingly normalised results.

This chapter sketches the history of unequal mobility as a project of modernity, in contrast to the more common story of modernity's quest for safer and faster ways to traverse the Earth. The opening parts of this chapter tell the story of the 'global colour line' through a focus on transatlantic slavery, plantation capitalism, and settler colonialism, and the continued consolidation of inequalities using a range of material and bureaucratic tools such as passports, visas and other border control mechanisms, such as Australia's Operation Sovereign Borders. I focus my attention on the histories of enslavement, emancipation and settler colonialism in the transnational creation of what WEB Du Bois called 'whiteness', and the subsequent replacement of explicit racial inequality with inequalities based on geography, nationality and notions of backwardness. I do so because they illustrate the histories of mobility injustice and because they were arenas for early humanitarianism, understood as the 'white man's burden', that continue to shape humanitarian work in the present.[4] They are a focus for this book, which is predominantly focused on the present and recent past, because of what anthropologist Ann Laura Stoler would call their 'colonial presence' or 'imperial duress'; the way 'colonial entailments . . . wrap around contemporary problems; adhere in the logics of governance; are plaited through racialised distinctions; and hold tight to the less tangible emotional economies of humiliations, indignities, and resentments that may manifest in bold acts of refusal to abide by territorial restrictions.'[5]

---

3   M Stevis-Gridneff, 'Protecting Our European Way of Life'? Outrage Follows New EU Role', *The New York Times*, 12 September 2019, nytimes.com.

4   WEB Du Bois, *Darkwater, Voices from within the Veil*, New York: Harcourt, Brace and Howe, 1920.

5   AL Stoler, *Duress: Imperial Durabilities in Our Times*, Durham, NC: Duke University Press, 2016, 4.

The second part of this chapter focuses on humanitarianism as a response to the violence of whiteness and inequality. In discussing the dominant humanitarian imaginary of relieving the suffering of strangers and the particular geographies therein, I highlight, in contrast, a range of caring measures that entail control mechanisms and mobility restrictions through policing, incarceration, and institutionalisation. In the final part of the chapter, I bring these various strands together and into the present. I introduce what I call humanitarian borderwork as a liberal response to the violence of mobility injustice that draws, to borrow from Edward Said, on particular geographical imaginations and hierarchies,[6] performs particular forms of control, (re)produces borders, and consolidates existing inequalities.

The Global Colour Line

Controls on movement are not inevitable but rather the product of particular policies and their implementation by those with power. Inequalities between who can and cannot move are not new. They did not exclusively emerge with the modern state consolidating its power within its territory and defining who belongs to its citizenry. Earlier forms of control, such as 'slavery, serfdom, and vagrancy laws', have all had an impact on people's freedom to move.[7] And, while controls are not new, the geographies of unequal mobility characterising the violent borders that foster death and suffering, which sit at the heart of this book, do have histories that we can trace to particular moments that continue to have, as Stoler would suggest, imperial duress.

In her recent work, mobilities scholar Mimi Sheller has argued that: 'the politics of mobility is deeply informed by colonial histories of coerced mobility, labour exploitation, sexual economies of bodily abuse, and the violent movement of white settler-colonialism.'[8] Alongside this, historians Marilyn Lake and Henry Reynolds have worked across colonial archives to shine a light on how WEB Du Bois's 'colour line' came to be transnationally, or in their words 'globally', produced through the

---

6   EW Said, *Orientalism*, London: Penguin, 1978.
7   R Jones, *Violent Borders: Refugees and the Right to Move*, London: Verso, 2016.
8   Sheller, *Mobility Justice*, 47.

aforementioned histories and subsequent immigration restrictions and border controls.[9] These immigration restrictions and border controls replaced explicit racist discrimination based on a belief in the natural superiority of white men, and, with it, white men's belief in an inalienable right to govern the globe, with less overtly racist bureaucratic forms of control. This reproduction of geographical hierarchies obfuscated their racist origins. As critical race studies scholar David Theo Goldberg argues: 'in disappearing, race reappears under other, less recognisable terms of reference. Migration is thought to have no racial dimension today because the terms of recognition, of identification, of reference themselves have been made to disappear.' But, he goes on, migrants' 'raciality becomes enigmatically self-evident in its non-referentiality'.[10]

Within histories of mobility, scholars have increasingly paid attention to the formative role of transatlantic chattel slavery in modern and late-modern regimes of unequal mobility that privileged white men's freedom of movement at the expense of others, 'whether female, animal, or slave'.[11] The freedom of movement accorded to white men was fundamentally linked to freedom of the sea and was taken advantage of by European colonial powers: the British, French, Dutch, Danes, Portuguese and Spanish. This freedom, political theorist Hagar Kotef points out, was inherently violent, accelerating as it did the movement of goods and people and spreading new forms of violence in the shape of chattel slavery, colonial extraction, dispossession and settlement around the world.[12] 'In this sense the foundational freedom of mobility of capital through which the modern world system was built was secured through limiting the mobilities of racialised others, and especially those who were enslaved in the service of plantation capitalism and its domestic reproduction.'[13] And it was through enslavement that race came to be constructed and white men developed 'mastery' built

---

9   M Lake and H Reynolds, *Drawing the Global Colour Line: White Men's Countries and the International Challenge of Racial Equality*, Cambridge: Cambridge University Press, 2008.

10   DT Goldberg, 'Parting Waters: Seas of Movement', in A Baldwin and G Bettini eds, *Life Adrift: Climate Change, Migration, Critique*, London: Rowman Littlefield, 2017, 113.

11   Sheller, *Mobility Justice*, 49.

12   H Kotef, *Movement and the Ordering of Freedom: On Liberal Governances of Mobility*, Durham, NC: Duke University Press, 2015, 121.

13   Sheller, *Mobility Justice*, 58.

upon, as Sheller argues, the 'repeated daily denial of others' personal freedom'.[14]

Importantly, differential capacity for movement led to different ideas about what it meant to be human and mobile, from 'free men' to 'slave girls'.[15] African American Studies scholar Alexander G Weheliye talks of racialised assemblages that discipline and order humanity into 'full humans, not-quite humans, and nonhumans',[16] whereby full humans benefit from freedom of movement at the expense of nonhuman others who are unentitled to, or incapable of, equal mobility. These racial hierarchies also intersected with gender. As Lake and Reynolds make clear, 'white men monopolised the status of manhood'.[17] Meanwhile, Caribbean philosopher Sylvia Wynter has argued that European conquests, enslavement and colonial encounters created the category of 'Man' in contrast to Black and Indigenous others.[18] With the end of the transatlantic slave trade and the abolition of chattel slavery, the mobility of newly emancipated enslaved people was, according to Sheller, 'experienced as especially galling and fearful to whites, leading to post emancipation systems of coercive control over free black mobilities'[19] that included particular humanitarian responses.

In a recent study examining present-day racist border controls in historical context, Martin Lemberg-Pedersen has drawn attention to the racist border controls instituted by US and European powers in response to the 1791 slave rebellion in Saint-Domingue, the subsequent creation of a free Haiti and the consequent fear of the spread of Black revolution. As Lemberg-Pedersen says, European media and politics at the time were dominated by discussions of 'Saint-Domingue refugees' and the

---

14   Sheller, *Mobility Justice*, 58. For a detailed account of how slavery and plantation capitalism came to construct race, see CLR James, *The Black Jacobins: Toussaint L'Ouverture and the San Domingo Revolution*, London: Penguin, 2001.

15   Sheller, *Mobility Justice*, 58.

16   AG Weheliye, *Habeas Viscus: Racializing Assemblages, Biopolitics, And Black Feminist Theories of the Human*, Durham, NC: Duke University Press, 2014, 4.

17   Lake and Reynolds, *Drawing the Global Colour Line*, 7.

18   S Wynter, '1492: A New World View', in V Lawrence Hyatt and R Nettleford eds, *Race, Discourse, and the Origin of the Americas: A New World View*, Washington, DC: Smithsonian Institution Press, 1996, 5–57; S Wynter, 'Unsettling the Coloniality of Being/Power/Truth/Freedom: Towards the Human, After Man, Its Overrepresentation – An Argument', *CR: The New Centennial Review*, 3(3), 2003, 257–337.

19   Sheller, *Mobility Justice*, 58.

(free Black) 'French Negro'. Those leaving Saint-Domingue 'typically consisted of the French plantation elite, artisans and blacksmiths in need of assistance, alongside their human property', with the Black people among them considered Haitian subversives 'contagious with revolutionary knowledge'. This 'gave rise to the further upscaling and securitisation of Western naval patrols in the Caribbean', with one outcome being 'the so-called Negro Seaman's Acts implemented between 1822 and 1848'. According to Lemberg-Pedersen, 'these Acts specifically prevented the arrival of free Black sailors by forcing ship captains to ensure that these were incarcerated during the ship's stay in port. Free Black sailors were threatened with whipping if they returned.' One estimate suggested that '10,000 Black seamen were imprisoned because of these laws'.[20]

The (im)mobility of enslaved and later emancipated peoples was not only a concern in plantation economies but also in white settler colonies, where Indigenous mobility was seen as undermining attempts to dominate territory for white exploitation. As historian Georgine Clarsen argues, 'foundational to settler colonialism are both the potential and actual capacities of settlers to roam as autonomous sovereign subjects around the world and across the territories they claim as their own – and conversely to circumscribe and control the mobilities of Indigenous peoples, to immobilise the former sovereign owners of those territories.'[21] Alongside this, exploitable Black and Brown migrant labour came to be seen as a threat to the white supremacy of newly settled white spaces. This led to the later introduction of racially restrictive immigration controls such as the White Australia policy supported by a number of Australian trade unions. 'In drawing the global colour line, immigration restriction became a version of racial segregation on an international scale',[22] and was, as the Australian case shows, often a racist response from white settlers to earlier brown-skinned migrant labour, whose work was central to the economic prosperity of the settler colony.

The global colour line was drawn through and a product of racial hierarchies of mobility. It also produced regimes of (im)mobility through particular transport infrastructures across land and sea. These

---

20 M Lemberg-Pedersen, 'Manufacturing Displacement. Externalisation and Postcoloniality in European Migration Control', *Global Affairs*, 5(3), 2019, 15.

21 G Clarsen, 'Special Section on Settler-Colonial Mobilities', *Transfers* 5(3), 2015, 41–8.

22 Lake and Reynolds, *Drawing the Global Colour Line*, 5.

aimed at connecting 'white men's countries', to ensure the smooth running of imperial trade and the opening of new markets. Infrastructures, such as the Canadian Pacific and Transcontinental railroads, were built using forced Indigenous and migrant labour in the service of continued white mastery over land and the means of movement. Sea routes, such as the 'All Red' route connecting Australia, New Zealand and Canada across the Pacific, were financed through an appeal to those in the core and periphery of the British Empire to preserve white hegemony over an empire on which the sun never set.[23] These new transport infrastructures, developed to consolidate white men's mastery of space and movement, created new forms of mobility injustice as they served the interests of capital and white men's mobility.

The importance of tracing this history of racial differentiation and its relations to mobility remains an urgent and necessary task. With the apparent end to colonial rule, the starkness of white supremacy appears to have given way to a liberal ideal of an equality of nations, while inequalities continue to be entrenched at the national level. As Lake and Reynolds argue, 'the imagined community of white men was transnational in its reach, but nationalist in its outcomes, bolstering regimes of border protection and national sovereignty.'[24] This was, in part, a response to calls for an end to racial discrimination premised on the basis of an equality of nations enshrined in international law. As a result, overtly racist exclusions have been replaced with a combination of geography and bureaucracy that have come to stand in for race. If the post–World War II liberal consensus recognised the need for a normative commitment to racial equality, white supremacy resisted, transplanting a commitment to exclusion, hierarchical division and a need to preserve 'white men's countries' onto bureaucratic tools such as passports and visas, and supposedly 'neutral' – or at least not overtly racist – categories such as nationality, labour skills and literacy.[25] At

---

23 See, for example: M Karuka, *Empire's Tracks: Indigenous Nations, Chinese Workers and the Transcontinental Railroad*, Berkeley: University of California Press, 2019; F Steel, 'The "Missing Link": Space, Race, and Transoceanic Ties in the Settler-Colonial Pacific', *Transfers* 5(3), 2015, 49–67.

24 Lake and Reynolds, *Drawing the Global Colour Line*, 4.

25 Labour and literacy are of course racialised, and it is not surprising to find that, for example, in the US the literacy test that was used to disenfranchise black voters in Mississippi in 1890 became the basis for US immigration restrictions. These same restrictions were also used across British Dominions including Natal, and later served as blueprints for apartheid. Ibid., 5.

the same time, as white supremacy came under attack from international treaties that affirmed the equal sovereignty of all nations and the right to self-determination of all people, immigration restrictions became the 'quintessential expression of the masculine sovereignty of "self-governing communities" '.[26]

The Tools of the Global Colour Line: Passports, Visas and Border Controls

When Malaysian Airlines flight 370 disappeared en route from Kuala Lumpur to Beijing on 8 March 2014, there was intense speculation about the presence on the flight of two men, Pouria Nour Mohammad, age 19, and Seyed Mohammed Rezar Delawar, age 29, originally from Iran and travelling on fake European passports. The story gained traction within a cultural environment in which the men, due to their nationality and assumed religion, were suspected of involvement in the plane's possible hijacking and disappearance. However, it is their use of fake Austrian and Italian passports that interests me here, in tracing the tools of the global colour line. While MH370 was headed to Beijing when it disappeared, the itineraries of the two men had them making an onward flight to Amsterdam, where Pouria Nour Mohammad had a connecting flight to Frankfurt and Seyed Mohammed Rezar Delawar had one to Copenhagen.[27]

But why were two Iranian men travelling on European passports? People online and on social media have, of course, put forward many theories, but only one concerns me here, and it relates to inequalities in the value of a passport. While it might be possible today for wealthy non-Europeans to buy European citizenship and thus a European passport,[28] reports at the time of MH370's disappearance suggested that the Iranians probably obtained their fake passports in Thailand for a price at least ten times higher than a legally obtained European pass-

---

26 Ibid., 8.

27 K Hodal et al., 'Italian's Passport Used to Board Flight MH370 Was Stolen in Phuket', the *Guardian*, 9 March 2014, theguardian.com; S Kamali Dehghan, 'Iranians Travelling on Flight MH370 on Forged Passports "Not Linked to Terror"', the *Guardian*, 11 March 2014, theguardian.com.

28 S Farolfi, L Harding and S Ophanides, 'EU Citizenship for Sale as Russian Oligarch Buys Cypriot Passport', the *Guardian*, 2 March 2018, theguardian.com.

port. However, a European passport has a much higher non-monetary value relating to the privileges of mobility it provides.

An Austrian or Italian passport grants the bearer privileged access to the entirety of the European Union without the need for expensive and hard-to-obtain visas. If José Matada had had a passport from a European Union country, he could have boarded the flight from Angola to London with nothing more than an airline ticket. And thus, in the case of MH370, what started as a story concerned with a potential hijacking – with some over-excited, politically motivated press reports declaring an Iranian plot[29] – became, according to the BBC, one concerning two men attempting to get to Europe to claim asylum.[30]

As Liza Schuster, a scholar with expertise on asylum seekers and European asylum policy, says:

> the absence of legal gateways for refugees has created a demand for agents and a very lucrative market for forged and stolen passports, or for genuine passports with fake visas. The more money the client is willing or able to spend, the better the product. Those with sufficient money can bribe embassy staff and effectively purchase a visa. European embassies are not exempt from such practices.[31]

Thus, the use of fake European passports reveals the unequal regimes of mobility that rest on a system of passports, visas, airlines and other legal transport providers policing who can move and how. That people criticised the Malaysian authorities in Kuala Lumpur for allowing men of Iranian appearance on a plane with European passports only further highlights the racial underpinnings of this regime. As the late director of the UK Institute of Race Relations, Ambalavaner Sivanandan, said: 'We wear our passports on our faces – or, lacking them, we are faceless, destitute taken from our children, voided of the last shreds of human dignity.'[32]

---

29 See, for example, D Kamin, 'Ex-El Al Expert: Iran Likely Involved in MH 370', *The Times of Israel*, 16 March 2014, timesofisrael.com.

30 M Hills, 'Mystery of Flight MH370 Raises Fears of Passport Fraud', *BBC News*, 11 March 2014, bbc.com.

31 L Schuster, 'Flight MH370 and the Desperate Demand for False Passports', *The Conversation*, 12 March 2014, theconversation.com.

32 A Sivanandan, 'Racism, Liberty and the War on Terror', *Race and Class* 48(4), 2007, 45–96.

The passport's now-universal usage as a way of governing who can move across borders gives it a starring role in the development of unequal mobility. This apparently simple document, measuring a globally standardised 125mm by 88mm and containing the same internationally agreed-upon information about the bearer, is a fascinating glimpse of how the world and its population have come to be governed and controlled through document technology and international treaties. The sociologist John Torpey, in his work on the passport's history, argues that, through their invention and now worldwide use, modern states have come to monopolise the legitimate means of movement in similar ways to the monopolisation of the legitimate means of violence, and capitalism's monopolisation of the means of production.[33] According to Torpey, the results of this process have deprived us of the freedom to move across certain spaces and make us dependent on states for the permission to move and for the formation of our 'identity'. Permission to move relies on having an identity and being identifiable, while this identity shapes our ability to access various spaces.[34] From the early 1800s to the present day, the passport has come to include and be dependent on a range of surveillance instruments. These included the then–newly developed techniques of photography and fingerprinting, and later biometric data such as iris scans, bar codes, computer chips and machine-readable standardised information.[35]

Alongside the passport as a tool to 'monopolise the legitimate means of movement', the use of visas permitting entry across borders has also grown. Visas play an increasingly crucial, material and legal role in determining who can gain access to the privileges of safe and legal travel. Meanwhile, the 'legality' of movement, or of the person moving, becomes a category through an assemblage of such documents.[36] The global colour line therefore rests not only on visible markers of race but also on the growth of state-sanctioned national-identity documents and

---

33 J Torpey, *The Invention of the Passport: Surveillance, Citizenship and the State*, Cambridge: Cambridge University Press, 2000.

34 Ibid.

35 Jones, *Violent Borders*, 82–3. See also L Amoore, 'Biometric Borders: Governing Mobilities in the War on Terror', *Political Geography* 25, 2006, 336–51; M Keshavarz, *The Design and Politics of the Passport: Materiality, Immobility, and Dissent*, London: Bloomsbury, 2019.

36 See, for example, NP De Genova, 'Migrant "Illegality" and Deportability in Everyday Life', *Annual Review of Anthropology* 31, 2002, 419–47.

passports. For example, the White Australia policy introduced in 1901 restricted Asian immigration until 1971, while Canada had restrictions on non-European migration until the 1960s.

But overtly racist policies of exclusion have been replaced with different measurements based on nationality, income levels, notions of risk and the ability to access the correct documentation. This has created what political geographer Henk van Houtum has likened to human blacklisting in a system of 'global apartheid'.[37] Today, visas and passports are not only for entry but, crucially, for access to safe and legal transportation. Legal mobility across borders works as a catch-22 here. Legal mobility status is all but impossible to obtain for the majority of the world's population, rendering the excluded 'illegal'.

In his book *Border Vigils*, Jeremy Harding has catalogued the growth of these controls, their effects on those wanting to move, and the smugglers willing to assist them.[38] His main focus is the European Union, and not without reason. Over the past two decades, the EU has developed a range of controls that make safe and legal travel into the EU increasingly exclusive. Borders have become what anthropologist Ruben Andersson calls 'extreme zones' of profit extraction that see human mobility or immobility as an economic resource to be exploited.[39] In this economy, purveyors of fake documents, like those used by Pouria Nour Mohammad and Seyed Mohammed Rezar Delawar, people smugglers and security companies operate and profit from border controls. Restrictive state policies have created conditions that facilitate the need for security companies and smugglers alike. Meanwhile, for those denied access to safe and legal routes, mobility becomes a matter of life and death.

Following the removal of its internal borders in 1995, the European Union introduced the Schengen Visa in 2004, limiting who can and cannot travel into the Schengen Area with only a passport. As well as European Union citizens, citizens of 62 other countries have visa-free access to Schengen for limited-time leisure trips. A further 111

---

37 H van Houtum, 'Human Blacklisting: The Global Apartheid of the EU's External Border Regime', *Environment and Planning D: Society and Space* 28, 2010, 957–76.

38 J Harding, *Border Vigils: Keeping Migrants out of the Rich World*, London: Verso, 2012.

39 R Andersson, *Illegality, Inc.: Clandestine Migration and the Business of Bordering Europe*, Berkeley: University of California Press, 2014.

countries (112 including the Occupied Palestinian Territories) require a Schengen Visa, including China and India, meaning that the majority of the world's population need a visa to travel legally to the EU. Citizens of a further twelve countries require a transit visa if they wish to change planes at a Schengen airport, including citizens from Bangladesh, Pakistan, Sri Lanka, Iran and Ghana, and large refugee-producing countries such as the Democratic Republic of Congo, Eritrea, Iraq and Somalia. Currently, Syrians do not require a transit visa but they do require a Schengen Visa. Such visas are similarly required for the United States, Canada, Australia and New Zealand. Visas are therefore a crucial factor in producing and maintaining unequal mobility as they not only grant or deny people entry to the EU but also determine how people can travel. Pouria Nour Mohammad and Seyed Mohammed Rezar Delawar travelled on fake European Union passports not only because they gave them visa-free access to the EU but because they gave them access to the relative safety and speed of air travel. If they had been travelling on Iranian passports without Schengen Visas, the two men would have not been allowed to board their second flight from Beijing to Amsterdam and they may have even been denied the right to board in Kuala Lumpur.

Privileged access to regular and safe forms of transportation including planes, trains, ferries and buses into the EU, US, Canada, Australia and New Zealand, as well as a range of other countries, is dependent on having the correct documentation. The European Union calls this 'carriers' liability', sometimes referred to as 'strict' carriers' liability and it is indeed strict. Strict carriers' liability results in the outsourcing of migration controls to private actors such as airlines and shipping companies. These actors are held legally and financially responsible for ensuring that those who use their services have the correct documentation, authorising not only their entry into states but also their ability to travel in the first place.

Carriers' liability, or Council Directive 2001/51/EC, is intended to supplement Article 26 of the Convention that implements Schengen. Article 26 of the Schengen Convention, signed in the Luxembourgish border town of Schengen on 14 June 1985 (and effective 26 March 1995), states:

> (a) If aliens are refused entry into the territory of one of the Contracting Parties, the carrier which brought them to the external border by air, sea or land shall be obliged immediately to assume responsibility for them again. At the request of the border surveillance authorities the

carrier shall be obliged to return the aliens to the third State from which they were transported or to the third State which issued the travel document on which they travelled or to any other third State to which they are certain to be admitted.

(b) The carrier shall be obliged to take all the necessary measures to ensure that an alien carried by air or sea is in possession of the travel documents required for entry into the territories of the Contracting Parties.[40]

This Council Directive supplements Article 26 of the Schengen Convention through harmonising the financial penalties imposed across the EU on carriers who breach their obligations, to ensure passengers possess the necessary travel documents, and 'where appropriate, visas'. Under the Schengen Convention, as outlined in section (a) of Article 26 above, a carrier is responsible for returning anyone travelling without the correct documentation. However, if the carrier is unable to carry out the return of the 'alien', they are additionally responsible for 'finding the means of his/her onward transportation' and, if this cannot be done immediately, the carrier becomes financially responsible for the costs of the 'alien's' stay and the subsequent return. Furthermore, a carrier may face fines up to €500,000 and individual EU member states may take additional action including the seizure of vehicles or the removal of operating licences.[41] This results in a shifting of responsibility for controlling the border (and subsequently also controlling mobility) to private companies and their individual employees.[42]

Importantly, to ensure that the European Union and its member states

---

40   The Schengen Acquis – Convention Implementing the Schengen Agreement of 14 June 1985 between the Governments of the States of the Benelux Economic Union, the Federal Republic of Germany and the French Republic on the Gradual Abolition of Checks at their Common Borders, *Official Journal* L 239, 22/09/2000 p. 19–62, eur-lex.europa.eu.

41   European Council Directive 2001/51/EC of 28 June 2001, supplementing the provisions of Article 26 of the Convention implementing the Schengen Agreement of 14 June 1985, eur-lex.europa.eu.

42   M Bosworth and M Guild, 'Governing Through Migration Control: Security and Citizenship in Britain', *British Journal of Criminology* 48, 2008, 703–19; G Lahav, 'Immigration and the State: The Devolution and Privatisation of Immigration Control in the EU', *Journal of Ethnic and Migration Studies* 24(4), 1998, 675–94. For more on the impact of historical carriers' liability in creating a racist mobility regime in the case of the UK, see N El-Enany, *(B)Ordering Britain: Law, Race and Empire*, Manchester: Manchester University Press, 2020.

are not in breach of their obligations under the 1951 Refugee Convention, 'these financial penalties do not apply to cases where the non-EU national is seeking international protection'.[43] However, this is a fudge. It does not mean that refugees and those seeking asylum can take an international flight to the EU. Carriers and their employees are not trained to make determinations about those in need of protection under International Humanitarian Law and therefore deny travel to anyone without the correct documentation. Furthermore, asylum and eventual refugee status is most often granted by state authorities many months, if not years, after an asylum seeker has entered and applied for asylum. This results in carriers not taking the risk of transporting anyone without correct documentation, as carriers are still held responsible for the costs and for deportation if an asylum seeker has had their request for international protection denied. Put simply this means, for example, that Syrian refugees without a Schengen Visa cannot catch a plane to a European airport or take the ferry costing just over €20 for a 90-minute journey from Turkey to the Greek island of Lesvos. Instead, we see how thousands of life seekers have travelled from Turkey to Lesvos in small, dangerously overcrowded rubber dinghies for prices up to €3,000, exemplifying what Andersson would call 'extreme profit extraction' based on unequal mobility.[44]

The use of irregular vessels like rubber dinghies or wooden fishing boats by life seekers is not restricted to the Mediterranean. In August 2001, the Norwegian cargo vessel the *MV Tampa* rescued 433 asylum seekers, predominantly Afghan Hazaras, from the sinking *Palapa 1*, a small wooden Indonesian fishing boat in the Indian Ocean close to Australia's Christmas Island. The demands of some of the rescued men to be taken to Australia – the closest port – rather than back to Indonesia and the refusal of the Australian authorities to let the *Tampa* dock at Christmas Island created a media storm around the world. Footage of the *Tampa*, its decks covered in tired and listless bodies attempting to keep out of the tropical sun between shipping containers, became a feature on the nightly news around the world. Arne Rinnan, the ship's captain, made impassioned pleas for the well-being of the life seekers he now housed on his ship's decks, drawing

---

43 European Council Directive 2001/51/EC of 28 June 2001, supplementing the provisions of Article 26 of the Convention implementing the Schengen Agreement of 14 June 1985, eur-lex.europa.eu.

44 Andersson, *Illegality, Inc.*

attention to the worsening conditions, the lack of food, water and basic sanitation as well as a lack of medical facilities to treat cases of dysentery. But the Australian authorities refused the *Tampa* entry to Australian waters and threatened Captain Rinnan with a charge of people smuggling. The ship was provided with some medical supplies and food but the ship remained under the watchful eye of the Australian navy. This stand-off continued for three days until, on 29 August, Captain Rinnan – acting for the well-being of his ship, his crew and the lives of those rescued – declared an emergency and proceeded to enter Australian waters. Captain Rinnan believed that international maritime law was on his side. The Australian authorities felt differently and forcibly boarded the *Tampa*. The boarding of the *Tampa* increased the international media storm and created a diplomatic storm alongside it. The Norwegian government accused the Australian government of attempting to force the *Tampa* back into international waters against Captain Rinnan's will, in contravention of international maritime law. Australia suggested that as the *Tampa* was a Norwegian vessel, Norway could take responsibility for the 433 life seekers on board. Meanwhile, Norway reported Australia to the United Nations High Commissioner for Refugees and the International Maritime Organisation.

However, the *Tampa* incident is also important because of the trail of policies that came in its wake that further consolidated the global colour line in repressive and new ways. These policies included the excising of islands from Australia's sovereign territory, meaning that future asylum seekers landing on such islands could not claim legal protection under Australian law; the outlawing of irregular boat arrivals; and the offshoring of asylum seekers intercepted in Australian waters to non-Australian island prisons on Papua New Guinea's Manus and Nauru. *Tampa* is also important for the substantial financial incentives subsequently given to authorities in Papua New Guinea, Nauru and Indonesia for housing Australia's unwanted asylum seekers and for preventing their journeys in the first place.[45] These policies, known as the 'Pacific Solution'

---

45 For more information Australia's border policies, see A Little and N Vaughan-Williams, 'Stopping Boats, Saving Lives, Securing Subjects'; L Weber and S Pickering, *Globalization and Borders: Death at the Global Frontier*, Basingstoke: Palgrave, 2011; for specific information on the use of third countries by Australia, see A McNevin, A Missbach and D Mulyana, 'The Rationalities of Migration Management: Control and Subversion in an Indonesia-Based Counter-Smuggling Campaign', *International Political Sociology* 10(3), 2016, 223–40.

and 'Operation Sovereign Borders', are seen by many policymakers and politicians around the world as something not to condemn but rather to emulate. Therefore, not only were the 433 asylum seekers rescued by the *Tampa* restricted by an Australian visa regime, but their irregular entry and the irregular entry by boat of those who came after have resulted in one of the most restrictive set of border controls governing 'illegalised' migration in the world. Such a regime not only produces unequal mobility, but actively punishes the irregular forms of travel that are such a regime's effects through a totalising system of oppression and control that Manus' most famous prisoner Behrouz Boochani calls the kyriarchal system.[46]

However, increased border controls extend not only before the borderline – determining, as we have seen, how and if people can board a plane or a ferry – but also beyond the borderline. For example, undocumented migrants in the EU live with the constant fear of random police checks determining their legal status and their right to be in Europe. In addition, in the UK the government has mandated a number of private actors, including banks, employers, universities, private landlords and now the National Health Service, with checking people's immigration status, resulting in a continuously widening regime of migration control that is known infamously as the 'Hostile Environment'.[47] Another tool of the global colour line, the Hostile Environment has come under increasing scrutiny due in part to the deportation of close to 100 Black members of the Windrush community – members or descendants of Black Afro-Caribbean post-war migrants to the UK at the time of Empire – to a number of now independent Caribbean states.[48] Beyond the monitoring of immigration status by non-governmental actors, charities are increasingly involved in the UK's structures of exclusion. For example, St Mungo's homeless charity has been working with the UK Home Office

---

46 B Boochani, *No Friend But the Mountains: Writing from Manus Prison*, Sydney: Picador, 2018.

47 The Hostile Environment came into effect in the Immigration Acts of 2014 and 2016. See M Goodfellow, *Hostile Environment: How Immigrants Became Scapegoats*, London: Verso, 2019, and El-Enany, *(B)Ordering Britain*.

48 See K Rawlinson and A Gentleman, 'Home Office Windrush Report Damns Hostile Environment Policy', the *Guardian*, 27 July 2019, theguardian.com; L de Noronha, 'Deportation, Racism and Multi-Status Britain: Immigration Control and the Production of Race in the Present', *Ethnic and Racial Studies* 42(14), 2019, 2413–30.

to target rough sleepers for deportation.[49] And in 2011, the children's charity Barnardo's took over the contract to run children's services in detention and deportation centres even after the UK was supposed to have outlawed the immigration detention of children.[50]

In the United States, Customs and Border Patrol agents are mandated to check people's immigration status anywhere within 100 miles of the border, including sea borders. Border checkpoints on roads extend inland into US territory, while agents routinely board Greyhound buses to check people's immigration status.[51] This targeting of Greyhound buses is not without reason; it is a calculated act of border patrol which combines both racial and class profiling. People of Latinx appearance claim racial profiling is a regular occurrence as they report being specifically targeted during such stops.[52] Meanwhile, Immigration and Customs Enforcement (ICE) perform immigration stops and raids anywhere across US territory with increasing regularity at migrants' places of work, during routine check-ins with immigration authorities, and at hospitals and schools. This broad range of border controls has an understandable impact on how people move within states as well as across borders, leading to further entrenchment of unequal mobility along racial and socio-economic lines.

Within the EU, member states are able to target policing to detect criminal activity and undocumented migrants.[53] In the Netherlands, the powers of interception are some of the most extensive in the world, as criminologist Paul Mutsaers has shown. The power to apprehend suspected undocumented migrants extends beyond the Koninklijke Marechaussee – or KMar for short – who are responsible for external

---

49   D Taylor, 'Homeless Charity Helped Target Rough Sleepers to Deport', the *Guardian*, 5 March 2018, theguardian.com.

50   F Webber, 'The Fading Red Line: Barnardo's Role in the Detention and Removal of Children', *Institute of Race Relations*, 15 May 2014, irr.org.

51   J Jarvie, 'Border Patrol Agents Spark Anger after Boarding Bus in Florida to Ask Passengers for Proof of Citizenship', *Los Angeles Times*, 23 January 2018, latimes.com; S Schmidt, 'Video Shows Border Patrol Officers Asking Greyhound Passengers for IDs, Taking Woman into Custody', *The Washington Post*, 23 January 2018, washingtonpost.com.

52   F Santiago, 'In the Hunt for Undocumented Immigrants, Border Patrol Agents Hassle Citizens, Too', *Miami Herald*, 26 January 2018, miamihearld.com.

53   C Rumford, 'Towards a Multiperspectival Study of Borders', *Geopolitics* 17(4), 2012, 887–902.

border control at, for example, Schiphol Airport, to all officers of the Dutch police as well as a host of other public and private institutions (as in the UK). Importantly, Dutch police are able to stop-and-search based only on the suspicion of a crime having taken place. In addition, all officers of the Dutch police have access to the 'Aliens Administration System', meaning, Mutsaers shows, that between 1997 and 2003, the majority (57 percent) of apprehensions of undocumented migrants were carried out by the regular police force. Furthermore, there is, according to Mutsaers, a strong element of racial profiling in the apprehensions made by Dutch police.[54] Similar forms of wide-ranging police powers relating to internal borders are also in effect in Australia.[55]

This results not only in a reinforcement of the global colour line but also increasing risks for those denied privileged mobility status. For example, the Missing Migrants Project of the International Organization for Migration recorded 1,456 deaths on the US-Mexico border between 2014 and 2017, with the top causes of death in 2017 being drowning, exposure and hypothermia from prolonged exposure to the desert.[56] This matters because the denial of safe and legal forms of transportation not only leads to deaths at the border, such as drowning in the Rio Grande, but also deaths far beyond the border as undocumented migrants are forced to walk long distances unable to access safe forms of travel like the Greyhound. In the EU, meanwhile, policing of internal borders has increased since the emergence of the 'migration crisis' in 2015. This has meant that life seekers not only lose their lives crossing the Mediterranean but that they also face unnecessary risks within the EU. For example, in the first six months of 2017, twelve people were reported to have died on the French-Italian border at Ventimiglia.[57] The Refugee Rights Data Project argues that 'by making the journey to

---

54 P Mutsaers, 'An Ethnographic Study of the Policing of Internal Borders in the Netherlands: Synergies between Criminology and Anthropology', *British Journal of Criminology* 54, 2014, 831–48; see also MJ Gibney, 'Asylum and the Expansion of Deportation in the United Kingdom', *Government and Opposition* 43, 2008, 146–67.

55 L Weber, ' "It Sounds Like They Shouldn't Be Here": Immigration Checks on the Streets of Sydney', *Policing & Society: An International Journal of Research and Policy* 21, 2011, 456–67.

56 '5,969 Missing Migrants Recorded in the Americas (since 2014)', Missing Migrants Project, US-Mexico Border, missingmigrants.iom.int.

57 A Quadroni and M Luppi, 'The Border Crossing Deaths in Como', *Open Migration*, 10 August 2017, openmigration.org.

France on trains more difficult, the closed border drives displaced people to take their chances via the so-called "Pass of Death" through the mountains, by walking through motorway tunnels or by resorting to smugglers and traffickers'.[58]

Meanwhile, increased border controls in certain areas have cascade effects on controls elsewhere, both on the routes taken by life seekers and the risks they face. As Ventimiglia has become more heavily controlled, life seekers cross the Italian-French border further north into the Hautes-Alpes region. They travel via the little-known Col de l'Échelle that sits between the Italian town of Bardonecchia – that lies at the Italian end of the Fréjus tunnel with its heavily policed rail and road route – and the French UNESCO heritage site city of Briançon, and via the Col de Montgenèvre between Oulx and Briançon. On the Oulx to Briançon route, life seekers eschew the regular bus service between the Italian ski resort of Claviere and its French counterpart Montgenèvre, where there is a near-permanent presence of Italian Guardia di Finanzia and French Gendarmerie. 'The path from Claviere is less difficult [than the Col de l'Échelle] but it is the easiest one to be intercepted on', says Silvia Gilardi, a representative of the NGO Rainbow for Africa. However, 'people arrive at Oulx station unprepared for the cold and the snow, with just a small rucksack and the clothes they're wearing'.[59] However, the danger of the Claviere route is evidenced by the death of twenty-nine-year-old Derman Tamimou from Togo in 2019 and the 2018 death of a Nigerian woman known as Blessing who drowned in a river while being pursued by the border police. Meanwhile, in 2018, three people lost their lives to hypothermia on the Col de l'Échelle, a route considered more treacherous than Claviere in part because it is more remote and subsequently less controlled.

I know these mountain passes intimately because I have spent many years cycling them freely during my summer holidays, passing between France and Italy and back with no more interference than an occasional wave from a Gendarme or the assistance of an agent of the Guardia di Finanzia as I try to negotiate a tricky junction on a steep climb. But why

---

58 A Lucas and M Welander, 'Dangerous Borderlands: Human Rights for Displaced People on the French-Italian Border', 3 October 2017, law.ox.ac.uk.
59 A Giuffrida, ' "We Have to Try": The Migrants Who Brave Frostbite in a Desperate Trek over the Alps', *The Observer*, 16 February 2019, theguardian.com.

do my holiday exploits matter? They matter because, while cycling may pose a small risk, I can cross this border without any risk to my life from the border itself. The global colour line and its attendant dangers are invisible to me as a white woman. In exercising my mobility across this border, I am not reduced to climbing the Col de L'Échelle at 1,762m above sea level, and some 12km on foot from Bardonecchia train station. I can drive a car or catch one of the regular warm buses that go from Oulx to Briançon over the regularly snowploughed road pass between Claviere and Montgenèvre, where the Police Aux Frontières sitting in their warm booth underneath a French flag do not give me – with my blonde hair and white skin – a second look. Like many other border zones and transit spaces, the Hautes-Alpes is made deadly by unequal mobility regimes that actively and violently discriminate against those who find themselves on the wrong side of the global colour line. And, like many other border zones and transit spaces, this deadly Alpine route has subsequently become a place of life-saving rescue and humanitarian compassion.[60]

The Politics of Saving Lives: from Colonial Amelioration to Structuring Violence

Humanitarianism has a history intimately linked to colonialism, abolition and whiteness. Understood as relieving the suffering of distant strangers and as a way of acting transnationally in the world, humanitarianism should not be taken for granted. Instead, it should be seen as the result of modernity's constituent parts, including the ability to feel compassion for the bodily suffering of strangers and to act on such compassion.[61] Importantly, mobility plays a constitutive role in humanitarianism. Historian James Vernon foregrounds the role of mobility in

---

60 A Camilli, 'Dodging Death Along the Alpine Migrant Passage', *Refugees Deeply*, 25 January 2018, newsdeeply.com.

61 Barnett, *Empire of Humanity*; Fassin, *Humanitarian Reason*; K Halttunen, 'Humanitarianism and the Pornography of Pain in Anglo-American Culture', *The American Historical Review* 100(2), 1995, 303–34; TL Haskell, 'Capitalism and the Origins of the Humanitarian Sensibility, Part I', *The American Historical Review* 90(2), 1985, 99–110; TL Haskell, 'Capitalism and the Origins of the Humanitarian Sensibility, Part II', *The American Historical Review* 90(3), 1985, 547–66; TW Lacquer, 'Bodies, Details, and the Humanitarian Narrative', in L Hunt ed., *The New Cultural History*, Berkeley: University of California Press, 1989.

the creation of the traditionally understood subject of humanitarianism: the distant stranger. Vernon charts how the increased mobility of people as a result of the industrial revolution created the conditions in which concern for distant strangers developed.[62] In his reading of modernity, the mobility of white men and their attendant capital across imperial space played a central role in the affective roots of humanitarianism.

As family and kinship ties came to be replaced with a society of strangers, a new set of problems developed concerning how to conduct economic, political and social life across time and space. This resulted in the creation of a number of abstract and bureaucratic ways of making relationships between distant strangers possible. One of these was humanitarianism itself. Through relieving suffering caused by the inequalities of an emerging capitalist system, humanitarianism became a form of liberal government.[63] Central to this was making saving distant strangers possible – it structures almost everything about the contemporary international humanitarian response industry. For instance, this industry mimics global logistics systems with their focus on reducing the problems of time and space through frictionless speed. Such humanitarian (logistics) systems are ready to be deployed anywhere in the world at a moment's notice because, while ever-increasing speed might be central to capitalism's pursuit of accumulation, in humanitarianism speed is central to saving lives.[64] Additionally, humanitarians themselves are understood as hyper-mobile, global subjects, zipping around the world to distant disaster zones to save distant strangers. Alongside a just-in-time humanitarian response industry which capitalises on existing unequal mobility, humanitarianism promotes neoliberal solutions based on an entrepreneurial individualism that contributes to an overall invisibilising of structural inequalities between populations and geographies.

Indeed, humanitarianism masks as much as it illuminates. Humanitarianism's history has allowed for an ethical commitment to distant

---

62   J Vernon, *Distant Strangers: How Britain Became Modern*, Berkeley: University of California Press, 2014.

63   SM Reid-Henry, 'Humanitarianism as Liberal Diagnostic: Humanitarian Reason and the Political Rationalities of the Liberal Will-to-Care', *Transactions of the Institute of British Geographers* 39(3), 2014, 418–31.

64   See Peter Redfield's work on the humanitarian kit in P Redfield, 'Vital Mobility and the Humanitarian Kit', in A Lakoff and SJ Collier eds, *Biosecurity Interventions: Global Health and Security in Question*, New York: Columbia University Press, 2008, 147–71.

strangers that allows white supremacy to go unchallenged. I trace the politics of humanitarianism through a focus on relieving the suffering of emancipated populations who were enslaved; caring for Indigenous communities under the violence of colonialism; the privileging of white mobilities; and the consolidation of racialised geographies. In exploring the intimate relationship between the global colour line and humanitarianism as, to borrow from geographer Derek Gregory, the 'velvet glove wrapped around the iron fist of colonialism',[65] I focus on the work of British colonial administrator George Arthur.

British abolitionist sentiment, transatlantic slavery, and the plantation economies of the Caribbean play a central role in the well-known story of William Wilberforce, whose work is given an almost mythical place in humanitarianism's origin story and the UK's false exceptionalism concerning its (anti-)colonial and (anti-)racist past. Wilberforce advocated for an end to slavery based on the humanity, if not equality, of enslaved people while advancing a conservative, anti-organised labour politics 'at home'. But we also find abolitionist sentiment and nascent humanitarian concerns in the work of colonial officials charged with overseeing the governance and stability of plantation economies and 'protecting' enslaved people from excessive working hours and punishments. Known as ameliorative codes, this protection was intended to appease both metropolitan abolitionists like Wilberforce and ensure slave economies continued to function profitably. Ameliorative policies, overseen by a 'Protector' – in reality, often a member of the slave-owning class – were, in addition, intended to prepare enslaved people for a freedom yet to come by encouraging both Christianisation and civilisation. As geographers Alan Lester and Fae Dussart suggest, 'through their instructive relationship with slave owners, the British government hoped, they would redeem cruel and aberrant British colonial societies at the same time that they reformed the benighted subjectivities of enslaved people.'[66]

Enter George Arthur, Lieutenant Governor of Honduras from 1814–1822, who 'came to be positioned at the forefront of a struggle between a

---

65 D Gregory, 'Counterinsurgency and the Humanitarian Present', *Geographical Imaginations*, 2012, geographicalimaginations.com.

66 A Lester and F Dussart, *Colonization and the Origins of Humanitarian Government: Protecting Aborigines across the Nineteenth-Century British Empire*, Cambridge: Cambridge University Press, 2014, 56.

humanitarian-inclined metropolitan lobby ... and slave-owning colonists'.[67] During his time as Lieutenant Governor of Honduras, Arthur had been exposed to a number of harrowing stories concerning the harsh treatment of enslaved people, both Black Africans and Indigenous peoples. The effect of these stories had stirred in him the need for ameliorative policies to protect the well-being of the enslaved but that stopped well short of advocating full emancipation. According to Seymour Drescher,

> amelioration was never about the revolutionary overhaul of West Indian societies in the interests of 'humanity'. It was about the more effective ordering and regulation of enslaved people, whose status in British colonies was now troubling to a large proportion of metropolitan society, but who were by no means considered ready for an experiment in individual freedom.[68]

Importantly, amelioration was tied to the 'good behaviour' and 'industrious disposition' of enslaved people, requiring them to demonstrate that they were using 'all means to improve their moral and religious condition'. Amelioration, therefore, was part of a 'controlled change deemed essential to post-abolition' and George Arthur found himself playing a central role in the experiment of how to incorporate humanity into colonial control.[69]

Following his tenure in Honduras, George Arthur was posted to Van Diemen's Land in 1824, where he attempted to use amelioration to govern both the convict and Aboriginal populations with differing levels of success. This geographical shift led to consequent continuities and changes in Arthur's governing techniques. Amelioration developed into a more explicit project he presented as 'protection' in the face of white-settler violence towards, and the resistance of, the Indigenous population. These changes make Arthur a vector through which we can trace the intersections and ambivalences of humanitarian sentiments and practices, and their development within various colonial spaces marked by white supremacy and underpinned by hierarchies of humanity and

---

67 Ibid., 56.
68 Ibid. See also S Drescher, *The Mighty Experiment: Free Labor versus Slavery in British Emancipation*, Oxford: Oxford University Press, 2004.
69 Lester and Dussart, *Colonization and the Origins of Humanitarian Government*, 57.

mobility. Through a study of Arthur's governance in Honduras and Van Diemen's Land, we can also better understand the importance of place in the dynamics of humanitarianism as well as the transnational systems of humanitarian knowledge that developed across the British Empire.

In his attempts to reconcile the violence of settler colonialism with a humanitarian concern for the well-being of Aborigines, George Arthur was assisted by George Augustus Robinson, a former builder and brickmaker from East London who had settled in Hobart in 1824. Robinson was hated and ridiculed by the white-settler population for both his humanitarian impulses and his class position. But he nevertheless gained the favour of the colonial powers in Britain and across the Empire through his humanitarian work, carving out a powerful position for himself and later becoming the Chief Protector of Aborigines in Port Phillip District. Robinson's main contribution to Arthur's humanitarian governance of Van Diemen's Land were proposals for protective spaces where Aborigines could be 'settled', civilised and safe from settler violence. Arthur's earlier attempt to use settler militias and regular troops to force Aborigines into protective reservations had failed. With Robinson as his on-the-ground man, displaced Aborigines were 'encouraged' – rather than forced – to seek sanctuary at the more modest Bruny Island settlement. Later, he and Robinson oversaw the removal of Van Diemen's Land's remaining Aboriginal population, decimated by settler violence, land dispossession and disease, to Flinder's Island under the logics of protection. Recounting the project of protection through removal, Arthur was clear: 'No! Their removal has been for their benefit, and, in almost every instance, with their own free will and consent. They have been removed from danger, and placed in safety in a suitable asylum . . . where they are brought under moral and religious inculcation.'[70]

What is immediately clear in the humanitarian work of Arthur and fellow colonial administrators is the ways in which humanitarian concern ran alongside and through systems of control. According to Stoler, protection of Indigenous peoples from the violence of colonial settlers was used for the legitimation of colonial government in newly colonised spaces.[71] Historian Kenton Storey has shown how logics of protection

---

70 Quoted in Lester and Dussart, *Colonization and the Origins of Humanitarian Government*, 74.

71 AL Stoler, 'On Degrees of Imperial Sovereignty', *Public Culture* 18(1), 2006, 125–46.

were used to bring about the expulsion of First Nation Salish from Vancouver Island. Here, protection of First Nation peoples from diseases, especially smallpox, brought by European colonisers came to perversely justify calls for and the execution of their expulsion from ancestral lands.[72] Meanwhile, Henry Reynolds, as well as charting the transnational drawing of the global colour line, has shown how the protection of Indigenous peoples from white settler violence created the Native Police and ushered in new policing practices. These not only sought to save Aborigines but had the subsequent effect of strengthening and expanding British control over the 'Terra Nullius' of Australian land.[73] All of this shows how humanitarianism is a flexible practice that can be put to work in the world for ends that seem to contradict and challenge the ideals of saving lives, relieving suffering and upholding human dignity.

We see how humanitarian modes of governance were laced with white supremacy as the discussions of backwardness and the need for civilising show. Attempts at providing care for, among others, those threatened by white settler violence, those thought unready to govern themselves, and those thought in need of civilising, deployed a range of mobility controls such as confinement, forced settlement and forced removal from Indigenous lands. Through a focus on George Arthur's policies, we can see how humanitarian sensibilities helped shape these controls when the freedom of enslaved people and Indigenous populations was a direct threat to white supremacy. As Sheller has discussed in relation to abolition, 'the personal mobility of the freed people was experienced as especially galling and fearful to whites, leading to post-emancipation systems of coercive control over free black mobilities.'[74] The life trajectory of George Arthur, the colonial administrator with a humanitarian sensibility, and those that followed in his wake, is one way in which the global colour line came to be transnationally produced through the movement of colonial officials and sharing of knowledge across imperial spaces.

This shows how humanitarianism does not run counter to the overt racism of white men's countries and the systems of 'mastery' that

---

72 K Storey, *Settler Anxiety at the Outposts of Empire: Colonial Relations, Humanitarian Discourses, and the Imperial Press*, Vancouver: UBC Press, 2016.
73 H Reynolds, *Forgotten War*, Sydney: Newsouth, 2013.
74 Sheller, *Mobility Justice*, 58.

underpin whiteness as a system of power. Humanitarianism is a product of the same paternalism we can observe in the global colour line by which, in both cases, there is an assumed hierarchy between those who can care for themselves and those who cannot. In fact, it highlights exactly how, while seeking to relieve racist violence, whiteness was not challenged but, in fact, strengthened through the introduction of a range of controls that worked through the logics of care. These controls through care left imperialism not just undisturbed but secured from any possible revolutionary impulses of emancipated Black and Indigenous populations.

A focus on humanitarian sensibilities in what Frantz Fanon called the 'European game' is important for understanding humanitarianism in the present, its role in structuring the limits of violence, and as an agent of violence itself. A focus on colonial humanitarianism shines a light on humanitarianism as a tool of control, a form of domination and a way to dominate, challenging the mainstream narrative of what humanitarianism scholar Michael Barnett calls 'twentieth-century humanitarianism'.[75] Twentieth-century humanitarianism involves an understanding of humanitarianism as promoted by the likes of the ICRC, and is based on their seven fundamental principles: humanity, impartiality, neutrality, independence, voluntary service, unity and universality – even though these grew out of a desire to humanise war rather than eradicate its violence in totality.[76] A focus on colonial humanitarianism complicates our understanding of not only who a humanitarian is, casting the net wider to include state actors, but also challenges the ICRC's seven fundamental principles around what humanitarianism is. It shows, as above, how humanitarianism is a liberal tool through which Du Bois's 'whiteness' works in the world, serving the global colour line, performing liberal politics, and creating capitalist markets through the need to save.

The anthropologist Didier Fassin suggests understanding this apparent ambivalence as the 'humanitarian reason' that 'serves to qualify the issues involved and to reason about choices made'.[77] In this reading,

---

75 M Barnett, *Empire of Humanity: A History of Humanitarianism*, Ithaca, NY: Cornell University Press, 2011.

76 J Pictet, *Proclamation of the Fundamental Principles of the Red Cross*, 1979, icrc.org.

77 D Fassin, *Humanitarian Reason: A Moral History of the Present*, Berkeley: University of California Press, 2012, 2. See also SM Reid-Henry, 'On the Politics of Our Humanitarian Present', *Environment and Planning D: Society & Space* 31, 2013, 753–60.

humanitarianism is a way of framing issues and addressing them. Deploying a humanitarian reason becomes a way of doing politics that reframes deeply political issues – colonial land expropriation, dispossession and genocide or unequal forms of mobility that cause death – as issues or problems that can be managed through saving lives, relieving suffering and upholding human dignity, based on a humanity that, as Sylvia Wynter argues, is the product of conquest, enslavement and colonisation.[78] This is a way of depoliticising deeply political issues through the management of 'bad things'. It suggests the unstoppable inevitability of these bad things and calls for immediate responses that do not allow for deliberation and debate.[79] In fact, under such a system, deliberation and debate that seek to understand the politics behind such suffering are often seen as endangering life and are charged as navel-gazing, rearranging the deckchairs on the *Titanic*, or fiddling while Rome burns. The humanitarian reason is, therefore, a way of exercising power in the modern world through normative concerns of care and instrumental concerns of control that come to structure responses as distinctly humanitarian.

Another anthropologist, Michel Agier, has extensively explored the uses of care and control in governing what he terms undesirable populations. With the exacting precision of an ethnographer, Agier has documented how the everyday practices of refugee camp design and management deploy a particular politics of control based on concerns with efficiency and order.[80] Similar practices have been uncovered in medical humanitarianism with its focus on triage and in the creation of particular 'humanitarian products', such as mid-upper arm circumference (MUAC) bands and personal protective equipment, intended to save more lives more efficiently.[81] In humanitarianism, then, there

---

78 Wynter, '1492'.

79 W Walters, 'Anti-Policy and Anti-Politics: Critical Reflections on Certain Schemes to Govern Bad Things', *European Journal of Cultural Studies* 11(3), 2008, 267–88. See also N Perkowski and V Squire, 'The Anti-Policy of European Anti-Smuggling as a Site of Contestation in the Mediterranean Migration "Crisis" ', *Journal of Ethnic and Migration Studies* 45(12), 2018, 2167–84.

80 M Agier, *Managing the Undesirables: Refugee Camps and Humanitarian Government*, London: Polity, 2011.

81 For an in-depth ethnography of medical humanitarian practice, see P Redfield, *Life in Crisis: The Ethical Journey of Doctors Without Borders*, Berkeley: University of California Press, 2013. For a specific exploration of life-saving humanitarian

appears a contradictory presence of a normative concern to save and an instrumental concern about rational and efficient order. However, these normative and instrumental concerns are not in contradiction. They form a way of doing politics that recognises both the provision of care and control as necessary for human security defined through white men's experiences. Alison Howell and Melanie Richter-Montpetit have recently argued that such understandings of security are the products of a hegemonic whiteness in which it is thought that disorder fosters insecurity and that such disorder and insecurity are distinctly racialised.[82] So, not only does humanitarianism deploy strategies of control to govern across time and space, including counting and identifying aid recipients and rationing food to make its work more efficient, but it also works in a broader way to restore and uphold the 'normal order of things' through aid provision.

This upholding of the normal order of things, or the swift restitution of normality in crises, is the very point of humanitarianism as a liberal technique of government that seeks to effectively manage problems rather than propose alternative and potentially revolutionary ways of doing politics. But humanitarianism is not without a politics. As a conservative, paternalistic way of bourgeois whiteness acting in the world, humanitarianism has very real political effects. By preventing revolution, structuring racialised hierarchies of humans between those who suffer and those who save, and through specific processes of medical and emergency triage that calculate and order suffering to better manage relief, humanitarians are created as powerful subjects who claim to speak on behalf of humanity. And, after all, who wants to be against or to challenge humanity? Furthermore, in proposing types of interventions and legitimating certain actions, such as search and rescue at sea, at the expense of other actions such as providing safe and legal routes, humanitarianism structures the exercise of power, empowering specific,

---

technologies, see P Pallister-Wilkins, 'Personal Protective Equipment in the Humanitarian Governance of Ebola: Between Individual Patient Care and Global Biosecurity', *Third World Quarterly* 37(3), 2016, 507–23; P Redfield, 'Bioexpectations: Life Technologies as Humanitarian Goods', *Public Culture* 24(1), 2012, 157–84; T Scott-Smith, 'The Fetishism of Humanitarian Objects and the Management of Malnutrition Emergencies', *Third World Quarterly* 34(5), 2013, 913–28.

82   A Howell and M Richter-Montpetit, 'Racism in Foucauldian Security Studies: Biopolitics, Liberal War, and the Whitewashing of Colonial and Racial Violence', *International Political Sociology* 13(1), 2019, 2–19.

most often already powerful, actors, including but not limited to humanitarian organisations.[83] However, humanitarianism's role in structuring and empowering happens not only in the pursuit of saving lives but can also be seen to have an effect in structuring violence and empowering those who would seek not to save but to kill.

We can trace a thread from humanitarianism's deployment in colonial forms of oppression to humanitarianism's use in attempted ethnic cleansing during the Ethiopian famine, its presence in the War on Terror and Israel's occupation of Palestine.[84] In talking about these continuities, the word trace itself is perhaps too benign as it, as Stoler argues, 'seems too easily unmoored from material damages and disseminated landscapes, or from border barricades installed as colonialism's parting gestures, now hardened and more intractable than stone'.[85] As a number of political geographers have argued in recent years, the idea that humanitarianism stands in opposition to violence is only a partial reading; rather, humanitarianism is deeply entangled with violence.[86] This entanglement happens not only in relieving the effects of violence but also in determining the limits of violence itself, through, for example, 'humane' weapons systems and counterinsurgency manuals that talk about social work with guns.[87] Beyond warfare, violence is broadly conceived as concerning not only physical harm but also structures of inequality and oppression. Therefore, humanitarianism, through practices of care in, for example, refugee camps and in search and rescue missions, also enacts processes of control that (re)produce and deepen inequalities between saviours and those in need. A discussion on the way humanitarianism comes to structure

---

83   See, for example, Fassin, *Humanitarian Reason*; I Feldman and M Ticktin eds, *In the Name of Humanity: The Government of Threat and Care*, Durham, NC: Duke University Press, 2012; Redfield, *Life in Crisis*; P Pallister-Wilkins, 'Médecins Avec Frontières and the Making of a Humanitarian Borderscape', *Environment and Planning D: Society and Space* 36(1), 2018; P Pallister-Wilkins, 'Hotspots and the Geographies of Humanitarianism', *Environment and Planning D: Society and Space* 38(6), 2020.

84   Gregory, 'Counterinsurgency and the Humanitarian Present'.

85   Stoler, *Duress*, 6.

86   See R Nisa, 'Capturing Humanitarian War: The Collusion of Violence and Care in US-Managed Military Detention', *Environment and Planning A: Economy and Space* 27, 2015, 2276–91; E Weizman, *The Least of All Possible Evils: Humanitarian Violence from Arendt to Gaza*, London: Verso, 2012.

87   D Kilcullen, 'Twenty-Eight Articles: Fundamentals of Company-Level Counterinsurgency', *Military Review*, 2006, 105–7.

violence might seem counterintuitive. However, it is of the utmost importance for understanding how humanitarian ideals are put to work not just for saving lives but also how saving lives structures and enables further processes of exclusion. These processes of exclusion enact what political scientists Laleh Khalili and Lisa Hajjar have termed an ethical commitment towards others who are not regarded as, and can never be, equal.[88]

Humanitarian Borderwork

'This is a mountain town, and the rules of the mountain say that everyone who is in danger must be rescued', said Joël Pruvot, a retired schoolteacher from Briançon.[89] The call to save lives at borders and in response to unequal mobility, like that articulated by Joël Pruvot, has been routinised in many places. In Europe it has been present since the 1990s but has become louder since the migratory events following the Arab Spring in 2011 and the worsening of the Syrian conflict; in the US it has been a refrain that has gone hand in hand with the ever-tightening restrictions on migration across the Mexican border; and in Australia it underpins resistance against the Pacific Solution and Operation Sovereign Borders and demands to close Manus and Nauru. All these calls build on popular understandings about our moral responsibilities when faced with the suffering of others regardless of borders and beyond the bounds of politics.[90] This universal appeal to humanity and action across and in spite of borders underpins humanitarian work and forms the basis of its legitimacy.

The humanitarian ideal offers a simple and powerful counterpoint to the violence of borders that divides us from each other. For many it is a powerful promise of a better world where we are all equal individuals, united by a common, shared humanity. For example, the name Médecins Sans Frontières/Doctors Without Borders appears to capture such a promise concerning the universal value of humanity above and beyond

---

[88] L Khalili and L Hajjar, 'Torture, Drones, and Detention: A Conversation between Laleh Khalili and Lisa Hajjar', *Jadaliyya*, 2013, jadaliyya.com.
[89] Ibid.
[90] J Orbinkski, 'MSF Nobel Peace Prize Lecture', 1999, nobelprize.org.

the international order of states.⁹¹ In many instances, humanitarianism offers an alternative way of approaching the world, one rooted in solidarity with humanity as a whole and thereby challenging the territorially and socially divisive state system and political policies that create and enforce inequality. But does humanitarianism provide this promise in practice? And what happens to humanitarianism when it responds to suffering produced by borders and the unequal mobility that results?

Poster in MSF-Greece's offices, Athens, 2015. © Polly Pallister-Wilkins

The amalgamation of borders, mobility and humanitarianism is most ably captured in the popular imagination by the global refugee regime which is argued to be failing by some commentators, scholars and politicians.⁹² The global refugee regime emerged in the mid-twentieth

---

91   P Pallister-Wilkins, 'Médecins Sans Frontières and the Promise of Universalist Humanitarianism', in R Jones ed., *Open Borders: In Defense of Free Movement*, Athens: Georgia University Press, 2019, 158–75.
92   See, for example, A Betts and P Collier, *Refuge: Rethinking Refugee Policy in a Changing World*, London: Allen Lane, 2017.

century and forms the basis for much of our normative understanding about refugees, their rights and our responsibilities. The framework set out by international humanitarian law and the Refugee Conventions of 1951 and the Protocol of 1967 mandates and governs the work of both state governments and the UNHCR in response to refugees.[93] This humanitarian response kicks into action in moments of displacement. Here, borders play a central, constitutive role as the category of refugee is dependent on the crossing of state borders. However, humanitarian responses do not only occur after people have crossed borders in search of protection. The refugee regime has evolved over time to recognise the need to assist internally displaced populations (IDPs). And yet still the logic of action underpinning the regime is too restrictive to understand the current relationship between mobility, border crossing and saving lives because the journeys themselves are a source of danger that require life-saving interventions.

Therefore, the life-saving efforts at borders witnessed in recent years are in addition to and/or different from the global refugee regime. They occur, in part, because such a regime fails to meet the needs of life seekers, as it is focused on upholding the global colour line by privileging the security of states, corralling refugees in camps, excluding them from work, and denying them political agency.[94] However, humanitarian responses to life seekers on the move are more diverse and involve a much wider constituency of actors mobilised by the dynamics of borders and unequal mobility.[95] According to Joël Pruvot, those rescuing life seekers journeying over the Alps to Briançon 'are doing what the government is supposed to be doing: preventing accidents from happening in the mountains, preventing people from dying.'[96] Such a pronouncement appears as common sense to Pruvot and the other residents of the Hautes-Alpes who have taken it upon themselves to save lives. Meanwhile,

---

93 For a discussion of the way the refugee regime came to produce refugees as a distinct category, separate from other forms of migration, and the ways this altered and humanitarianised responses to people seeking safety through mobility, see K Long, 'When Refugees Stopped Being Migrants: Movement Labour and Humanitarian Protection', *Migration Studies* 1(1), 2013, 4–24.

94 For an excellent example of how the current refugee regime works to imprison and exclude, see S Hoffmann, 'Humanitarian Security in Jordan's Azraq Camp', *Security Dialogue* 48(2), 2017, 97–112.

95 Pallister-Wilkins, 'Médecins Avec Frontières'.

96 Ibid.

governments have mobilised search and rescue missions and routinely use the need to save lives as justification for the imposition of stronger border controls.

However, the compulsion to help strangers and relieve their suffering, or expecting the government to do so, is not common sense. Instead, it is one way of understanding our, or our governments', role in the world in relation to others and a way of acting with compassion towards fellow human beings. As charted above, the compulsion to save lives has a history, a politics, and different constituencies and effects. Additionally, as we have seen, humanitarian ideals and practices are much broader than those encoded in the 1951 Convention and enacted through the work of the UNHCR and other refugee agencies. As other scholars have argued, the focus on the Refugee Convention as the expression of humanitarian sentiment regarding mobile, displaced, migrant populations leads us to forget the formative role of colonialism, the slave trade, abolition and emancipation in the formation of both the global colour line and humanitarianism.[97]

Let us return briefly to transatlantic slavery. Not only did the trade see the creation of new regimes of racialised (im)mobility, but its humanitarian aftermath ushered in new border controls based on attempts at stopping the trade in human beings and humanitarian concerns for the wellbeing of the emancipated. Lemberg-Pedersen discusses what he calls the 'suppressionist border control of the slave trade' enacted initially by the British in the Atlantic and along the African coast to prevent the now-illegal trade in human beings. This border control included the recapturing of enslaved people at sea by the British Navy, as well as the US and Haitian navies, alongside their relocation and resettlement to other colonial territories. A number of extra-territorial camps were set up in the West Atlantic where enslaved people who had been recaptured were disembarked by the UK and US, in order to 'appease the racialised fears on their own territories'.[98] Alongside this, the UK engaged in military

---

[97] See, for example, BS Chimni, 'The Geopolitics of Refugee Studies: A View from the South', *Journal of Refugee Studies* 11(4), 1998, 350–74; El-Enany, *(B)Ordering Britain*; L Mayblin, *Asylum After Empire: Colonial Legacies in the Politics of Asylum Seeking*, London: Rowman and Littlefield International, 2017; D Vigneswaran, 'Europe Has Never Been Modern: Recasting Historical Narratives of Migration Control', *International Political Sociology* 14(1), 2020, 2–21.

[98] Lemberg-Pedersen, 'Manufacturing Displacement', 17.

campaigns and increased colonial expansion on the African continent in an attempt to suppress the trade. These humanitarian moves responding to the suffering of mobile enslaved populations through enacting forms of border control can be understood as an early form of what I term humanitarian borderwork.[99]

Humanitarian borderwork concerns the work of saving lives in border spaces. Borderwork is an idea stemming from border studies, arguing that borders are continually (re)produced through the work of border guards, bureaucrats and state officials, among others.[100] Borderwork – concerned with stopping, defending and securing territory – is infused with life-saving sentiments and actions creating humanitarian borderwork. In this symbiotic relationship between violent borders, unequal mobility regimes and the humanitarian relief of suffering that results, both humanitarian action and borders themselves come to be (re)structured in particular ways. These particular ways represent approaches to politics around both the creation and consolidation of the global colour line through borderwork, or what Van Houtum calls global apartheid, preserving privileged ways of life to the (sometimes fatal) detriment of the excluded, and how we respond to suffering in limited ways that attend to the wound rather than cure the disease. Humanitarian borderwork is diverse. It serves different constituencies of ideas and people and is used for the pursuit of different and often divergent goals that appear, at least at first glance, like Australia's offshore island prisons for asylum seekers, to be far from humanitarian. With a focus on emergency life-saving, humanitarian borderwork remains rooted in operational responses rather than structural solutions capable of challenging the unequal mobility upon which it rests, all while continuing to uphold white supremacy.

---

99   P Pallister-Wilkins, 'Humanitarian Borderwork', in Cengiz Günay and Nina Witjes eds, *Border Politics: Defining Spaces of Governance and Forms of Transgressions*, New York: Springer, 2017, 85–103; R Jones, C Johnson, W Brown, G Popescu, P Pallister-Wilkins, A Mountz and E Gilbert, 'Interventions on the State of Sovereignty at the Border', *Political Geography* 59, 2017, 1–10.

100   C Rumford, 'Introduction: Citizens and Borderwork in Europe', *Space and Polity* 12(1), 2008, 1–12.

3
Care and (Border) Control

... how to explain what we do when we discover their lay-up spots stocked with water and stashed rations. Of course, what you do depends on who you're with, depends on what kind of agent you are, what kind of agent you want to become, but it's true that we slash their bottles and drain their water into the dry earth, that we dump their backpacks and pile their food and clothes to be crushed and pissed on and stepped over, strewn across the desert and set ablaze. And Christ, it sounds terrible, and maybe it is, but the idea is that when they come out from their hiding places, when they regroup and return to find their stockpiles ransacked and stripped, they'll realize their situation, that they're fucked, that it's hopeless to continue, and they'll quit right then and there, they'll save themselves and struggle toward the nearest highway or dirt road to flag down some passing agent or they'll head for the nearest parched village to knock on someone's door, someone who will give them food and water and call us to take them in – that's the idea, the sense in it all.[1]

How to explain the above quote from former US Border Patrol agent Francisco Cantú? How to pick apart the apparent perversity of destroying people's belongings? Of crushing, pissing on, and setting alight the

---
1 F Cantú, *The Line Becomes the River*, London: Penguin Random House, 2018, 33–34.

supplies on which people's lives depend in order to save them? Welcome to the intersection of humanitarianism and border control in the hands of the state and the abominable logic of stopping through saving. But Cantú's soul-searching account of why the US Border Patrol behaves as it does not only hints at the way in which humanitarian logics of saving are folded origami-like into securing and strengthening the border. His account also highlights the ways border control is a deeply human endeavour determined in large part by the individual behaviour of officers and the exercise of their professional discretion.[2]

Narratives of rescue have become repeated and common refrains in policy announcements concerned with managing migration. As borders have become ever more exclusive, and as deaths have risen, so too has rhetoric around the need to save lives. The EU, its member states, Australia and the US all use the rhetoric of needing to save lives and stress the importance of rescue. Entire policy decisions, like the EU-Turkey 'Deal' that is designed to keep refugees in Turkey and out of Europe, have been justified and defended on the grounds of saving lives. However, saving lives is more than just rhetoric. In the everyday working lives of those responsible for policing borders, border police do more than pay lip service to activities of rescue. Rescue structures their daily activities and, as it does so, has an impact not only on the type of borderwork they undertake, but also on the border itself, where it is located, and how it comes to be (re)produced.

The Good, the Bad and the Invisible

'The only thing that can stop a bad guy with a gun is a good guy with a gun.' We have become used to this saying in response to recent gun massacres and subsequent discussions around gun control in the US.

---

2 D Bigo, 'The (In)securitization Practices of the Three Universes of EU Border Control: Military/Navy – Border Guards/Police – Database Analyst', *Security Dialogue* 45(3), 2014, 209–25; K Côté-Boucher, 'The Paradox of Discretion: Customs and the Changing Occupational Identity of Canadian Border Officers', *British Journal of Criminology* 56(1), 2016, 49–67; N El Qadim, 'Postcolonial Challenges to Migration Control: French-Moroccan Cooperation Practices on Forced Returns', *Security Dialogue* 45(3), 2014, 242–61; B İşleyen, 'Transit Mobility Governance in Turkey', *Political Geography* 62, 2018, 23–32.

Care and (Border) Control   55

Likewise, in border control, the narrative of good guys stopping bad guys has both substantive analytical purchase and serious impacts on daily operations. The bad guys in the world of border control are the people smugglers, and the good guys who will stop them are, of course, the border control agents whose task it is to prevent and police illicit 'goods'. Such characterisations are more than simple metaphors I have attached to these actors in a border play. They are terms that I have heard repeated by those involved in the policing of Europe's borders, at the headquarters of Frontex (the EU's Border and Coast Guard Agency) and by border police in the field.[3]

The pivotal role of people smugglers in enticing migrants to make journeys, or worse, trafficking people to their deaths on unsafe routes over land and sea is a constant refrain from Brussels to Canberra.[4] But, as Moisés Naím somewhat cynically observed when he pitched organised crime as the threat majeure: borders are big business and organised criminal networks are often more skilled in finding, testing and exploiting gaps in border security than the police are in either stopping networks or securing borders.[5] In discussing the current relationship between smugglers and the increase in border controls, Jeremy Harding recalls one of the opening exchanges in *Casablanca* that also touches on a key idea in humanitarianism known as the lesser evil, in which there are no good solutions, only less bad ones.[6] It is 1942 and Casablanca is full of refugees fleeing the horrors of Nazism. Peter Lorre's Ugarte asks Humphrey Bogart's Rick to mind two sets of safe-conduct papers until his clients arrive, saying to Rick: 'You despise me don't you? You object to the kind of business I do, huh? But think of all those poor refugees who must rot in this place if I didn't help them. But that's not so bad. Through ways of my own, I provide them with exit visas'. To which Rick

---

3   P Pallister-Wilkins, 'The Humanitarian Politics of European Border Policing: Frontex and Border Police in Evros', *International Political Sociology* 9(1), 2015.

4   B Frelick, 'Tone Down the Scaremongering Over Migrants'. New York: Human Rights Watch. 2015, hrw.org.

5   M Naím, *Illicit: How Smugglers, Traffickers and Copycats are Hijacking the Global Economy*, London: William Heinemann, 2006.

6   For a comprehensive discussion and critique of the lesser evil, see E Weizman, *The Least of All Possible Evils: Humanitarian Violence from Arendt to Gaza*, London: Verso, 2012. For a liberal defence of the lesser evil and its importance in a post-9/11 age more specifically, see M Ignatieff, *The Lesser Evil: Political Ethics in an Age of Terror*, Princeton, NJ: Princeton University Press, 2004.

replies: 'For a price, Ugarte, for a price.' Here, in Ugarte's world full of refugees and the controls made up of passports, visas and lists, it is the organised criminal networks who provide a lesser-evil service 'for a price' to migrants for whom other avenues have been closed.[7]

But, in the world of law enforcement and border policing, even if, off the record, officials will acknowledge the complementary relationship between prohibition and organised crime, smugglers are the bad guys. In the work of European border police, both in the Warsaw HQ of Frontex and at the external borders of the EU in Greece and Italy, the term 'bad guys' communicates quickly and simply 'what the border police do'. 'Bad guys' references a form of what William Walters calls 'anti-policy' designed to combat bad things.[8] The use of the term 'bad guys' is especially noticeable among those who work in Risk Analysis and out in the field of operations, where stopping these 'bad guys' is, I was told, the 'most fundamental part' of 'what we do'.[9]

However, this discourse of 'bad guys', and its partner 'good guys', is interspersed with humanitarian considerations, so that the job of border policing becomes not only one of regular law enforcement but one that elides with humanitarianism. During my time interviewing border police and observing the work of those at Frontex HQ, at national police ministries, and in the field, I was repeatedly informed that the job of the border police was not to simply stop the 'bad guys' exploiting weaknesses in member state and European border controls but to prevent the bad guys exploiting migrants for their own criminal ends. I have been told repeated stories about organised criminal networks exploiting the vulnerabilities of migrants and harming them in multiple ways, so much so that it has become a familiar script in a well-rehearsed play involving: overloaded migrant boats crossing the Mediterranean; leaving migrants to freeze to death; forcing migrants from boats at gunpoint; deliberately scuppering vessels to interrupt interception efforts or to ensure rescue by European agencies and thus delivery of their human cargo; or, most routinely, exploitation through the large sums of money migrants pay to facilitate their journeys. In all of these stories, however, the migrant is a

7   J Harding, *Border Vigils: Keeping Migrants out of the Rich World*, London: Verso, 2012, 14.

8   W Walters, 'Anti-Policy and Anti-Politics: Critical Reflections on Certain Schemes to Govern Bad Things', *European Journal of Cultural Studies* 11(3), 2008.

9   Pallister-Wilkins, 'The Humanitarian Politics of European Border Policing'.

victim, cynically exploited by the criminals for their own personal gain. They have no speaking part in this play; they are the spoils in a heroic fight between the bad guys of organised crime and the good guys of law enforcement. Aside from creating heroes and villains and staking out powerful subject positions for the heroic storytellers, this discursive construction of the organised criminal networks as 'bad guys' has another logic. It calls upon a humanitarian ideal premised on a victim and a perpetrator.

When I have pushed those officials who reference the 'fight against bad guys', I ask them that if they are fighting 'bad guys', does this make them the 'good guys'? While no one has ever wholly rejected the nomenclature of 'good guys' (who would?), I am usually told that their job is more nuanced. In nuancing their work, the border police recognise 'how people like me' see their work as uncaring, cruel and inhumane, because 'all we see is the stopping', the 'detaining', the 'deporting' and we 'read bad things in those human rights reports'. But they are keen to stress that the violence or the threat of violence underpinning their mandate is a regulated and limited violence, and that the evil they are often perceived as doing is a lesser evil than that perpetuated by the 'bad guys', who do not have the same codes of conduct in their exploitation of migrants' misery.

The border police are good guys then, but good guys who believe that what they are doing, while necessary, is tempered by the rule of law and a liberal order that respects the right to life. And their work, as terrible as it can appear, is better than the alternative of a world where the bad guys are left unchecked, free to exploit whomever they will. Therefore, they are good guys in relation to the bigger evil of the organised criminal networks. Of course, this narrative spectacularly fails to recognise or even consider the structures that enable bad guys to take advantage of migrants as they attempt to circumvent border restrictions, let alone consider an alternative world of fewer or abolished border controls and a subsequent destruction of the smugglers' business model.

In describing their work in terms of law enforcement that references the lesser evil of much humanitarian work, border police and the officials back at HQ actively depoliticise their work. They further depoliticise their role and reinforce the notion that their work is about policing and not politics by stressing how they are carrying out the wishes of politicians and citizens across the EU, and that it is in these spheres that political discussions of their work should take place. They do not do politics. However, policing and borders are political. In removing themselves from politics, border police officers work to reinforce border control as a form of a necessary and uncontested lesser evil. Presenting border policing as an arena free of politics adheres to the relationship between the violence that underpins borders and structures unequal mobility, and the concomitant alleviation of such violence via a humanitarian approach to protecting life. Promoting their work through lesser-evil rhetoric and appealing to wider humanitarian approaches to saving lives shifts discussion of border control, the violence it produces and any subsequent attempt to address such violence to a discussion about preventing 'bad things', and a swift restitution of normality that importantly fails to address the political underpinnings.[10]

The policing of 'bad things' by the good guys of the border police may conjure visions of heroic endeavours more reminiscent of police work in films in which the police are 'distant, exotic, and heroic'.[11] However, in my research of the everyday work of the border police, I found that the policing of bad things caused by the bad guys also contains the mundane and the absurd. When I was in Evros, Greece, shadowing the work of the Greek border police and the Frontex Joint Operation Poseidon Land, I fell into conversation with a Greek police officer working with the border control division in the Orestiada district. As we were walking the borderline where the Greek government were constructing their 12km border fence, we were accompanied on our journey by a Turkish farmer ploughing his field on the other side of the fence. Over the drone of his tractor, the officer, who had risen swiftly through the ranks to become a local commander, exchanged pleasantries with the farmer – 'I speak some Turkish', they informed me – and asked him how things were. The farmer replied by saying his family was well and that his crops were doing much better now that people were not using his fields to hide from the police before attempting to cross into Greece.

---

10   P Pallister-Wilkins, 'Humanitarian Rescue/Sovereign Capture and the Policing of Possible Responses to Violent Borders', *Global Policy* 8(S1), 2017. See also, J Jeandesboz and P Pallister-Wilkins, 'Crisis, Routine, Consolidation: The Politics of the Mediterranean Migration Crisis', *Mediterranean Politics* 21(2), 2016, 316–20.

11   D Fassin, *Enforcing Order: An Ethnography of Urban Policing*, London: Polity Press, 2013, and Pallister-Wilkins, 'The Humanitarian Politics of European Border Policing'.

The officer went on to explain to me how this part of the border (the only part of Greece's land border with Turkey not marked by the Evros river) was simply fields intersected by the dusty track that we were walking along before the fence was built. They explained to me how they knew the farmer well and how their family had come from 'that side' before the founding of the Turkish Republic in the aftermath of the First World War. 'We're probably cousins', they joked, waving at the farmer. 'Doesn't that make all this seem a bit silly?' I asked. The officer agreed but explained that their family had been in the police for generations and that, with their constant responsibility for the border, it was a good, secure job in an area with little else but farming. For this officer, the border was their source of employment, and the prevention of border crossing by life seekers was the main focus of their daily work. 'But, of course, my father and grandfather did this work for Greece, I do it now for the European Union. This is the front line and I have a duty to protect this part of the border on behalf of the rest of Europe.' They stopped and turned to me: 'But I'm not a bad person. I know that's what many people think. There were journalists from your country[12] here last month and they kept asking me questions about how I stop migrants, why I stop migrants, how it makes me feel, if I feel bad, if I read the reports from the human rights groups that criticise us? You have to understand that sometimes it's very hard. I know that we can be seen as heartless.'

This officer continued by stressing that they were 'a human with feelings and were not heartless' and that it was 'impossible not to be moved by the things that you see and to want to reach out and help'. Our conversation neatly encapsulated what critical security studies scholar Claudia Aradau has identified as the dual discourse of 'risk and pity' in border control and law enforcement.[13] The officer went on: 'One night we were patrolling this part of the border, it was the winter and it was very cold, when we spotted a group of migrants waiting in the field there, across

---

12   My country, in this instance, being the Netherlands. I subsequently watched the documentary made by those who had been to Evros a month before me and was shocked by the officer's hostile attitude displayed towards Bram Vermeulen, the journalist asking questions on camera. The questions hinted at judgement and complicity in the work of this particular officer. See *Langs de Grenzen van Turkije*, made by NRC Weekend and VPRO and aired on VPRO, 21 October 2012; available at npostart.nl and (as 'Along the Borders of Turkey') at youtuveb.com.

13   C Aradau, 'The Perverse Politics of Four-Letter Words: Risk and Pity in the Securitisation of Human Trafficking', *Millennium* 33(2), 2004, 251–78.

the border where they had been left by the smugglers. They were waiting for our patrol to pass, waiting to cross, but we saw them and stopped them. We obviously couldn't let them cross into Greece. But we could not cross to get them either. They did not know where else to go because they had been left there by the smugglers and they were so close to the border, five metres away, they were waiting in the field and they were freezing cold and thirsty. We couldn't cross to them so we threw them some blankets and some water. There were not enough blankets to go around so we tried to explain to them that they would be warmer if they grouped together like penguins and shared the blankets between them. They had been left there in the freezing cold by the smugglers, they did not know where to go, they were scared to go back. We waited, guarding them for hours.'[14]

This apparent standoff ended when the migrants eventually decided to cross into Greece and be arrested by the border police, whereupon they were taken to the Fylakio detention centre, infamous at the time for its poor conditions.[15] This incident, as absurd as it seems with discussions about penguins and the ridiculous image it conjures of Greek border police guarding a small huddle of people in a field on the other side of a border that they, the police, cannot cross, is illustrative of the wider relationship between caring and controlling in both humanitarianism and policing. Furthermore, it shows the tension between policing mobile people and protecting fixed space. The language used by the officer to recount the story, and the actions of the officers themselves, were influenced by humanitarian compassion while also being a form of humanitarian performance. The border police, by giving blankets and water, showed what they believed to be a concern for the welfare of the migrants while simultaneously denying them entry to Greece. When the migrants did enter, they were stopped and arrested, thereby fulfilling the border police's role as securers of the European border.

The presence of this dual logic of care and control should not come as a surprise to those familiar with the political sociologies of

---

14   This quote is also found in Pallister-Wilkins, 'The Humanitarian Politics of European Border Policing', 61.

15   Human Rights Watch, *The EU's Dirty Hands: Frontex Involvement in Ill-Treatment of Migrant Detainees in Greece*, 2011, hrw.org.

policing more broadly. Policing has a long history of both upholding law and order and providing care, both with the aim of creating and maintaining overall societal well-being. Miriam Ticktin, an anthropologist specialising in humanitarianism and its relationship to migration, has argued that humanitarianism and policing are two sides of the same coin, 'intimately linked, with policing often accompanied by a gesture toward the humane, and toward the ethical, where force is justified in the name of peace and right'.[16] In turn, as the cultural sociologist Jane Zavisca explains, the narrative of good guys and bad guys also relies on the victimisation of migrants, who are 'preyed' on and 'lured' into unsafe situations by smugglers. This narrative in turn reinforces the good guy/bad guy dichotomy by 'depicting border police as humane shepherds tending to a flock'.[17] This image of the shepherd has a long history in humanitarian thought and action. Known as pastoralism, this idea underpins modern humanitarian practice, which sees the world as its space of operation, borders as mere lines on a map and their flock as the whole of humanity.[18] According to Zavisca, the depiction of border police as shepherds tending to their flock 'reinforces the humanity of the Border Patrol as "saviours"'.[19]

But what of the life seekers in this good guy/bad guy narrative? Who are they as the victims and the subjects of protection? Where are they? What happens to the lives and stories of those border crossers whose mobility must be policed and in turn whose lives must be saved? The discourse and practice of 'good guys' and 'bad guys' at the border renders life seekers as objects to be controlled or cared for, at best, or invisible, at

---

16 M Ticktin, 'Policing and Humanitarianism in France: Immigration and the Turn to Law as State of Exception', *Interventions: International Journal of Postcolonial Studies* 7(3), 2005, 359.

17 JR Zavisca, 'Metaphorical Imagery in News Reporting on Migrant Deaths', in R Rubio-Goldsmith et al, eds, *¿No Vale Nada la Vida? La Vida No Vale Nada: Political Intersections of Migration and Death in the U.S.-Mexico Border*, Tucson: University of Arizona Press, 2016, 167–89.

18 On pastoralism in humanitarianism, see D Fassin, *Humanitarian Reason: A Moral History of the Present*, Berkeley: University of California Press, 2012.

19 Zavisca, 'Metaphorical Imagery in News Reporting on Migrant Deaths'. For a view about smugglers from migrants themselves, see N Perkowski and V Squire, 'The Anti-Policy of European Anti-Smuggling as a Site of Contestation in the Mediterranean Migration "Crisis"', *Journal of Ethnic and Migration Studies* 45(12), 2018.

worst. Treating life seekers as the objects of care and/or control cloaks the reasons why people are seeking life in the first case. By treating life seekers as a 'problem' within the logic of policing bad things, they can be reduced to defective objects, without agency, to be dealt with through care and control. As a 'bad' thing to be policed, life seekers become stripped of their humanity, their names, stories, hopes, and dreams. Meanwhile, the deeper politics of why they are seeking life – wars, injustice, inequality, human rights abuses, endemic poverty and lack of opportunities, sustained more often than not by the relatively peaceful and prosperous Global North – go unobserved, unremarked upon and unchallenged.

Through this dehumanisation and obfuscation, life seekers remain only a problem to be addressed through a series of interventions as opposed to a living, breathing embodiment of global injustice. An end to such global injustice would require considerably more than the liberal, technocratic and humanitarian solutions that are currently deployed that ensure life seekers remain (mostly) alive but also politically invisible. And, like the facile 'solution' to gun violence in the United States, the discourse of good guys stopping bad guys ignores the elephant in the room. In this case it is not the lack of gun control, the holy grail of the Second Amendment in US culture, and a history of racist violence, but instead the network of racist global border controls that create and compound unequal mobility.

Extending the Line

The need to save lives stakes out powerful positions for law enforcement operatives and state officials, while reducing life seekers to mere objects needing to be saved from smugglers. This need to save lives, inscribed into the everyday working practices of border and coastguard agents, has an impact on where the border actually is. That is, such work has geographic, spatial effects that result in borders no longer being found at the edges of territory. The idea that the border is more than a line on a map, separating two countries, is not new to political geographers. The argument that the border is everywhere, following the bodies of those the border seeks to include in or exclude from the privileges of citizenship, has almost become clichéd among border scholars.[20] However, the extension of the border beyond or before the line marking the edge of territory, where most border policing was traditionally assumed to take place, happens through specific practices, including those involved in saving lives.

In late April 2015, the Director of Amnesty International UK, Kate Allen, made an impassioned plea for an increase in EU rescue efforts in the Central Mediterranean. This came after the Italian Navy's Mare Nostrum efforts to rescue life seekers had been wound down the previous year, and while increasing numbers of people were setting off from Libyan shores. Allen argued that the EU needed to step up to the plate and do more:

> The EU's response does not go far enough. Europe's leaders have committed more resources, but the geographical limit in place means that those resources are still not enough. The yellow on this map [see below] is the area covered by Triton – the border patrol that the EU announced increased support for, following their crisis talks. But the orange is where the majority of shipwrecks happen. The two do not match up. The red shows the area covered by Italy's search and rescue mission – Operation Mare Nostrum – which rescued tens of thousands. But other EU governments, including the UK, refused to support it and it ended last October. We won't stop pushing until leaders agree to the search and rescue operation beyond the 30 nautical mile limit currently in place. Unless the boats go further, we can expect more men, women and children to drown this summer.[21]

---

20   Paradigmatic work in border studies and political geography that has led to the idea that 'borders are everywhere' include: L Amoore, 'Biometric Borders: Governing Mobilities in the War on Terror', *Political Geography* 25, 2006; M Coleman, 'Immigration Geopolitics Beyond the Mexico-US border', *Antipode* 39(1), 2007, 54–76; D Lyon, 'The Border is Everywhere: ID Cards, Surveillance and the Other', in E Zureik and MB Salter eds, *Global Surveillance and Policing: Borders, Security and Identity*, London: Willan, 2006; C Rumford, 'Rethinking European Spaces: Territory, Borders, Governance', *Comparative European Politics* 4, 2006, 127–40; C Rumford, 'Towards a Multiperspectival Study of Borders', *Geopolitics* 17(4), 2012.

21   K Allen, 'Mediterranean Crisis: "We Don't Let People Drown" ', Amnesty International UK, 29 April 2015, amnesty.org.uk.

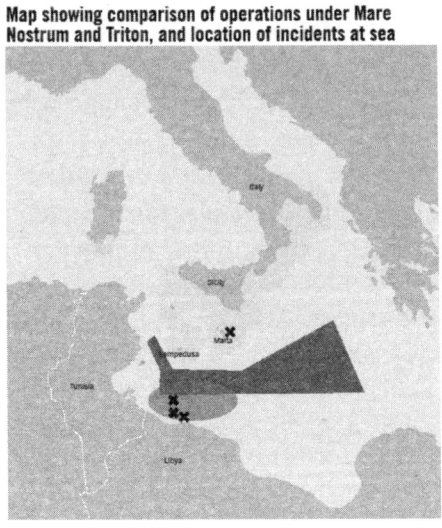

Map from
Amnesty International Report calling for increased
rescues. © Amnesty International

Allen's request is interesting for a number of reasons, especially in regard to the demand that Europe use border control missions for the purposes of saving lives and, in so doing, extend its efforts beyond European territorial waters. As can be clearly seen in the map that was used to illustrate Allen's argument, Joint Operation Triton, the EU-funded border policing operation co-ordinated by Frontex was restricted to intervening in the territorial waters of Italy and Malta only. Meanwhile, the Italian Navy's Mare Nostrum operation, operating officially as a search and rescue operation – and not a border policing operation – was able to operate in international waters under the Safety of Lives at Sea (SOLAS) directive. What Allen was calling for in the need to save lives was an extension of the zones of European operation in the Mediterranean and the extension of European efforts into international waters. Through the worthy and just demand to save lives, Allen was asking for an alteration of where European interventions occur. This request for a change in the geography of Europe's border resulted in the hardening of the border and further endangerment of lives.[22]

---

22   Pallister-Wilkins, 'Humanitarian Rescue/Sovereign Capture'; J Watkins, 'Bordering Borderscapes: Australia's Use of Humanitarian Aid and Border Security Support to Immobilise Asylum Seekers', *Geopolitics* 22(4), 2017, 958–83.

Italy's Operation Mare Nostrum (Our Sea) began in October 2013 as an ostensibly humanitarian mission of search and rescue. In the framing of those like Kate Allen, who called for more SAR missions, Mare Nostrum represented a humanitarian logic of rescue that was in contrast and opposition to the control purposes of border policing. But such a framing of care versus control, of humanitarian SAR missions standing in contrast to more traditional border policing missions designed to apprehend and capture, is far too simplistic. Migrant safety and border security in the Central Mediterranean instead became two mutually achievable goals. With Mare Nostrum framed as a humanitarian mission, migrants were intercepted at sea and came under the immediate 'sovereign gaze' of the Italian state. Finger-printed, photographed and with their details uploaded onto databases, those rescued were also subject to the full power of Italian and by extension EU border control. As political geographer Paolo Cuttitta has documented, Mare Nostrum was not only an Italian naval mission. Alongside Italian sailors, members of the Italian coastguard, Carabinieri, and the Guardia di Finanza (the main institution responsible for border policing in Italy) contributed with personnel and hardware.[23] Meanwhile, legal scholar, Violeta Moreno-Lax, has mapped the evolution of maritime responses to the 'migration crisis' in the Mediterranean and calls these processes 'rescue through interdiction'.[24] This has led Cuttitta and Moreno-Lax to the same conclusion as me, that Mare Nostrum was as much a mission of identifying and screening migrants, as it was one of humanitarian concern.[25]

Meanwhile, looking at who funded the Mare Nostrum operation undermines the idea that the operation ever sat apart from wider European Union border control efforts. As well as the Italian government, the EU contributed €1.8 million to the operation from their External Borders Fund.[26] Furthermore, the wider political narrative at

---

23 P Cuttitta, 'Humanitarianism and Migration in the Mediterranean Borderscape: The Italian-North African Border between Sea Patrols and Integration Measures', in C Brambilla, J Laine and Gianluca Bocchi eds, *Borderscaping: Imaginations and Practices of Border Making*, London: Routledge, 2016.

24 V Moreno-Lax, 'The EU Humanitarian Border and the Securitization of Human Rights: The "Rescue-Through-Interdiction/Rescue-Without-Protection" Paradigm', *Journal of Common Market Studies* 56(1), 2018, 119–40.

25 Pallister-Wilkins, 'Humanitarian Rescue/Sovereign Capture'.

26 European Commission, 'Frontex Joint Operation "Triton" – Concerted Efforts to Manage Migration in the Central Mediterranean', Press Release, 7 October 2014,

the time articulated humanitarian concerns in response to migratory movements across the Mediterranean Sea and elsewhere. The November 2015 Valletta Summit on Migration's political declaration stated the following, with bold in the original:

> We are deeply concerned by the sharp increase in flows of refugees, asylum seekers and irregular migrants which entails suffering, abuse and exploitation, particularly for children and women, and unacceptable loss of life in the desert or at sea. Such an increase places the most affected countries under severe pressure, with serious humanitarian consequences and security challenges. **We agree that the first priority in this context is to save lives** and do everything necessary to rescue and protect the migrants whose lives are at risk.[27]

The need to save lives is boldly stressed as being the first priority, and such a priority is then clearly linked to the politics of emergency that suggests saving lives entails and subsequently enables 'everything necessary to rescue and protect the migrants whose lives are at risk'.[28] In looking at the role of mobility, death, and rescue in the Mediterranean, sociologist Rogier van Reekum argues that humanitarian concerns and greater knowledge of suffering has collapsed what he calls the 'firewall' between rescue and border policing. With such rescues being possible through a combination of what is possible (for example, the use of naval resources for search and rescue/interception) and who is made responsible, or what van Reekum calls responseable (those capable of saving, like the Italian navy).[29] Here, the architectures of border control, such as the European Border Surveillance System (EUROSUR)[30] make visible not only irregular border crossing but also the suffering and death such irregular crossing produces.

---

europa.eu.

27 European Council, *Political Declaration Valletta Migration Summit 11–12 November, EUCO 809/15, Brussels*, 2015, consilium.europa.eu.

28 Ibid.

29 R van Reekum, 'The Mediterranean: Migration Corridor, Border Spectacle, Ethical Landscape', *Mediterranean Politics* 21(2), 2016, 336–41.

30 For more on EUROSUR, see J Rijpma and M Vermeulen, 'EUROSUR: Saving Lives or Building Borders?', *European Security* 24(3), 2015, 454–72, and J Jeandesboz, 'EU Border Control: Violence, Capture and Apparatus', in Y Jansen, R Celikates and J de Bloois eds, *The Irregularization of Migration in Contemporary Europe: Detention, Deportation, Drowning*, London: Rowman & Littlefield, 2015, 87–102.

Such knowledge of suffering compels powerful actors – responseable actors in van Reekum's terminology – to intervene to save lives.

Staying with the Valletta Summit, its Action Plan is clear on how the need to save lives not only shifts Europe's responsibility for life into the Mediterranean, but into countries beyond Europe. The Action Plan talks of enhancing the humanitarian capacities of 'host countries' and commits to the implementation of initiatives in the Horn of Africa and North Africa by mid-2016. In this, the EU and its asylum service office EASO are involved, along with the UNHCR, in conducting training and improving asylum facilities in 'countries of origin, transit and destination'.[31]

Meanwhile, the EU has developed further tools and instruments for extending its control of mobility into African space, including the Horn of Africa Regional Action Plan and the accompanying Khartoum Process, which aim to tackle displacement, irregular migration and migrant smuggling. Alongside this, the EU Emergency Trust Fund for Africa, or to give it its full title, 'The European Union Emergency Trust Fund for Stability and Addressing Root Causes of Irregular Migration and Displaced Persons in Africa' (EUTF for Africa), is attempting to do what its name suggests through the use of a range of practices, including the provision of humanitarian assistance. The slick website of the EUTF for Africa says it aims

> . . . to provide emergency protection, life-saving assistance, evacuation to refugees in Libya in the framework of the Evacuation Transit Mechanism (ETM). Furthermore, it will contribute to provide resettlement and complementary pathways for refugees living in/or transiting Niger, Burkina Faso, Cameroon and Chad.[32]

In practice, this has resulted in the EUTF for Africa providing €40 million to Sudan under the Better Migration Management program – it is believed that the €5 million of these funds allocated to the judiciary and law enforcement have gone to the Rapid Support Forces (RSF). The RSF is a

---

31 European Council, *Action Plan Valletta Migration Summit 11-12 November, EUCO 810/15, Brussels*, 2015, consilium.europa.eu.

32 EUTF for Africa, Protection and Sustainable Solutions for Migrants and Refugees along the Central Mediterranean Route, 2017, ec.europa.eu.

counterinsurgency force that has grown out of the Janjaweed militia famous for carrying out the Sudanese regime's genocidal counterinsurgency policies in Darfur during the 2000s.[33] Alongside Sudan, the EUTF has implemented a €46 million programme to fund and train the Libyan Border and Coast Guard to rescue/intercept the vessels of life seekers as they head to Europe.[34] This €46 million from the EUTF is increased by Italy also pledging financial and technical assistance to Libya with the estimated total amount pledged until 2023 standing at €285 million, some of which is going towards a planned search and rescue centre.[35]

Alongside the use of European funds to facilitate Sudanese, Libyan and other African states' border control and rescue efforts, the border is also extended through reforming EU border control itself. In making the case for the new European Union Border and Coast Guard Agency, the new and improved Frontex 2.0, the EU Commission produced a handy fact sheet full of infographics, linking increased numbers of life seekers crossing European borders, their protection needs and the ability for the new agency to 'send liaison officers and launch joint operations with neighbouring third countries, including operating on their territory'.[36] The infographic visualises this clearly with a map including North Africa, Turkey and the Middle East. What this means, in practice, is EU experts and equipment operating in non-European territory for the purposes of policing European borders and containing life seekers.[37] And such activities occur alongside and through complementary narratives of rescue.

Though Italy's Mare Nostrum operation ended in 2014, according to Chatham House in 2018, Italian naval vessels are back in Libyan waters to rescue life seekers through the interception of their vessels, and in

---

33   S Baldo, 'Border Control from Hell: How the EU's Migration Partnerships Legitimizes Sudan's "Militia State" ', *The Enough Project*, April 2017, enoughproject.org.

34   European Commission, *Press Release, EU Trust Fund for Africa Adopts €46 Million Programme to Support Integrated Migration and Border Management in Libya*, Brussels, 28 July 2017, europa.eu.

35   N Nielsen, 'EU and Italy Put Aside €285m to Boost Libyan Coast Guard', *EU Observer*, 29 November 2017, euobserver.com.

36   European Commission, *Securing Europe's External Borders: A European Border and Coast Guard Agency*, 2015.

37   For more on how this externalisation works and what it means for life seekers and the societies in which practices of externalisation take place, see D Howden and G Zandonini, 'Niger: Europe's Migration Laboratory', *Refugees Deeply*, 2018, newsdeeply. com.

turn disrupt the business model of smugglers.[38] Therefore, it appears as if the 'geographical limit' that Kate Allen referred to as impeding the possibilities of rescue is no longer an impediment. Through the imbrication of universal concerns for life and exclusive and exclusionary border control practices, the possibilities for rescue have been extended, politically and spatially, with the geographical limit being extended almost exponentially to encompass the possibility of interventions across Africa, through the EUTF for Africa, and beyond. The securing of life comes to support and consolidate the securing of privileged spaces through paternalistic European rescues that are intended to exclude and contain; as I have argued elsewhere, 'to care at a distance for those who are not quite equal and never will be'.[39] In a world where the need to save lives has been mobilised and works alongside and through border controls that produce and protect privilege, interventions that act to both rescue and intercept can conceivably happen wherever a life seeker is at risk, and is thus without geographical limit.

It should be noted that extending the possibility for interception through rescue is not Europe's preserve alone. For many years, the US Customs and Border Patrol (CBP) resisted calls for more humanitarian-informed policies to reduce the border deaths caused by their 'prevention through deterrence' policies that purposefully used the harsh elements of the desert environment.[40] These policies came into existence in 1994 while in 1998 the BORSTAR (Search, Trauma and Rescue) unit of the CBP was created. The implementation of the prevention through deterrence policy had an immediate knock-on effect on the numbers of lives lost in spite of the subsequent creation of BORSTAR. That trend held until the early 2000s, when, as the political geographer Jill Williams argues, there was a realisation that care could be mobilised for the purposes of control. According to Williams: 'Rather than simply ignoring or dismissing deaths, what emerges in the early 2000s is a much more complicated geopolitical discourse that reconciles border enforcement with transnational human rights by discursively linking migrant

---

38   A Gray Meral, *Migration Deals Risk Undermining Global Refugee Protection*, 13 April 2018, chathamhouse.org.

39   P Pallister-Wilkins, 'Hotspots and the Geographies of Humanitarianism', *Environment and Planning D: Society and Space* 38(6), 2020, 991–1008.

40   V Squire, 'Desert "Trash": Posthumanism, Border Struggles, and Humanitarian Politics', *Political Geography* 39, 2014, 11–21.

safety to greater border security'. Williams points to the arguments made by then CBP Commissioner Robert Bonner in 2004 arguing that 'a secure border is a safe border, and a safe border saves lives', resulting in what Williams calls a safety/security nexus – and what I have referred to as care and control – in which 'greater border security is the solution to, not the cause of, migrant deaths'.[41]

The use of humanitarian concerns to restructure what intervention becomes possible, and where that intervention becomes possible, is what Eyal Weizman refers to when he discusses the role humanitarianism plays in structuring not just life-saving in response to violence, but the tools and limits of violence itself.[42] In the context of life saving in the Mediterranean or at the US-Mexico border, life-saving occurs in response to border violence, while simultaneously working to (re)structure border violence through underpinning a range of new technologies and techniques designed to simultaneously rescue and capture. As Francisco Cantú makes clear at the start of this chapter, despicable acts of vandalism and violence against the very things migrants need to stay alive are carried out to save lives through pressuring life seekers into giving themselves up. Such life-saving thus becomes a way of policing the border while (re)inscribing its violent character more deeply with every water barrel drained, every pile of food set alight and every blanket pissed on.

Deepening the Line

As well as extending the geographical limit of life saving, or potentially abolishing it all together, the humanitarian concern in border control also deepens existing border policing practices. The Netherlands is at the 'cutting edge' of such deepening.[43] Early proponents and adopters of what is known as Integrated Border Management (IBM), the Netherlands

---

41   J Williams, 'The Safety/Security Nexus and the Humanitarianisation of Border Enforcement', *The Geographical Journal* 182(1), 2014, 31, and Pallister-Wilkins, 'The Humanitarian Politics of European Border Policing'.

42   Weizman, *The Least of All Possible Evils*.

43   See P Mutsaers, 'An Ethnographic Study of the Policing of Internal Borders in the Netherlands: Synergies between Criminology and Anthropology', *British Journal of Criminology* 54, 2014.

has integrated a number of separate security agencies for the purposes of border security. In the shadow of 2015's 'refugee crisis' and during the Dutch presidency of the European Union, the Netherlands launched their new Border Security Teams (BSTs), Grensbewaking in Dutch, made up of units from the Dutch Border Police (KMar), the Sea Ports Police, members of the Royal Marines, the Royal Land Forces, the Commando Service Centre, interpreters from the Immigration and Naturalisation Service (IND), and experts from the Repatriation and Departure Service (DT&V). The BSTs are presented as a 'complex solution to a complex problem' and attempt to both secure the borders of the EU and secure the lives of refugees and migrants.[44]

The BSTs are illustrative of what criminologist Bethan Loftus has called the 'intensification, deepening, and diversification' of border policing.[45] The institutional complexity of the BSTs is supposed to, according to those responsible for envisioning them, reflect the complexity of current migratory phenomena.[46] They also continue what, in the early 2000s, international relations scholar Peter Andreas called the militarisation of border control, bringing Dutch military units into the border policing assemblage.[47] But what is interesting here is why such a 'complex solution to a complex problem' has been realised. Andreas argued that the militarisation of border security has gradually taken place in response to what he calls 'clandestine transnational actors': the bad guy smugglers and the invisible life seekers already discussed. However, in Andreas's formulation, the militarisation of border control in response to 'clandestine transnational actors' is focused solely on securing borders and territory and containing mobile, transnational, clandestine actors in a world of increased risk and uncertainty. What

---

44 Koninklijke Marechaussee, *Factsheet: Border Security Team Chios*, Den Haag: Ministerie van Defensie, 2016. See also P Pallister-Wilkins and J Smeekes, 'The Dutch Border Security Team in Chios and the Intensification, Diversification and Deepening of Border Policing' in Theodoros Fouskas ed., *Immigrants and Refugees in Times of Crisis*, European Public Law Organization (EPLO) Publications, 2021.

45 B Loftus, 'Border Regimes and the Sociology of Policing', *Policing and Society* 25(1), 2015, 115–25.

46 See Marechaussee, *Factsheet*; and Pallister-Wilkins and Smeekes, 'The Dutch Border Security Team in Chios and the Intensification, Diversification and Deepening of Border Policing'.

47 P Andreas, 'Redrawing the Line: Borders and Security in the Twenty-First Century', *International Security* 28(2), 2003, 78–111.

has changed, and what the BSTs are representative of, is the addition of the need to save lives within this changing border security assemblage. In addressing these changes, the then Minister of Defence Jeanine Hennis-Plasschaert was keen to stress, 'the refugees are not our enemies. People smugglers are.'[48]

In discussions held with those responsible for the BSTs at the Ministries of Defence, and Justice and Security, and with commanders of deployed BSTs in Chios and Lesvos, the need for a new, flexible and diverse response was a repeated refrain, resting on the foundation of a two-fold reality in deployment: one border control, one humanitarian.[49] I was repeatedly told that the BSTs need to be complex not just to address the changing nature of migratory routes, pressures and quick-witted people smugglers. They also have to be 'ecosystems' made up of a range of agencies carrying out a range of tasks because their responsibilities extend into caring for those life seekers caught in their operations. These caring tasks extend from carrying out rescues at sea and ensuring camp security, to a range of other 'humanitarian'-related tasks in between, including co-ordinating humanitarian distribution efforts by non-state humanitarian actors.

While the Dutch might be at the forefront of the deepening of border policing within Europe, perhaps influencing the wider European Union approach to carrying out effective integrated border management, they are not alone. For all the success of calls for new, technocratic, complex solutions to complex problems, such changes at the European Union level also rest on a bedrock of rescue. The 2015 'refugee crisis', like all crises, was productive, bringing the BSTs into being and giving weight to calls for and the eventual birth of a new and improved Frontex. This new Frontex has a mandate that now explicitly makes provision for 'search and rescue operations', whereas previously such missions had remained the responsibility of individual member states. Here, deepening the policing of the border not only means the inclusion of new activities in the daily life of border police and new conglomerations of actors and agencies, but also a deepening of the

---

48 See Government of the Netherlands, *Dutch Naval Vessel to Join NATO Operation in Aegean Sea*, March 2016, government.nl.

49 See Pallister-Wilkins and Smeekes, 'The Dutch Border Security Team in Chios and the Intensification, Diversification and Deepening of Border Policing'.

EU's pockets, as another handy infographic of piles and bags of money makes clear.

The need for search and rescue, therefore, has an impact on the mandate of the new European Border and Coast Guard agency. But it also affects the EU's relations with its member states and structures joint cooperation. As an illustration, the EU's 2015 Internal Security Fund's National Programme for Greece is explicit in stating the need for investment and enhancement – or what Loftus might call 'intensification, deepening, and diversification'[50] – in the Hellenic Coast Guard (HCG) to better rescue those at sea. 'In order to continue protecting efficiently the external south-eastern maritime borders of the EU controlling border crossings and saving lives at sea, the renewal of the operational fleet of the HCG is of utmost importance.'[51] The EU Internal Security Fund National Programme is clear that the 'protection of human life at sea is a priority not only for GR [Greece] but also for the EU'.[52] The deepening of Greek capacity involves the provision of two new 'Coastal Patrol Vessels' (CPV) at a cost of €27m. According to the Internal Security Fund National Programme, these CPVs will have 'over 2 days autonomy and a range of about 1,500 nm' and are 'equipped with state-of-the-art surveillance equipment for day and night observation as well as the appropriate Search & Rescue equipment to cope with emergency SAR situations'. Moreover, the CPVs will have a faster boat 'for tactical or SAR operations and shall have the capability to operate under demanding weather conditions'.[53] Greece's surveillance capacity must also be deepened in order to make them 'responseable', as van Reekum would have it,[54] with the Internal Security Fund providing €540,000 for a Thermal Vision Vehicle equipped with a maritime radar with the specific capability to detect 'small moving targets on the sea at a minimum range of 5nm',[55] or in other words the small, rubber dinghies most commonly used by life seekers crossing the Aegean.

---

50   Loftus, 'Border Regimes and the Sociology of Policing'.
51   EU Internal Security Fund's National Programme for Greece, 2015, 19, statewatch.org.
52   Ibid., 14.
53   Ibid., 20.
54   Reekum, 'The Mediterranean'.
55   EU Internal Security Fund's National Programme for Greece, 20, 2015.

To 'allow the Union to grant protection and humanitarian assistance in a swift manner to those in need',[56] the European Commission has allocated €506m to the Asylum Migration Integration Fund (AMIF) and the Internal Security Fund. When this is coupled with further contributions from European member states, as well as private donations to NGOs, it is estimated around €751m have been allocated for life seekers in Greece. The majority of this €751m has been used to meet the needs of, at the time of this writing, over 60,000 people who have become stranded in Greece since the implementation of the EU-Turkey 'Deal' that prevents onwards movement and uses the Aegean Islands as effective prisons.[57] The EU and Greece have spent most of this money on increased border policing and providing basic needs. Additionally, money has been shared among humanitarian organisations in receipt of EU funds. As it currently stands, the Greek Directorate of Reception and Social Integration at the Ministry of Interior is responsible for the longer-term reception of life seekers in the hotspots. The Greek army is tasked with the construction, logistics and management of the spaces as well as the provision of food that is subsequently sub-contracted to private catering companies.

Hotspots are another instrument in the EU's Integrated Border Management, and a key device and site of the 'intensification, deepening, and diversification' of border control.[58] Intended as 'one-stop interoperable shops',[59] hotspots are poorly defined by the EU but are presented as the EU's technical answer of how to manage what Michel Agier has termed 'the undesirables'.[60] In policy documents and pronouncements, the EU is unclear about what a hotspot actually is and does, referring instead to a 'hotspot approach' intended to 'provide a platform for the agencies to intervene, rapidly and in an integrated manner, in frontline Member States when there is a crisis due to specific and disproportionate migratory pressure at their external borders'.[61] However, in practice, hotspots are sites containing a combination of

56   Ibid.

57   D Howden and A Fotiadis, 'Where Did the Money Go? How Greece Fumbled the Refugee Crisis', the *Guardian*, 9 March 2017, theguardian.com.

58   See A Vradis, E Papada, J Painter and A Papoutsi, *New Borders: Hotspots and the European Migration Regime*, London: Pluto, 2019.

59   Pallister-Wilkins, 'Hotspots and the Geographies of Humanitarianism', 2.

60   M Agier, *Managing the Undesirables: Refugee Camps and Humanitarian Government*, London: Polity, 2011.

61   Statewatch, 'Explanatory Note on the "Hotspot" Approach', 2015, statewatch.org.

functions for the purpose of controlling or interrupting people's mobility, collecting their personal and biometric data and making them readable – and thus pliable – to the EU and its member states, so as to better manage the 'bad things' of crisis. Hotspots are also humanitarian sites that aim to provide life seekers with basic needs while reflecting the 'interests of both states and humanitarian agencies for whom the concentration and segregation of refugees are politically and logistically expedient'.[62] As the EU Parliament's Committee on Civil Liberties, Justice and Home Affairs (LIBE) makes clear, hotspots are intended to 'allow the Union to grant protection and humanitarian assistance in a swift manner to those in need'.[63]

Meanwhile, the hotspots on the Greek islands of Lesvos and Chios – two key sites for the operation of the Dutch BSTs – are made up of many different components to more efficiently manage migration in an age of technocratic solutions and outsourcing. Neoliberal outsourcing is a common practice in border control in Europe, the US and Australia. Visa services are contracted to private agencies, detention centres are run by controversial private security companies, such as G4S, Serco and Mitie, and security companies promote ever-more-elaborate technological systems as solutions for securing borders – what Ruben Andersson has called an 'illegality industry'.[64] However, just as the UK children's charity Barnardo's was contracted to run children's services in detention and deportation centres, the hotspots also see the subcontracting of humanitarian services, such as food to private caterers.

Economic geographer Anja K Franck argues that this sub-contracting is fuelled by a form of disaster capitalism, in which market logics of efficiency and rationalisation are mobilised to manage 'bad things' and restore order, while simultaneously expanding the market.[65] The ability

---

62   LS Newhouse, 'More than Mere Survival: Violence, Humanitarian Governance, and Practical Material Politics in a Kenyan Refugee Camp', *Environment and Planning A: Economy and Space* 47(11), 2015, 2292–307.

63   D Neville, S Sy and A Rigon, 'On the Frontline: The Hotspot Approach to Managing Migration', European Parliament, Brussels, May 2016, europarl.europa.eu.

64   R Andersson, *Illegality, Inc.: Clandestine Migration and the Business of Bordering Europe*, Berkeley: University of California Press, 2014.

65   AK Franck, 'The Lesvos Refugee Crisis as Disaster Capitalism', *Peace Review: A Journal of Social Justice* 30(2), 2018, 199–205. For more on the privaisation/neoliberalisation of humanitarian care provision, see T Scott-Smith, 'Humanitarian Neophilia: the "innovation turn" and its implications', *Third World Quarterly* 37(12), 2016, 2229–51.

of humanitarian practices of care to aid the expansion of the market and the ability of the market to aid the practice of humanitarianism has a long-running history. The historian Thomas L Haskell has argued that humanitarianism as a Eurocentric, Western practice intent on saving distant strangers emerged alongside capitalist market logics that enabled the effective mobilisation of moral sentiments. Moral sentiments that, prior to the creation and accumulation of excess profit among a new middle class – who had been made sentimental to the bodily suffering of distant others through new forms of communication – would have been rendered useless without the resources to enact them. But, at the same time, the enactment of such moral sentiments concerned with others, and now enabled under capitalism, was effective exactly because they did not seek to upset or overturn the capitalist order; rather, they maintained and strengthened an emerging liberal order through deepening processes of rationalisation.[66] The mobilisation of humanitarian sentiments therefore has the effect of deepening the border through increasing: the number of actors involved in both policing and rescuing; the available resources, both monetary and technological; and the types of practices, including search and rescue and the provision of basic needs that are the result of border violence. However, such deepening also involves practices that blur the line between care and control in the everyday work of those state actors, such as the BSTs who are tasked with controlling the border while also providing care.

Blurring the Line

I cleaned her feet one at a time with a disinfectant wipe, swabbing the fluid from the edges of her broken blisters and smearing them with ointment. Slowly, I unraveled a roll of white gauze around each pallid foot, then covered them gently with an elastic wrap. As I looked up, I saw that the woman had been watching me with her head resting on

---

66   TL Haskell, 'Capitalism and the Origins of the Humanitarian Sensibility, Parts I and II'. On the mobilisation of compassion through knowledge of bodily suffering, see TW Lacquer, 'Bodies, Details, and the Humanitarian Narrative', in L Hunt ed., *The New Cultural History*, Berkeley: University of California Press, 1989. On knowledge, compassion and saving distant strangers in the history of the modern state, see J Vernon, *Distant Strangers: How Britain Became Modern*, Berkeley: University of California Press, 2014.

Care and (Border) Control   77

her shoulder. Eres muy humanitario, oficial, [you are very humanitarian, officer] she told me. I looked down at her feet and shook my head. No, I said, I am not.[67]

Francisco Cantú, the former US Border Patrol agent turned author, may not consider himself a humanitarian, and it may seem from the actions of many border agents, working to reinforce violent borders, unequal mobility regimes, and protect the privileged, that the work of border policing is focused only on control at the expense of care of any sort. However, such an understanding of policing generally fails to consider the central role that population security has played in the genealogy of policing more generally, in which the security of the population is upheld through acts of care alongside forms of control. As Brigadier Salamagas of the Greek Police in Orestiada made clear to me: 'All our operations and all our actions have one common axiom – the protection of human life!'[68]

In thinking through the blurred line between care and control, it is important to think about how the dynamics of the border create certain risks that the border police have to attend to in their daily work. Put simply, the border matters in creating the conditions of border police work. The border matters not only in the border police's role in guarding territory and defending the line, but also in how guarding and defending creates particular risks for those excluded from safe and legal forms of travel.[69] Border control, from visa regimes and fingerprinting to stopping boats, that produces and reproduces the border enables the need for care.[70] This means that the border as a space of inclusion and

---

67   Cantú, *The Line Becomes the River*, 154 [translation from Spanish my own].

68   Interview with Brigadier Georgios Salamagas, Orestiada Police Station, Evros, Greece, 8 October 2012.

69   The work of feminist geopolitics has been important in drawing attention to the ways that borders, policing and other modes of control have very real bodily effects on those they seek to control and that these effects are differentiated along lines of race, gender and class. See, for example, J Hyndman, 'Towards a Feminist Geopolitics', *The Canadian Geographer* 45(2), 2001, 210–22; J Hyndman, 'The Geopolitics of Migration and Mobility', *Geopolitics* 12(2), 2012, 243–55; VA Massaro and J Williams, 'Feminist Geopolitics', *Geography Compass* 7(8), 2013, 567–77.

70   In thinking through borders as making certain things possible and other things impossible, the work of Keller Easterling on multipliers, switches and remotes is interesting to consider. For Easterling, certain infrastructures and technologies act as multipliers, switches and remotes shaping and reshaping particular spaces through the

exclusion regulating unequal and risky mobility makes care necessary in the first instance, blurring the line between care and control.

Unequal mobility puts people at risk who – through their exclusion from safe and legal travel – become a risk when they encounter the border. As both a risk and at risk, life seekers become the subject of the border police tasked with both protecting territory and protecting life. And this paradox of protection, between the protection of the individual against harm and the protection of borders and the internal space of the state, manifests itself in the daily activities of the border police. This is the seemingly vicious cycle of humanitarianism – it relieves the worst excesses of state violence to make such violence palatable in a liberal order.[71]

This blurring of the line between care and control is visible during search and rescue at sea, where border police can be engaged simultaneously in acts of rescue and acts of capture, and where such simultaneity helps to reinforce the other. As already discussed, processes of rescue extend the border into new territory and can, in theory, remove the geographical limit entirely, as policing becomes not only about protecting the line of the border but about protecting life. In the everyday work of the Dutch BSTs, this paradox of protection sees them engage in food distribution, the provision of blankets and clean clothes, and various pieces of medical equipment. In one instance, an individual officer bought land for the creation of an Islamic graveyard, with the idea that it was important to uphold human dignity in death.[72] Meanwhile, on the other side of the Aegean, Turkish border police also

---

possibilities they open up and foreclose, or the accidents they bring into being. For my argument, it is interesting to think about the border itself as a multiplier of needs, or as a switch that generates particular effects, both intended and not. Additionally, it is possible to think of humanitarian action as a multiplier and/or switch in terms of the border, making certain actions possible and foreclosing others. See K Easterling, *Extrastatecraft: The Power of Infrastucture Space*, London: Verso, 2016, 73–75. The idea of a border as multiplier has been discussed by Mimi Sheller in a lecture on 'Mobility Justice' at the Centre for Urban Studies at the University of Amsterdam, 20 April 2018.

71 This argument has been made by a number of scholars of humanitarianism. See, for example, M Duffield, 'The Liberal Way of Development and the Development–Security Impasse: Exploring the Global Life-Chance Divide', *Security Dialogue* 41(1), 2010, 53–76; Fassin, *Humanitarian Reason*; SM Reid-Henry, 'Humanitarianism as Liberal Diagnostic: Humanitarian Reason and the Political Rationalities of the Liberal Will-to-Care', *Transactions of the Institute of British Geographers* 39(3), 2014.

72 See Pallister-Wilkins and Smeekes, 'The Dutch Border Security Team in Chios and the Intensification, Diversification and Deepening of Border Policing'.

Care and (Border) Control

express humanitarian sentiments while being tasked with preventing the onward movement of Syrian, Iraqi and Afghan life seekers to Europe. Beste İşleyen, an international relations scholar, has argued that Turkish border officials make sense of their everyday interactions with life seekers through humanitarian sentiments and practices, alongside those of honour (namus in Turkish). Honour, here is both a respect for life and a respect for their professional work in guarding the territorial integrity – or honour as purity – of the Turkish state.[73]

However, geography matters in acts of protection. In the popular imagination, humanitarian crises and the responses to them happen in 'other' far-away places, where people who are not quite equal, and can never be equal, reside. In the humanitarian imagination, those with the resources and capacity to help travel to distant places; for example, setting out on SAR missions into international waters, or undertaking missions in other countries, like the Dutch BSTs. Meanwhile, the act of saving itself can involve acute closeness, such as when border police bandage the blisters of border crossers in the deserts of the southern US, or pull life seekers from the Evros river. Elsewhere, I have used the term 'distant-while-proximate' to talk about the contradictory geographies of distance structuring humanitarian borderwork.[74] But the 'refugee crisis' in Europe has meant that the strangers are no longer distant to Europeans. The strangers are in European towns and cities. They can be found walking along European roads, taking a variety of European modes of transport, using European supermarkets, and trying to cross European borders. However, while the strangers are no longer distant geographically, they must remain distant socio-politically, and therefore humanitarian logics of saving become mobilised alongside and entwined within bordering processes that uphold exclusivity.

The hotspot approach is one of the key European instruments for keeping life seekers distant-while-proximate when the need to save comes up against the need to exclude. The hotspots, such as Moria on Lesvos or Vial on Chios, like violent borders more generally, create the very conditions for the need for care. The hotspots are sites where the mobility of life

---

73   B İşleyen, 'Turkey's Governance of Irregular Migration at European Union Borders, Emerging Geographies of Care and Control', *Environment and Planning D: Society and Space* 38(5), 2018, 849–66.

74   Pallister-Wilkins, 'Hotspots and the Geographies of Humanitarianism'.

seekers is controlled through registration in EU systems of surveillance. In turn, this system not only registers, but also aggregates and calculates, and these processes of registration, aggregation and calculation go on to enable the efficient provision of basic needs.[75] These include the provision of water, sanitation and hygiene (WASH) facilities, shelter, food and physical security, provided through a conglomeration of actors including the local authorities, various agencies of the EU, border policing agents, such as the Dutch BSTs and Frontex, and non-governmental humanitarian agencies. Through these processes the hotspots work to keep life seekers alive 'while forming them as a "displaced population" – a known, calculated mass' that can be controlled.[76]

Moria Hotspot, Lesvos, Greece, October 2015. © Polly Pallister-Wilkins

Moria is a paradigmatic example of the ways care and control exist simultaneously, creating an uneasy politics modulating life. But Moria is also an example of how border controls and the particularities of the border create and exacerbate the need to care. Moria is a terrible site for

---

75 See D Bulley, 'Inside the Tent: Community and Government in Refugee Camps', *Security Dialogue* 45(1), 2014, 63–80.

76 Ibid., 71.

a camp of any sort, let alone one catering to the needs of displaced and potentially vulnerable populations. Its location on the side of a steep hill amid an olive grove makes it unsuitable for the adequate provision of basic needs, produces constant sanitation problems, and makes the provision of adequate shelter difficult, both in terms of the steep terrain and in terms of the small size, approximately 1 square km, of the space.[77]

In 2020, there were 20,000 people residing in and around Moria, a site built for 3,000 people. This means that there is simply not enough room in Moria for the number of people who are forced to call it 'home', resulting in the camp spilling outside of its high walls and fences, with people now camped among the olive grove in which Moria sits. The overcrowding and lack of adequate facilities feeds a vicious cycle of insecurity necessitating ever-greater levels of humanitarian intervention. Fire is one particular risk due to the lack of adequate shelter. On 19 September 2016, large parts of the residential area of the hotspot were destroyed in a fire,[78] while, on 25 November 2016, a woman and child were killed after a gas canister attached to a hot plate exploded inside their small nylon tent. It was reported by MSF that they were using the hot plate to try and keep warm. Later that month, three young men died and a fourth was taken to hospital in a critical condition. Survivors and friends reported that the deceased had no pre-existing medical conditions, and to keep warm, the men had been burning cardboard, plastic and scraps of wood in the tents they shared.[79]

More recently, Moria has been accused by humanitarian organisations of producing trauma through its poor conditions. The number of cases of people suffering from psycho-social illnesses has increased over time and the poor conditions in the hotspot are directly blamed by those such as Dr Alessandro Barberio, a clinical psychiatrist working for MSF:

In all of my years of medical practice, I have never witnessed such overwhelming numbers of people suffering from serious mental

---

77 P Pallister-Wilkins, 'Moria Hotspot: Shelter as a Politically Crafted Materiality of Neglect', in T Scott-Smith and ME Breeze eds, *Structures of Protection: Rethinking Refugee Shelter*, New York: Berghahn Books, 2020, 71–80.

78 H Smith, 'Thousands Flee as Blaze Sweeps through Moria Refugee Camp', the *Guardian*, 20 September 2016, theguardian.com.

79 MSF, 'One Year on from the EU-Turkey Deal: Challenging the EU's Alternative Facts', 2017, msf.org.

health conditions, as I am witnessing now amongst refugees on the island of Lesbos. The vast majority of people I see are presenting with psychotic symptoms, suicidal thoughts – even attempts at suicide – and are confused. Many are unable to meet or perform even their most basic everyday functions, such as sleeping, eating well, maintaining personal hygiene, and communicating . . . The asylum seekers include people who have been subjected to extreme forms of torture and violence, both in their countries of origin and during their journey. They have been severely traumatised, both mentally and physically. In their island prison on Lesbos, they are forced to live in a context that promotes frequent violence in all its forms – including sexual and gender-based violence that affects children and adults. This constant violence serves as a recurrent trigger for the development of severe psychiatric symptoms . . . While these vulnerable people await the conclusion of their asylum application, it strikes me that the appalling living conditions and the exposure to constant violence, the lack of freedom and rights accorded to migrants, the severe deterioration of health and mental health, and the everyday stress and pressure placed on all inhabitants of the island, has caused Lesbos to resemble an old-fashioned mental asylum, not seen in parts of Europe since the mid-20th century.[80]

Moria was first intended as a registration point for life seekers. It is first and foremost a space of border control, checking the identities of life seekers excluded from regular forms of travel, a space built with the infrastructural capability to record biographical and biometric entries on databases such as the EURODAC system and to perform police checks to catch potential smugglers. Such controls require a large portion of Moria be given over to housing the complex computer systems. These systems require their own power generators, air conditioning systems, and secure communication links, to ensure the security of the databases being simultaneously curated and mined in the fight against bad guys while making life seekers into a 'known calculated mass'.[81] The centrality of control as a function of Moria means that the

---

80 A Barberio, 'Moria Is in a State of Emergency', MSF, 17 September 2018, msf. org.

81 D Bulley, 'Inside the Tent'.

computer systems have the most luxurious conditions in Moria; meanwhile they are separated from the residential areas by yet more fencing and are thus safe from the ever-present threat of fire.

The stark differentiation between the space as one of control and one of care may have been manageable when Moria was a transit point in the journeys of life seekers. However, as control on onward movement has hardened and following the EU-Turkey 'Deal', life seekers are now 'stuck' on the Aegean islands, permitted only to return to where they came from and denied onward movement. Therefore, Moria's controls, both in terms of the databases the space has produced from those who have passed through and the very architecture of the site itself, have necessitated the need for increased levels of care within the space for those now forced to call the space 'home'.

Therefore, as a registration point in the EU's border control arsenal, Moria is not a traditional refugee camp. For humanitarians, care in traditional refugee camps is primary and control a necessary part of providing care. Moria is a space of a different kind. It exists first and foremost for the purpose of control. This turns the mainstream understanding of humanitarianism on its head, and instead supports the argument that refugee camps are also spaces where states assert their control over non-citizen populations, keeping them distant-while-proximate, under the gaze of a suspicious sovereign.[82] Care in Moria provides basic needs to a captive population, contingent on and constituted by the hotspot itself, its architecture and its systems of control.

Care and control become blurred in border control in other ways. Care and access to it have come to control who can move and who cannot. Within the format of the EU-Turkey 'Deal', certain types of vulnerability and suffering, and the need to access certain types of predominantly medical care, control who is allowed to leave the Aegean Islands for mainland Greece.[83] Meanwhile, Greek law currently allows

---

82 For an insightful exploration of this, see S Hoffmann, 'Humanitarian Security in Jordan's Azraq Camp', *Security Dialogue* 48(2), 2017. See also L Khalili and L Hajjar, 'Torture, Drones, and Detention: A Conversation between Laleh Khalili and Lisa Hajjar', *Jadaliyya*, 2013, jadaliyya.com.

83 See R Jones, C Johnson, W Brown, G Popescu, P Pallister-Wilkins, A Mountz and E Gilbert, 'Interventions on the State of Sovereignty at the Border', *Political Geography* 59, 2017; P Pallister-Wilkins, 'Im/mobility and Humanitarian Triage', in Katharyne Mitchell, Reece Jones and Jennifer Fluri eds, *Handbook on Critical Geographies of Migration*, Northampton, MA: Edward Elgar, 2019, 372–83.

for certain categories of vulnerable people to be exempt from possible deportation to Turkey. Here, suffering and the assumed ability to better provide care on the mainland comes to control the mobility of life seekers on and off the Aegean Islands. Vulnerabilities are determined according to strict categories: pregnant women, unaccompanied minors, single parents with children, victims of torture, and people with disabilities.[84]

Within the context of Europe, the use of violence to save lives might not be as extreme as the examples laid out by Francisco Cantú, in which destruction of property, food and water is seen as a way of saving migrant lives in precarious border environments. The blurred line between care and control, or control through care, is oftentimes subtler in the European experience. However, it does not make the use of rescue and saving lives in upholding the violence of an exclusive European border regime any less real. The moral imperative to save lives enables and facilitates a range of measures that help to consolidate the power of the border while alleviating its worst effects. But, more than this, rescues at sea, or linking mobility to particular types of suffering, come to structure the very limits and violence of the border itself. The imperative to save lives has such power that humanitarian borderwork can occur even in the absence of an immediate threat to life, through pre-emptive notions of risk management and pre-emptive forms of rescue.

Pre-emptive Rescue

'The only way you can stop the deaths is in fact to stop the boats,'[85] said Tony Abbott, former prime minister of Australia. Though such use of humanitarian sentiment to justify border control might seem perverse, it has come to structure border control efforts in Europe as well as Australia. Saving people by stopping boats and/or stopping smugglers is a common refrain from politicians, policymakers, think tanks and certain corners of academia. Such an argument deploys the use of considerable force in the shape of military and border policing assets to

---

84   Human Rights Watch, 'Greece: A Year of Suffering for Asylum Seekers', 2017, hrw.org.

85   R Ackland, 'If Europe Listens to Tony Abbott, the Future for Refugees Will Be Cruel', the *Guardian*, 21 April 2015, theguardian.com.

fight a war on smugglers. It aims to re-write International Humanitarian Law and European human rights law to make Europe a less attractive destination for asylum seekers while colonising developmental discourse and policy implementation.[86] And it is all done under the umbrella of saving lives, in which saving lives enables those calling for the deployment of naval forces to 'destroy the boats'.[87] After all, as anthropologists Ilana Feldman and Miriam Ticktin have argued, who is against saving lives?[88]

Recent EU efforts in Libya might be the clearest example of the ways that pre-emptive rescue is used to further harden Europe's borders. However, the EU-Turkey 'Deal' operates using similar logic but in an altogether subtler and, I argue, more dangerous way. Its main proponents purposefully and habitually use the language and sentiment of humanitarianism to launch an assault on human rights frameworks and humanitarian law in the name of saving lives and securing the border, rationally and efficiently. The EU-Turkey 'Deal' highlights the power of humanitarian ideals and how they can be put to work for the taking of life and the undermining of freedoms rather than the well-being and dignity of humanity as a whole.

The 'Deal' is claimed to be the brainchild of Gerald Knaus, the founder of the 'European Stability Initiative' think tank based in Berlin. 'Deal' here is in inverted commas because it is nothing of the sort – it is simply a short statement between the EU and Turkey, for the very

---

86   See for example recent calls to push for greater levels of development in countries of origin or 'transit' in the Global South to tackle 'root causes'. A paradigmatic example of such work is the recent book by Alexander Betts, a migration scholar, and Paul Collier, a scholar of development and African political economy, *Refuge: Rethinking Refugee Policy in a Changing World*, Oxford: Oxford University Press, 2017. In policy circles this approach has been taken up and pushed by the IOM (International Organization for Migration). For a critique, see PM Frowd, 'Developmental Borderwork and the International Organization for Migration', *Journal of Ethnic and Migration Studies* 44(10), 2017, 1656–72, and by the EU with its EUTF for Africa.

87   See, for example, Euronews, 'EU Set to OK Plan to Destroy Smugglers Boats', 18 May 2015, euronews.com. For a critique of such a plan, see comments made by then UN secretary-general Ban-Ki Moon, who said that 'there is no military solution to the human tragedy playing out in the Mediterranean. It is crucial that we take a holistic approach that looks at the root causes, at security and the human rights of migrants and refugees, and have legal and regulated immigration networks', reported by Reuters, 'No Military Solution to Boat Migrant Crisis: U.N. Chief to Paper', 26 April 2015, reuters.com.

88   Feldman and Ticktin eds, *In the Name of Humanity*.

important reason that any official deal would have required the democratic oversight of the European Parliament, where it would have faced fierce opposition from MEPs critical of its attack on fundamental rights and International Humanitarian Law.[89] The 'Deal' has been criticised by a number of human rights organisations, including the Council of Europe, arguably Europe's leading human rights organisation, who argues that the 'Deal' 'at best strains and at worst exceeds the limits of what is permissible under European and international law'.[90] If the EU-Turkey Statement undermines human rights, it is clear from how its sets out its nine-point plan that this undermining is done to save lives. As the Statement says, 'in order to break the business model of the smugglers and to offer migrants an alternative to putting their lives at risk, the EU and Turkey decided in March 2016 to work together to end the irregular migration from Turkey to the EU'.[91]

Here, risks to life are invoked as a justification and a foundation for a plan that seeks to keep life seekers outside of Europe, by either preventing their movement in the first instance, or by returning those deemed not in need of protection. The statement continues to justify its actions in the name of 'ending human suffering' and 'policing bad things' in its first of nine points:

1) This will take place in full accordance with EU and international law, thus excluding any kind of collective expulsion. All migrants will be protected in accordance with the relevant international standards and in respect of the principle of non-refoulement. It will be a temporary and extraordinary measure which is necessary to end the human suffering and restore public order . . .[92]

The second point of the plan claims that 'for every Syrian being returned to Turkey from Greek islands, another Syrian will be resettled from

89   The full statement can be found here: European Council, 'EU-Turkey Statement', 18 March 2016, consilium.europa.eu.

90   Council of Europe, Committee on Migration, Refugees and Displaced Persons, Rapporteur Tineke Strik, 'The Situation of Refugees and Migrants under the EU-Turkey Agreement of 18 March 2016', Doc 14028, 19 April 2016, semantic-pace.net.

91   European Council, 'EU-Turkey Statement'.

92   Ibid. The statement is able to claim it is in accordance with existing legal frameworks by its use of the term 'irregular migrants' and its claims that it will only return those found not to be eligible for protection under the refugee regime.

Turkey to the EU taking into account the UN Vulnerability Criteria'.[93] However, this is where the aims of the statement start to fall apart. The idea that Syrians are not in need of protection and can be returned to Turkey is one of the 'Deal's' biggest failures, or at least an area that has led Knaus to call for changes to Greece's asylum system, in order to speed up returns of those whose claims are found inadmissible.

The EU-Turkey Statement is effectively unworkable under current International Humanitarian Law, European fundamental rights and Greek Law, all of which incorporate the 1951 Refugee Convention and the 1967 Protocol. Syrians and many other life seekers are indeed eligible for asylum in Greece. Meanwhile, Turkey has repeatedly been ruled a non-safe third country by Greek asylum hearings, meaning people cannot be returned there.[94] However, when one considers the Statement to be about keeping people outside of European space, this is clearly a problem. According to arguments made by Knaus in 2017, Greece needs to be made an unattractive destination for those seeking asylum by reducing chances for appeal and accelerating returns to Turkey. And, perversely, this is to be done in order to save lives.[95]

Knaus has argued that the EU-Turkey Statement and the hotspot approach that exists alongside it must enact a liberal ethical commitment to care for others while keeping them distant and unequal. Through this ethical commitment that works to enforce exclusion, Knaus argues that the EU-Turkey Statement can operate not only to save migrant lives, but also to save Europeans from the potential harm brought by migrants. Here, the name of Knaus' think tank, the European Stability Initiative, is not incidental. A non-expert in refugee or migration issues, Knaus betrays his real use of humanitarianism as being about the swift restoration of the status quo and the protection of existing order. For

---

93   Ibid.

94   See Amnesty International, 'The EU-Turkey Deal: Europe's Year of Shame', 2017, amnesty.org.

95   Gerald Knaus made these arguments in a public event hosted by the University of Amsterdam on 23 March 2017. For a critique of the suffering caused by the EU-Turkey Deal, see MSF, 'One Year on From the EU-Turkey Deal'. See also Moreno-Lax, 'The EU Humanitarian Border and the Securitization of Human Rights', on how interdiction by border authorities is used with the express purpose of making Europe appear to be an unattractive destination. For a greater discussion of Knaus argument in relation to exclusionary humanitarianism see P Pallister-Wilkins, 'Hotspots and the Geographies of Humanitarianism'.

Knaus, life seekers must be kept outside of European space through processes of exclusion justified on the grounds of pre-emptive rescue, in order to save Europe from the return of fascism that he sees as the inevitable result of the presence of migrants in European space.[96]

In order to carry out pre-emptive rescues, the EU-Turkey Statement empowers the Turkish border police and coastguard 'to prevent new sea or land routes for illegal migration opening from Turkey to the EU'.[97] Through calling for interventions before the European border line, either to save lives or to exclude life seekers, the involvement of Turkey becomes necessary and central. In order to enact care and control outside of European space, in this instance, local authorities have to be brought into the European border control assemblage. Unlike in other situations, when intervention is justified on humanitarian grounds that override state sovereignty, respect for Turkish sovereignty sees Turkish border police and coastguard enact a range of pre-emptive practices designed to interrupt onward mobility of life seekers and to effectively prevent risky boat crossings.

Beste İşleyen has explored how the Turkish police engage in various forms of intervention to govern transit mobility in Turkey. For example, she has documented the use of checkpoints and ID cards designed to prevent the movement of life seekers within Turkey, meaning that the Turkish-European border stalks the bodies of life seekers within Turkish territory.[98] Meanwhile, she has also explored the twenty-one state-run 'Temporary Protection Centres' in the south-east of Turkey, close to its borders with Syria and Iraq. These, she argues, are both humanitarian camps offering basic needs to displaced Syrians, Iraqis and Afghans, and places of control, aimed at keeping them geographically distant from Europe and the possibilities of onward mobility.[99]

In Turkey, then, we see the ways humanitarian concerns for saving lives come to be clearly enacted in attempts to control and limit the mobility of life seekers. On Turkey's western coast, the Turkish coastguard are charged with rescuing life seekers in Turkish territorial waters, and subsequently returning them to Turkey. In order to carry out these

---

96 Knaus, University of Amsterdam, 23 March 2017.

97 European Council, 'EU-Turkey Statement'.

98 İşleyen, 'Transit Mobility Governance in Turkey'.

99 İşleyen, 'Turkey's Governance of Irregular Migration at European Union Borders'.

practices of capturing through rescue, they have been assisted by the UN Migration Agency (IOM) and the European Union, with funding and equipment, such as six new SAR boats. Even the design of the six new boats stresses the role of safety. The boats were made by Damen, a Dutch shipyard, with the input of the Royal Netherlands Sea Rescue Institution (KNRM) and are designed to hold up to 120 survivors and to operate in all weather and sea conditions. Meanwhile, the EU is clear about the purpose of the vessels, with the EU ambassador to Turkey Christian Berger saying upon the delivery of the first two boats:

The strenuous efforts by the Turkish Coast Guard have been crucial in saving human lives in the Aegean Sea and the Mediterranean. The EU is proud to be able to contribute to the efforts of the Turkish Coast Guard through these first two state-of-the-art search and rescue vessels delivered today.[100]

Pre-emptive rescue underpins ongoing European policies in the central Mediterranean and Libya, where EU attempts to keep life seekers out of European space lead to calls for interventions by the Libyan coastguard with the assistance of the UNHCR and the IOM. Such practices have been widely criticised, with the Libyan coastguard being accused of opening fire on life seeker vessels,[101] while the policies of detention in Libya have been condemned by a variety of organisations, including European governments, as being inhumane.[102] The hypocrisy of European governments condemning Libyan border control practices and detention conditions, while simultaneously supporting them through funding and calls for saving lives and a reduction in the number of life seekers crossing European borders, speaks to the tensions between a belief in universal humanity and the exclusivity of territorial states.

---

100   Damen, 'Turkish Coast Guard Command Takes Delivery of First Two (of Six) Damen Search and Rescue Vessels', 6 July 2017, damen.com/en/news/2017/07/turkish_coast_guard_command_takes_delivery_of_first_two_of_six_damen_search_and_rescue_vessels.

101   J Belhumeur, 'Libyan Coastguard Opened Fire at Refugee Boats: NGOs', Aljazeera, 25 May 2017, aljazeera.com.

102   NL Times, 'Dutch Minister Horrified by Conditions in Libyan Detention Centers', 29 March 2018, nltimes.nl.

Current policies of pre-emptive rescue and hardened border control, in Libya and elsewhere, build on and are intended to replace older, now seemingly routine SAR operations in the central Mediterranean. These older SAR operations are carried out by a range of state and non-state actors. And these organisations were initially praised by a European public and political culture keen to reward itself for acts of humanity that bolstered a European sense of self based on paternalistic ideals around the desire to help. However, such praise has slowly given way to resistance against life-saving taking place within European space and has been replaced with a hardened exclusivity and calls for even greater restrictions on the mobility of life seekers. The political response to these calls for more restrictive policies has been pre-emptive forms of rescue, such as border control in Libya and increasing support for Turkey's policing of the European border. However, the increasingly criticised life-saving work of non-state actors does not stand in stark contrast to the humanitarian borderwork of states. Though the border-work of non-governmental humanitarian organisations exists in a different political register, driven by humanitarian ideals and the desire to make the violence of unequal mobility visible, such work also structures the border.

Four
Médecins Avec Frontières

You see this Somali guy in Somalia, now you see this Somali guy in South Sudan, now you see this Somali guy in Brussels, and what's the difference? It's the same Somali guy. And it was really this simple thing. If this is really about people, why do you care where that person is? And that really opened up looking at the notion of the route, connecting the dots. What's the difference? What makes the person vulnerable? Maybe the person is more vulnerable in Brussels? That was very difficult for MSF to refuse, you know Doctors Without Borders, but now that the guy has crossed a border, what we don't treat you?[1]

We need new ways of working. The old ways are not good enough for addressing the needs of people on the move.[2]

The need to save lives in response to unequal mobility complicates the picture of who does borderwork. Additionally, responding to the risks posed by unequal mobility requires new ways of saving lives. This chapter explores the role of humanitarian organisations in borderwork as they respond to the suffering caused by unequal mobility regimes and

---

1   Interview with a key architect of MSF's SAR operation, Amsterdam, 10 July 2018.

2   A humanitarian practitioner shares their thoughts with me during an informal interview, 12 May 2016.

border violence. Sometimes this humanitarian borderwork fosters new spatial configurations, public interventions and debates, while sometimes it consolidates existing orders. Simultaneously, it creates new visualisations of the humanitarian subject and reaffirms racialised categories of victimhood and hierarchies of suffering. As a result, I also explore the ways humanitarian borderwork facilitates and includes new multi-scalar, multi-sited and temporally limited ways of working and some of the operational hurdles and ethical questions that arise.

In this chapter, I draw on my research engagement with the medical humanitarian organisation Médecins Sans Frontières (MSF)/Doctors Without Borders, who have been active agents in responding to the suffering caused by unequal mobility in a range of places across the Mediterranean region, Western Balkans, North Africa, northern France, Central America, and in the Australian detention centres in Manus and Nauru. They have engaged in a range of new and experimental practices for a medical humanitarian organisation, including running search and rescue vessels at sea and bus routes, mobile clinics, and transit camps on land, and a highly active Twitter account, @MSF_Sea, used to raise awareness and general advocacy.

Mobile Humanitarians

Unequal mobility underpins humanitarian practice. Our dominant conception of humanitarianism is most often of non-state actors intervening in distant places. This has emerged and reinforced itself over the last century, but has roots in older, colonial 'civilising' missions. In all of these understandings and enactments, humanitarians are the ones who exercise mobility. They are the ones that move across borders and travel to faraway, 'desperate' locations to relieve the suffering of strangers, driven by a sense of purpose and a desire to help.

This ability of humanitarian practitioners and their 'kit' to exercise mobility, to transcend the borders of states, forms a key component of the humanitarian imaginary. It is seen as something central to the humanitarian mission, and at its heart rests on structures of deep inequality.[3]

---

3 Ilana Feldman and Miriam Ticktin eds, *In the Name of Humanity: The Government of Threat and Care*, Durham, NC: Duke University Press, 2012; J Hyndman, *Managing*

Humanitarians are mobile not only to exercise compassion and provide care but because they can be. Help is facilitated by both a belief in the intellectual superiority of such help and a practical ability to provide help. These two factors are, in turn, underpinned by enormous socio-economic, political and military structures, highlighting the deeply Eurocentric and colonial origins of humanitarianism and what political sociologist of humanitarianism Monique J Beerli calls 'hierarchies of competency'.[4]

The assumed ability to be mobile as a central, structuring force of humanitarianism in the past and present manifests in the idea of ingé-rence (the right to interference) in the work of MSF. Here, human suffer-ing requires and even demands that the normal rules of state sovereignty do not apply based on the ideal that suffering is a universal human expe-rience and thus suffering's relief should also be universal, transcending political divisions and state borders.

In 1999, when collecting the Nobel Peace Prize on behalf of MSF, then–international president James Orbinski was clear when he said: 'National boundaries and political circumstances or sympathies must have no influence on who is to receive humanitarian help'.[5] There are, of course, practical limitations on this right to interfere – states can and do regularly deny humanitarian practitioners access or revoke their rights to operate within their territory. However, the very name Médecins Sans Frontières speaks to the idea of mobility for humanitarians being at the heart of humanitarian practice. In this formulation, borders should not get in the way of a doctor's obligation to relieve suffering, and borders can be transgressed and disrespected when the need to help demands this.

But this right to intervene, based as it is on the ability to exercise mobility, is hierarchical and unidirectional, iterating Khalili and Hajjar's aforementioned conception of humanitarianism as an 'ethical

---

Displacement: Refugees and the Politics of Humanitarianism, Minneapolis, MN: University of Minnesota Press, 2000; P Redfield, *Life in Crisis: The Ethical Journey of Doctors Without Borders*, Berkeley: University of California Press, 2013.

4 On the hierarchies of competency, see MJ Beerli, 'Blurring the Boundaries Between In/Formal Knowledges of the Global: Tracking the Itinerary of Report Production Within International Aid Bureaucracies', EISA Conference, Prague, 14 September 2018.

5 J Orbinkski, 'MSF Nobel Peace Prize Lecture', 1999, nobelprize.org.

commitment towards others who are not quite equal'.[6] Humanitarianism as an unequal mobility regime, in and of itself, is enabled and sustained not only by normative ideals about the right to intervene in the face of misery and the universality of humanity, but also by particular forms of expert knowledge and vast infrastructures. As an example, humanitarian logistics is now a recognised specialism in which one can study for an advanced degree. The importance of logistics in the ability to practice ingérence cannot be overstated, and it concurrently highlights the uneasy politics of mobility within humanitarianism. Logistics is considered 'vital' in humanitarian practice. The social anthropologist Peter Redfield has called humanitarianism's reliance on logistics and the various ways logistics shapes humanitarian practice 'vital mobility'.[7] This clever use of the dual meaning of vital, as both essential and life-giving, pinpoints the key role of transporting practitioners and their life-saving 'kit'; in fact, an MSF logistics specialist boasted to me that MSF can get anything anywhere in the world in 48 hours, and joked that MSF is in reality a 'logistics organisation with a humanitarian mission'.[8] Meanwhile, Lisa Smirl's work on the role of the different spaces of aid, including cars, compounds and hotels, shows how the Toyota Land Cruiser has come to stand for the life-saving, go-anywhere, can-do attitude of contemporary humanitarianism.[9]

Meanwhile, for those hard-to-reach places – not accessible by plane or Toyota Land Cruiser because they are too far from an air strip or road – the sphere of humanitarian innovation is focused on conquering the problems of distance-in-aid delivery. We see such efforts, for example, in the use of what have been termed 'good drones' for the delivery of aid and the extraction of information necessary for effective intervention.[10] This good drone has the potential to expand the scope of caregiving, enabling humanitarians to access neglected communities and overcome the limits placed on the desire to help by

6   L Khalili and L Hajjar, 'Torture, Drones, and Detention: A Conversation between Laleh Khalili and Lisa Hajjar', *Jadaliyya*, 2013, jadaliyya.com.

7   P Redfield, 'Vital Mobility and the Humanitarian Kit', in A Lakoff and SJ Collier eds, *Biosecurity Interventions: Global Health and Security in Question*, New York: Columbia University Press, 2008.

8   Interview with humanitarian logistics officer, MSF, Greece, 30 November 2015.

9   L Smirl, *Spaces of Aid: How Cars, Compounds and Hotels Shape Humanitarianism*, London: Zed Books, 2015.

10   KB Sandvik and MG Jumbert eds, *The Good Drone*, London: Routledge, 2017.

Médecins Avec Frontières 95

more 'conventional' transport infrastructures and the limit of their knowledge.[11]

However, this unequal mobility regime between humanitarian practitioners and those they seek to help is no longer adequate for understanding the role of mobility in constituting and enabling humanitarianism. In today's highly mobile, yet unequal world, we have seen how those in need of humanitarian help are no longer 'distant' or staying put 'over there', out of sight of the Global North. Increasingly, the right to move is exercised by life seekers unsettling the traditional mobility regime underpinning humanitarian practice, and the various ways of working that have been developed over time that rely on life seekers remaining in the Global South, close to their places of origin. As a result, the hierarchies between practitioners and subjects of protection, created in part by these unequal geographies underpinning humanitarian practice, come into question. Such unsettling results in humanitarians having to face the politics of mobility head-on. These problems include the deaths and injuries that result from unsafe forms of transportation and the wider political injustices. The inherently political nature of mobility regimes and violent borders is forcing humanitarians to reassess their relationship to politics more broadly.

Pop-Up Humanitarianism

The fertile agricultural fields outside the small Greek village of Idomeni extend north to the chain-link border fence marking the Greek border with Macedonia. Through these fields a railway line cuts a straight path through the border fence. Further to the east, a short 2.5km away, the E75 highway links Athens and Thessaloniki to Skopje, Belgrade and Budapest. On the Macedonian side of the border, the E75 passes between the Flamingo and the Rendez Vous casinos where weary travellers can fill their tanks with petrol and (they hope) their pockets with coins from the slot machines. On the Greek side, there is the standard and ubiquitous 'Hellenic Duty Free' shop. On either side of the border there are large hangers through which the E75 passes, funnelling trucks and cars

---

11   S Healy and S Tiller, 'Be Near a Road: Humanitarian Practice and Displaced Persons in North Kivu', *Refugee Survey Quarterly* 35(2), 2016, 56–78.

through both Greek and Macedonian customs and border control. Back towards Idomeni, the railway line passes through the border unimpeded by such controls, and as a result the fields alongside the railway between the village and the borderline became a central node in the journeys of life seekers for twelve months between 2015–16.

According to humanitarian affairs advisors, medical staff and displacement specialists working for MSF in Athens, the 'ghostly' presence of life seekers passing through Idomeni was first noticed in the spring of 2015 by local farmers.[12] These farmers kept finding discarded clothes and water bottles in the woods and in the old abandoned railway station, where life seekers had been keeping out of sight and getting some sleep before attempting the crossing into Macedonia further along the railway line. As the presence of these discarded items grew to an amount that suggested the route was becoming well established, MSF was confronted with a conundrum of what to do.

Summer was coming and with it an intense heat that heralded the possibilities of dehydration for life seekers keen to remain out of sight, to avoid possible interception by the Greek police. MSF was already running a mobile clinic for those in need but it was decided that simple water taps would be installed to ensure that those heading across the border were well hydrated. These water taps were made 'light-touch' enough to ward off undue attention. Any attention from the authorities risked shutting the route down and displacement specialists working for MSF understood that movement was the principal 'thing' life seekers needed access to, and this movement was something that could at least be made safer if not actively facilitated.

As spring turned into summer, the numbers of life seekers using the route increased and so too did the border controls. Macedonian border police now patrolled the border crossing where the railway line passed through the border fence, intermittently interrupting and preventing border crossings. This interruption changed the dynamic of assistance between MSF and life seekers on the move, requiring increases in intervention and the provision of more than just water taps. Over the summer, and into the early autumn of 2015, as arrivals to the Aegean Islands grew steadily and life seekers continued their journeys to other parts of Europe via northern Greece, a transit camp for 1,000 people emerged.

---

12   Interview with MSF humanitarian affairs advisor, Athens, 14 January 2016.

Médecins Avec Frontières   97

Idomeni and the Greek-Macedonia border,
January 2016. © Polly Pallister-Wilkins

The events of 21 August 2015 were particularly critical in stimulating the construction of the space. On this day, Macedonia decided to temporarily shut its border at Idomeni, with armed border police violently preventing crossings. The closure of the border resulted in 3,000 people becoming stuck with little access to decent sanitation, shelter, or adequate hygiene facilities. An MSF humanitarian displacement advisor was quick to point out that the Macedonian closure of the border 'just provokes a humanitarian crisis on the other [Greek] side'.[13]

As a result of this 'humanitarian crisis' on the Greek side of the border, the ground was levelled, tents were erected, clinics established, other WASH (water, sanitation and hygiene) facilities, including toilets and showers, provided and a Wi-Fi hotspot installed. An MSF co-ordinator in Idomeni stated at the time: 'With other European countries closing borders, we fear a domino effect leading to FYROM closing its borders as well. The new camp is a positive step towards the

---

13   Humanitarian displacement advisor quoted in: MSF, *Greece: MSF Help Create a Refugee Transit Camp in Idomeni*, 28 September 2015, msf-me.org.

improvement of accommodation and hygiene facilities in case people get stuck here.'[14] Throughout the autumn of 2015, the camp at Idomeni was slowly consolidated as it responded to the basic needs of increasing numbers of people passing through the border. Alongside the four large tents that provided short-term sleeping quarters for 240 people, porta-cabins were introduced to the space to provide housing for clinics and office space. However, these facilities soon proved inadequate as the numbers continued to rise, resulting in an expansion of the site and facilities.

Over the winter of 2015 and into 2016 the Macedonian border police closed the border crossing at Idomeni. Meanwhile, after violent push-back from Afghan refugees, MSF closed the transit camp while they discussed whether to allow the Greek police access.[15] In response to the closure of Idomeni, MSF developed a satellite site at the EKO petrol station in nearby Polykastro, some 20km south along the E75. White tents sitting next to a petrol station forecourt, with their wood stove chimneys to help ward off the cold winter, were a strange sight when I was driving north from Thessaloniki towards the border. When I visited in January 2016, the Greek police were forcing the buses transporting life seekers to stop at Polykastro, where they made people disembark before determining whether people would be allowed to travel to Idomeni to cross the border. These determinations were based on people's country of origin – for example, Afghans were prevented from travelling to the border while Syrians were allowed onwards to Idomeni.

As people were forced to wait at the EKO petrol station, similar needs that had been present at Idomeni were now present on the petrol station forecourt, resulting in MSF and other humanitarian agencies providing a range of basic needs at the site. Idomeni reopened in late January 2016, but Polykastro remained as an overflow space – a desperate place of waiting. Both sites continued to grow in terms of residents, with anywhere between 6,000 and 9,000 people using the space at Idomeni. This increase in numbers was the result of the slow closure of the Balkan Route to more and more categories of refugees. Slowly, further along the

---

14   Ibid.; the co-ordinator in Idomeni confirmed this story to me during an interview on 12 January 2016 in MSF's office in nearby Polykastro. See also P Pallister-Wilkins, 'Médecins Avec Frontières and the Making of a Humanitarian Borderscape', *Environment and Planning D: Society and Space* 36(1), 2018.

15   Interview with MSF humanitarian affairs advisor, Athens, 14 January 2016.

Médecins Avec Frontières

EKO service station, E75, Polykastro, January
2016. © Polly Pallister-Wilkins

line of people's flight, borders closed depending on countries of origin:
Afghans, then Iraqis and eventually all life seekers. This turned Idomeni
from a place of transit, where life seekers might be stopped and forced
to wait for a night or a few days before getting the chance to cross, into
a space of indefinite waiting.

The 'official' shelters provided by MSF and the UNHCR were no
longer sufficient for the number of residents, even as more and more
were erected. Small dome-style camping tents filled the gaps both
spatially and organisationally as crossings got harder and harder and the
border was shut for all life seekers in March 2016. As spaces of transit
became spaces of indefinite waiting, MSF, alongside a number of other
humanitarian organisations and a groundswell of volunteers, continued
to provide what basic needs they could amid worsening conditions. And
then, in late May 2016, Idomeni was gone. So too was the camp at the
EKO petrol station. As quickly as they had emerged, they disappeared.

The temporality of these spaces is inextricably and intimately linked
to the politics of the border and the forces of unequal mobility. As was
repeatedly made clear to me in interviews and discussions about

Idomeni and elsewhere, these spaces emerged in response to migrant agency in identifying routes and lines of flight, but also in response to the particularities of the border and the harms that it created. Meanwhile, the border and the limits it placed on movement created the very conditions that necessitated the need for humanitarian assistance, as people were left requiring shelter, food, medical assistance and suitable sanitation facilities.

I call this 'pop-up humanitarianism' in recognition of the constitutive relationships between the particular conditions of the border over time and the subsequent need and, importantly, possibilities created by interruptions and waiting for humanitarian assistance. All humanitarianism is thought to be pop-up in nature, in that it responds to particular emergencies of a limited duration. In the humanitarian imaginary, an emergency occurs, and humanitarian organisations arrive to provide assistance and relief until the emergency is over or more long-term state responses can be established. However, in practice, the duration of an emergency is not fixed, and systemic emergencies and humanitarian responses have become a common feature; for example, the seventy-year displacement of Palestinian refugees, still managed by the United Nations Relief Works Agency (UNRWA), and more recent displacements in East Africa and the building of large refugee camps like Kakuma and Dadaab in Kenya, both of which resemble small cities. Even if Idomeni no longer exists, life seekers remain warehoused in other facilities around Greece with their mobility tightly controlled and border crossing to other parts of Europe denied.

The particularly pop-up nature of Idomeni and Polykastro occurred elsewhere along the 'corridors and narrow bands' that life seekers were forced to navigate.[16] The cases of Idomeni and Polykastro serve as an illustrative example here, even while each similar site along the migratory chain remains unique, structured as they are by the particularities of the border conditions and mobility of life seekers. In Europe alone, similar pop-up sites emerged and continue to emerge across Greece, Italy, the Western Balkans, Eastern Europe and France, at border sites, along transport corridors and in places of waiting. Pop-up humanitarianism appears markedly different in its temporality from other refugee

---

16   J Whittall, 'Layers of Siege: The Chain of Complicity from Syria to Europe', *MSF Analysis: Reflections on Humanitarian Action*, 2 June 2016, jadaliyya.com.

and displacement emergencies because of the constitutive role of the border and unequal mobility in creating spaces, finite times and particular conditions for the provision of limited forms of care.[17]

The dynamics of unequal mobility – but mobility nonetheless – unsettles the traditional ways displacement has been mapped and responded to. In her groundbreaking work on the constitutive role of the spatio-temporal and material aspects of aid, Smirl highlights the importance of how providers of aid think about the 'space of crisis'. These ways of thinking concern spaces 'distant' from the Global North, or at least from humanitarians themselves when they are deployed in the field, and these spaces are assumed to be spatially fixed. Smirl makes clear that humanitarian ways of working reinforce the 'location and categorisation of victims and beneficiaries from a Cartesian perspective where space is flat, mappable and static'. These approaches, she goes on to argue, are 'consistent with the dominant approach to space within international politics, where what is called the "territorial trap" assumes physical geography and political territory are coterminous, can be mapped out, carved up, bordered and defended', and that territorial states are containers for their citizens and societies.[18] The mobility of life seekers through the Aegean, Greece, the Western Balkans and beyond in 2015–16 fundamentally challenged this Cartesian understanding of space as static. And it subsequently challenged the humanitarian responses as actualised through the building of static spaces, such as camps, clinics and compounds. While tents were erected in Idomeni and Polykastro to address shelter needs, the space, from the perspective of life seekers, was one of transit, a resting place en route to a more permanent, settled and secure future elsewhere.

Therefore, unequal mobility impacts not only the need for aid but also the spaces and times of aid provision. In Idomeni, Polykastro and elsewhere, the mobility of refugees and migrants freed the spaces and times of aid provision from the dominant Cartesian understanding of spatial relations. These Cartesian understandings of static spaces and

---

17   Pallister-Wilkins, 'Médecins Avec Frontières'.

18   Smirl, *Spaces of Aid*, 6. The 'territorial trap' is an important work by geographer John Agnew that has challenged many of the assumptions made about the territorial spatiality of the world. See J Agnew, 'The Territorial Trap: The Geographical Assumptions of International Relations Theory', *Review of International Political Economy* 1(1), 1994, 53–80.

fixed times of aid were replaced with other spatio-temporal logics that produced pop-up humanitarian spaces and the identification of new needs and approaches to the delivery of assistance.

Humanitarianism on the Move

The spatial limitations in the humanitarian imaginary not only impact the practice of humanitarianism but also studies of humanitarianism. Academic literature has paid attention to the spatialities and materialities of the camp, and the mobility of humanitarians and their kit, as well as the movement of the affective emotions and logics that underpin the desire to help.[19] As Smirl argues, 'the differential rates of mobility and speed between the international community and the target population are rarely examined, yet lie at the heart of some of the ineffectiveness of humanitarian assistance.'[20] But, aside from this, little attention has been paid to the mobility of humanitarian subjects themselves and how this impacts the delivery of humanitarian assistance. The discussion of pop-up humanitarianism showed how the assumed spatial logics of humanitarianism are unsettled and reconfigured by the mobility of life seekers and the humanitarian borderwork that results. Yet, what happens when the assumed logics of mobility in humanitarianism are unsettled and, in some cases, turned on their head?

19   On the spatialities and materialities of the camp, see N Abourahme, 'Assembling and Spilling-Over: Towards an "Ethnography of Cement" in a Palestinian Refugee Camp', *International Journal of Urban and Regional Research* 39(2), 2015, 200–17; I Katz, ' "The Common Camp": Temporary Settlements as a Spatio-Political Instrument in Israel-Palestine', *The Journal of Architecture* 22(1), 2017, 54–103; I Katz, 'Spreading and Concentrating: The Camp as the Space of the Frontier', *City* 19(5), 2015, 722–35; A Ramadan, 'Spatialising the Refugee Camp', *Transactions of the Institute of British Geographers* 38(1), 2013, 65–77; S Turner, 'What Is a Refugee Camp? Explorations on the Limits and Effects of the Camp', *Journal of Refugee Studies* 29(2), 2016, 139–48. On the mobility of humanitarians and their kit, see Redfield, 'Vital Mobility and the Humanitarian Kit', and Smirl, *Spaces of Aid*. On the movement of affective emotions and logics, see K Mitchell and KP Kallio, 'Spaces of the Geosocial: Exploring Transnational Topologies', *Geopolitics* 22(1), 2017, 1–14, and M Mostafanezhad, 'Celebrity Humanitarianism and the Popular Geopolitics of Hope along the Thai-Burma Border', *Political Geography* 58, 2017, 67–76.

20   Smirl, *Spaces of Aid*, 11.

In his attempt to have studies of migration take transport and transportation infrastructures seriously, William Walters has argued:

The vehicle, its road, its route – these particular materialities are not entirely missing from scholarship on migration politics. But . . . they rarely feature as a central focus in theorisation and investigation of migration worlds. This is surely a paradox. All migrations involve journeys and those journeys are more often than not mediated by complex transport infrastructures, authorities and norms of transportation. Granted, in many instances those journeys may be rather uneventful and not in the least bit life-changing or politically salient . . . Nevertheless, in many other instances, the journey is politically salient, perhaps even a life-or-death experience.[21]

Taking Walters's plea seriously opens up possibilities to examine new sites of power and intervention in the governing of mobility, the consolidation of unequal mobility and the hardening of borders. But it also prompts me to ask further questions. If, as Walters says, 'the journey is politically salient, perhaps even a life-or-death experience', what does this mean for the work of those whose job it is to save lives? If studies of migration have not taken the journey seriously enough, how have humanitarians responded to the journey itself and the mediating effect of transport and transport infrastructures?

In the early summer of 2015, the numbers of life seekers journeying across the Aegean Sea from Turkey to Lesvos started to rise to such a level that it garnered the attention of large, international humanitarian organisations, such as the International Rescue Committee and MSF. The dangers of the 10km sea crossing, in overcrowded, rubber dinghies mass-produced in Chinese factories, were clearly visible to the attendant media and an interested public keen on spectacle.[22] What was less visible were the journeys life seekers took after arriving on the beaches.

Out of sight and out of mind for the media was the 70km journey on foot across the island from north to south. In the rising summer heat,

---

21 W Walters, 'Migration, Vehicles, and Politics: Three Theses on Viapolitics', *European Journal of Social Theory* 18(4), 2015, 470.

22 See P Pallister-Wilkins, 'There's a Focus on the Boats Because the Sea Is Sexier than the Land', *The Disorder of Things*, 9 December 2015, thedisorderofthings.com.

migrants walked along narrow, winding and mountainous roads in order to register with the waiting Greek and European border authorities so that onward passage off the island to Athens could be secured.[23] The vehicle (or lack thereof), the road, the route, and the infrastructures of transportation – or to be more precise, the active denial of transportation – were sites and causes of potential life or death.

The KTEL bus takes around one hour and thirty-five minutes to cross the island from Molyvos to Mytilene and at the time of writing costs €7.50 for a full, adult fare. However, the public transport network of Lesvos was denied to life seekers due to their arrival as irregular migrants. This meant that they had no choice but to walk the 70km across the island. As Thalia, an MSF team member, remarked in a blog post published by MSF UK:

> As we were driving, we met people walking – families with children, older people. They looked exhausted after walking for who knows how many hours, some of them all night. We had some bottles of water, so we opened the window. It seemed like thousands of hands reached through the window just trying to get a small bottle of water. Then we saw people lying down in the middle of the road, unable to go on walking in the heat. One was a boy of about 18. He couldn't walk even another metre. Further on, I saw a father dragging a rope attached to a plastic crate with his two-month-old baby inside. He was too tired to carry the child any further, so he was dragging her in a crate. He had cut a branch from an olive tree and fixed it onto the crate to give the baby some shade.[24]

Thus, in the early summer of 2015, MSF's emergency team on Lesvos determined that the most urgent need was for transportation. 'I never expected to be running a bus company when I came here', was how Florence, an MSF medical coordinator, put it when MSF began a bus

---

23   For more on the dynamics of registration, see K Rozakou, 'Nonrecording the "European Refugee Crisis" in Greece: Navigating through Irregular Bureaucracy', *Focaal – Journal of Global and Historical Anthropology* 77, 2017, 36–49. For more on the use of registration/deportation documents for onward mobility, see AK Franck, 'Im/Mobility and Deportability in Transit: Lesvos Island, Greece, June 2015', *Tijdschrift voor economische en sociale geografie* 108(6), 2017, 879–84.

24   MSF UK, *Bus Drivers Without Borders*, 3 September 2015, blogs.msf.org.

service across the island.[25] Meanwhile, MSF migration specialists from the Operational Centres in Amsterdam and Brussels were talking about how to operationally 'improve [the] conditions for people in flight [on] all stages of their journey'.[26]

MSF bus route, Lesvos, November 2015. © Polly Pallister-Wilkins

The journey then became the focal point for MSF activity on Lesvos, requiring, according to one displacement specialist, significant 'adaptation'.[27] A medical humanitarian organisation is not a transportation organisation, and if they engage in the logistics of transportation at all, it has historically been in relation to medical emergencies in the form of ambulances, or in moving patients to and from clinics for routine medical interventions during systemic emergencies. In 2015, however, adaptation and a focus on improving conditions for people on all stages of their journey required not only the provision of buses, but also the adjacent infrastructures of running such a service. And, while

---

25 Ibid.

26 Conversation with MSF migration and displacement specialists from Amsterdam and Brussels, 12 September 2015.

27 Interview with MSF displacement specialist, Brussels, 14 November 2016.

adaptation might be necessary, the existing logics of operational efficiency in which helping the greatest number of people with the most effective use of resources played a central role.

The decision to run a bus service based on a recognition of the dangers of walking across the island also shows how interventions intending to save lives follow the endangered life seekers wherever they may be found. This echoes much of the work on contemporary borders that argues that borders are no longer found at the edges of state territory but are differentially embodied, spatially disaggregated and potentially anywhere. The risks faced by mobile life seekers led to new spatialities of humanitarian practice configured through and around mobility. The buses and the roads along which they travelled became spaces and infrastructures facilitating humanitarian action while the bus became a humanitarian device via which MSF could provide care.

In asking us to take transport infrastructures seriously as mediators of migration, William Walters mobilises the word 'via' and offers three meanings that he suggests can help us to see migration differently. Firstly, via refers to 'the in-between, the en-route, the places on the way', and Walters suggests 'all sorts of political phenomena become newly thinkable once we approach the migration complex from the angle of its vehicles'. Secondly, via also draws our attention to 'the specific *means* of transportation' in question, unsettling the idea in 'a great deal of talk about global migrations or mobile flows . . . that movement is rather generic'. Here, a 'greater attentiveness to the materials, infrastructures, knowledges, economies and authorities that both facilitate and constrain, sort and shape, accelerate and impede movement is warranted'. Different forms of transportation, such as ships, planes and buses, not only 'generate different experiences and cultures of mobility; they also have different affordances for political action'. And, thirdly, 'via can refer to the Latin word for road or way' which Walters uses to 'observe the emergence of different problematizations . . . that allow us to plot the different ways that questions of life on the road have been assembled', and provides us with 'a locus for problematizations of the human and for the possibility of politics'.[28]

What Walters mobilises with a discussion of via was actualised in MSF's humanitarian response to the unsafe journeys of life seekers in

---

28   Walters, 'Migration, Vehicles, and Politics', 471–72.

Médecins Avec Frontières

the summer and autumn of 2015 on Lesvos. The in-between and en route played a role, and places on the way, such as the bus stop created by MSF at Mantamados, materialised. The bus service and the bus stop facilitated, accelerated, constrained, sorted and shaped life seekers' journeys and governed their encounters with the provision of basic needs and access to medical care. Approaching the journeys of life seekers from the perspective of the route and the role of vehicles, MSF's response offered unconventional services and introduced new ways of working. Meanwhile, the specific means of transportation were important in affording MSF the possibility to exercise a particular humanitarian politics that centred both the physical well-being and the mobility of life seekers in contrast to the politics of unequal mobility barring irregular migrants from accessing public transport.

However, the buses also worked to transport life seekers to Moria, the hotspot, where, as was discussed in the previous chapter, irregular border crossers are registered and their details uploaded onto various databases. Importantly, here, once on the bus, life seekers were not free to leave before they reached Moria, and so the buses worked as a mobile part of the EU border regime, capturing people and holding them for the short period of time between landing on the beaches and registering with the police authorities. But, while the buses may have assisted with a smoother and more efficient running of the EU's border control regime, speeding up the transfer of arrivals to the registration facility, transport infrastructures also enabled the denial of medical care at the Mantamados bus stop.

Viscose Velocity in Humanitarian Medical Care

Infrastructure acts as a 'connective tissue' between the desire to help and the provision of life-saving work. In discussing the differences between those who suffer and those who care, the anthropologist and former humanitarian practitioner Didier Fassin has argued that the lofty and universal ideals of humanitarianism are often in contradiction with the 'concrete terms under which humanitarian agents have to operate'.[29]

---

29 KP Donovan, 'Infrastructuring Aid: Materializing Humanitarianism in Northern Kenya', *Environment and Planning D: Society and Space* 33(4), 2015, 733, and D Fassin, 'Humanitarianism as a Politics of Life', *Public Culture* 19(3), 2007, 499–520.

This is quite literally the case when we consider MSF's bus service – a bus service firstly made necessary and secondly enabled by the roads people had to travel. The role of infrastructure is central both to producing unequal mobility regimes and the provision of humanitarian relief itself. However, humanitarianism does not just use infrastructure – roads, air corridors, shipping routes, hospitals and sanitation systems – but also provides and builds it.

The provision of infrastructures became a central aim of MSF's 2015 intervention on Lesvos. These infrastructures moved beyond the traditional provision of camps most readily associated with humanitarian assistance and moved into what is more readily called infrastructuring, which takes account of the contested and negotiated – simply put, the messy context in which these 'connective tissues' operate. In the case of MSF's work on Lesvos, infrastructuring saw the provision of a bus service and an attendant bus stop. Here, mobility required particular material interventions, while such material interventions had particular types of effects on what type of care became possible to provide within the limited time and space of the bus stop at Mantamados.

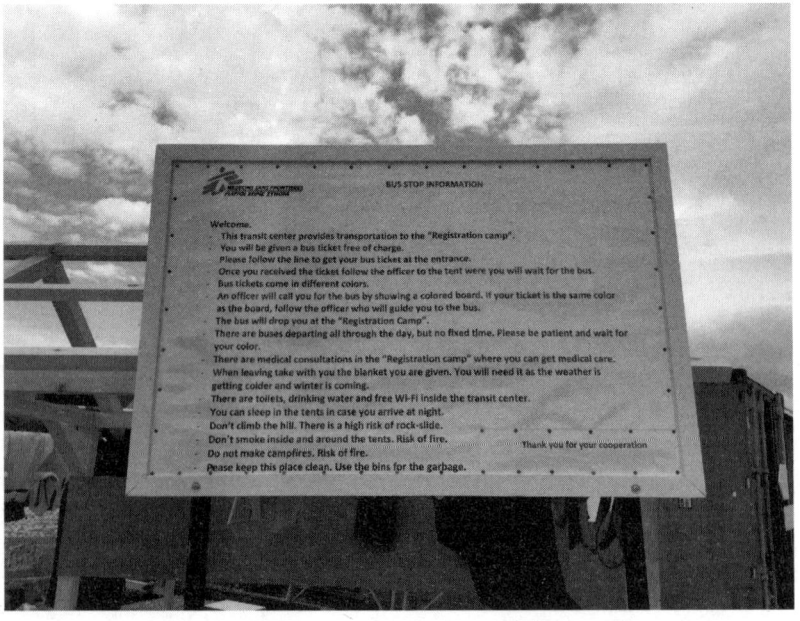

Sign at an MSF-run transit space at Mantamados,
Lesvos, November 2015. © Polly Pallister-Wilkins

Médecins Avec Frontières 109

Logics of efficiency and the intricacies of Lesvos' physical geography and road network resulted in MSF breaking the bus journey in two through the creation of a staging post. This staging post, or bus stop, sat on a hillside overlooking the village of Mantamados, approximately 20km from the northern shore of the island and 50km from the registration point at Moria, near the capital of Mytilene. The bus stop's role was to regulate the movement of people between the landing beaches and the registration point, working as a sort of pressure valve regulating the demands placed on MSF practitioners located at various points along the migratory chain. Mantamados was designed and built to allow people to rest, wait and perhaps stay the night while regulating onwards mobility and pre-emptively avoiding problems of congestion further down the line.

The role of Mantamados as a bus stop and transport space was clear from the sign welcoming arrivals in English, Arabic and Dari. The sign is illuminating in a number of ways, including the careful outlining of the transportation system developed by MSF to manage mobility and the application of triage-like processes involving sorting, categorising and issuing tickets that replicated practices more normally associated – at least for MSF – with emergency waiting rooms.[30] Additionally, the materialisation of the bus stop's purpose is also interesting in what it tells us about the relationship – at least at that time – between MSF, as a provider of basic needs in border spaces, and the border regime authorities. The sign makes clear that the buses from Mantamados will transport people to the 'Registration Camp' of Moria. Here they are then subjected to the border control and asylum processes and of the EU designed to filter life seekers through processes of inclusion and exclusion.

According to Lisa Smirl, 'the built environment changes behaviour by making certain options more or less efficient, desirable, noticeable or palatable'.[31] But we can also say the reverse: that certain options centred around efficiency, desirability, noticeability and palatability shape the built humanitarian environment. In the case of Mantamados, we cannot trace easy, linear processes from the built environment to particular ways of working. Instead, what we see is a more complex relationship

---

30   For more on this, see Pallister-Wilkins, 'Médecins Avec Frontières'.
31   Smirl, *Spaces of Aid*, 153.

between the dynamics of uneven mobility, operations intended to facilitate that mobility, such as the bus service, logics of operational efficiency, and the influence of medical ethics. On this last point, the bus stop sign contains the clear instruction that 'there are medical consultations in the "Registration Camp" where you can get medical care'. Coming from MSF, the world's leading medical humanitarian organisation, the idea that an MSF space would not provide medical care seems at first glance to be strange – but is it?

In order to understand the absence of medical consultations at Mantamados, it is necessary to explore two things: one, the particularities of mobility that were occurring on Lesvos at that time; and two, the relationship of medical ethics to space and time. When thinking about the mobility of life seekers on Lesvos, there is much talk among MSF of congestion and decongestion.[32] This talk of congestion and decongestion suggests neither a smooth movement of people, nor a complete stasis, but instead something sticky or viscous. This stickiness or viscosity is intimately related to the role of border crossing points like that at Idomeni, and transport infrastructures like MSF's bus service.

Work on 'stickiness' and viscosity in humanitarian action has focused on the necessary stickiness of certain technologies, most notably therapeutic foods. Scholar of humanitarian technologies Tom Scott-Smith has advanced the importance of viscosity in his work on the role of feeding technologies that require stickiness in order to be effective. In these instances, if the food, in this case a foodstuff called Plumpy'nut™, flows too quickly, it fails to administer its life-giving properties. If it flows too slowly, it does not administer these properties fast enough.[33] In the case of the uneven mobility exercised by life seekers, their sticky mobility calls for and conditions a particular type of humanitarian caregiving. The need to administer care is premised on the risks associated with and generated by life seekers. Particular forms of mobility and the speed of that mobility impact how and what type of care can be administered. If

---

32   Conversation with MSF Humanitarian Affairs Officer, Mytilene, 10 October 2018.

33   T Scott-Smith, 'Sticky Technologies: Plumpy'nut™, Emergency Feeding and the Viscosity of Humanitarian Design', *Social Studies of Science* 48(1), 2018, 3–24. See also P Pallister-Wilkins, 'Im/mobility and Humanitarian Triage', in Katharyne Mitchell, Reece Jones and Jennifer Fluri eds, *Handbook on Critical Geographies of Migration*, Northampton, MA: Edward Elgar, 2019, 372–83.

Médecins Avec Frontières 111

life seekers move too fast, there is in many cases no need for the provision of care and no opportunity to provide it. If life seekers move too slowly, new risks emerge and different forms of humanitarianism – for example, more traditional refugee camps – result. As life seekers on Lesvos (and elsewhere) did not move 'fast' but in a way that was modulated by the rhythms of infrastructure, in a sticky sort of syncopation, the conditions for sticky care responding to the dynamics of mobility, space and time were created.

In discussions with MSF specialists during the 'height' of the 'refugee crisis', the problem of velocity on operations was repeatedly raised. 'Speed of movement prevents good care' was how one displacement specialist put it to me.[34] Time and again, concerns were raised over whether proper care could be administered in conditions of im/mobility. These were concerns centred on operational ability. But, more than this, concerns were raised over whether care should be administered in such conditions. These were concerns centred on medical ethics and they are key to understanding why there was no medical care available at the Mantamados bus stop.

When talking to a public health advisor at Mantamados about why there were no medical doctors present, they bluntly stated, 'people are not going to die on the beaches or on the journey across the island unless they have pre-existing medical conditions'.[35] There was no immediate medical emergency on Lesvos and what risks were there were related to mobility, impacting the operational possibilities for a medical humanitarian organisation like MSF. Those with medical needs were considered to be those with pre-existing conditions for which the emergency humanitarian medical infrastructures that MSF specialise in were not needed. A field hospital is not necessary to refill a prescription for hypertension, especially in a highly developed context such as Greece, where fully functioning medical facilities exist, even if life seekers were sometimes denied access to such services for political reasons. In later meetings, those with oversight for medical operations stressed the tensions that exist between effective care and appropriate care in particular contexts.[36]

---

34   Interview with MSF displacement specialist, Brussels, 14 November 2016.

35   Discussion with MSF public health specialist, Mantamados, 25 November 2015.

36   Repeated discussions and correspondence with an MSF medical director, 2016–18.

Medical care has a different velocity to that of the bus service. Care targeted at the human body requires a different spatial and temporal repertoire, built around fixed infrastructures, such as hospitals to enable effective and suitable treatment. A bus stop built around the facilitation of movement is clearly not a space (or a time) for the effective provision of care. In addition, the ethics of specifically medical humanitarian practitioners were in tension with operational logics aimed at fostering mobility. For instance, in medical ethics, diagnosis should only be attempted when continuity in care can be guaranteed. How would this have been possible at a bus stop intended to facilitate movement? The need for continuity and follow-up in medical practice was therefore in conflict with the desires of life seekers to carry on their journeys to a place of ultimate safety, and with other MSF operations designed to facilitate those journeys.

Therefore, the Mantamados bus stop did not offer medical care. Instead, sticky forms of mobility and viscous concerns over congestion and decongestion modulated where, when and how medical care was provided. This meant providing buses as a form of pre-emptive risk management, creating Mantamados as a pressure valve regulating congestion and decongestion on the island, and offering medical consultation at the 'Registration Camp', where registration dynamics gave time for providing limited medical facilities.

The EU-Turkey Statement – popularly and erroneously known as the EU-Turkey 'Deal'[37] – that came into effect on 20 March 2016 has resulted in the mobility of life seekers becoming more and more viscous and congestion becoming the order of the day. Following the EU-Turkey 'Deal', medical consultations in the 'Registration Camp', more popularly known as Moria Hotspot, ceased and the bus service ended. MSF refused to be complicit with what they saw as a repressive border regime, with the Head of Mission in Greece at the time publicly stating:

We took the extremely difficult decision to end our activities in Moria because continuing to work inside would make us complicit in a system we consider to be both unfair and inhumane. We will not

---

37   The agreement is little more than a statement of cooperation between the two bodies, and as the European Parliament has not approved the agreement it is not a deal in the constitutional sense.

Médecins Avec Frontières

allow our assistance to be instrumentalised for a mass expulsion operation and we refuse to be part of a system that has no regard for the
humanitarian or protection needs of asylum seekers and migrants.[38]

Mantamados continued for a few more months as a first assistance
point, but it too slowly came to a sputtering end.

These changing dynamics of mobility and the growing congestion on
Lesvos has again caused a change to MSF's operations. Between 2016–
18, medical services on the island were provided through a combination
of mobile clinics and a semi-permanent clinic in the island capital of
Mytilene. However, as congestion grew and, with it, conditions wors-
ened, MSF made a compromise in 'returning' to Moria. While the
organisation remains outside the walls of the dangerously congested
hotspot, in the winter of 2018 it decided to set up shop in an olive grove
across the road from the entrance.[39] The congestion of life seekers on
Lesvos has resulted in both the emergence of public health risks and the
subsequent possibility for MSF to operate in a more traditional medical
humanitarian fashion, offering vaccination programmes, sexual and
reproductive health services and psycho-social trauma support.[40]

The clinic opposite Moria has a relatively fixed patient population (at
the time of this writing) engaging in work such as vaccination drives
and psycho-social care that is more in tune with MSF's regular operational routine. Meanwhile, repeated talk about the dangers of congestion on the overcrowded island and the need for decongestion shows a
continued concern with the dynamics of and interrelationship between
mobility and well-being. Calls for decongestion and calls to 'open the
island' aim to prevent the emergence of a long-term, systemic need for

---

38   MSF, *Greece: MSF Ends Activities inside the Lesvos Hotspot*, 22 March 2016, msf.
org.
39   For more information about the conditions in Moria, see A Barberio, 'Moria Is
in a State of Emergency', MSF, 17 September 2018, msf.org; Liz Clark, ' "It Is Difficult to
Believe This Is Europe": The Mental Health Crisis in Moria Camp', *Blogs from Doctors
Without Borders*, 21 September 2018, blogs.msf.org.; MSF, 'No Roof, No Recovery', 17
October 2018, msf.org; MSF, 'Self-Harm and Suicides Increasing for Child Refugees in
Lesbos', 17 September 2018, msf.org; MSF, 'Confinement, Violence and Chaos: How a
European Refugee Camp Is Traumatising People on Lesbos', 18 July 2018, msf.org; MSF,
'Overcrowded, Dangerous and Insufficient Access to Healthcare in Moria', 4 May 2018,
msf.org.
40   MSF, 'MSF Activity Update – March 2018', 16 March 2018, msf.org.

the provision of humanitarian assistance on what has ostensibly become an island prison.[41] MSF's current concerns are structured by and focused on the lack of mobility. Fears of the need for a long-term humanitarian presence on Lesvos, as the period of emergency becomes years rather than weeks, changes the operational dynamics of the organisation not only in how they respond on the ground but also in how they engage in another of MSF's core missions: témoignage, or bearing witness. As the crisis on the islands becomes systemic and has been exacerbated by the Covid–19 pandemic, MSF has engaged in evermore outspoken forms of critique about what they understand to be EU-made conditions of neglect which further threaten lives and consolidate violent borders.

Search and Rescue, Visibility and the Making of Publics

When you think of the work of MSF in response to the so-called refugee crisis in Europe since 2015, perhaps your mind immediately goes to their search and rescue vessels operating in the Mediterranean rather than a transitory, doctorless bus stop next to a small Greek village on the island of Lesvos. And this would not be without foundation, but this visibility in the minds of the public is exactly why I have chosen not to start my discussion of MSF's humanitarian borderwork with a discussion of search and rescue at sea. My decision to focus first on the less 'glamorous' practices of transit camps and bus services is to challenge what I have discussed elsewhere as the 'sexy and spectacular' nature of search and rescue that conjures images of David Hasselhoff in a pair of red swim shorts running along a beach.[42]

It cannot be denied that MSF's SAR missions were something of a 'media sensation', with journalists from all over the world wanting to get on the SAR boats to cover what they saw as the source of the 'refugee crisis'.[43] This interest was used by MSF in their SAR missions that

41   See P Pallister-Wilkins, 'Hotspots and the Geographies of Humanitarianism', *Environment and Planning D: Society and Space* 38(6), 2020,, 991–1008.

42   Pallister-Wilkins, 'There's a Focus on the Boats Because the Sea Is Sexier than the Land'.

43   Interview with a key architect of MSF's SAR operation, Amsterdam, 10 July 2018.

intended to save lives at sea and make visible the realities of unequal mobility, or what they termed in reports and in public statements as a lack of safe and legal routes. MSF used SAR to increase the visibility of their rescue missions to make public, and make a public around, what became the #safepassage campaign.

Visibility for MSF operations and, most importantly, humanitarian advocacy and communications, worked differently from how it has been discussed by many scholars studying search and rescue or border practices at sea. In these accounts, visibility is discussed as relating to the ability to 'see' being a central facilitating and structuring component of search and rescue, alongside Europe's border regime.[44] This is not to say that visibility has not played a role in structuring MSF operations at sea – in fact, it is central in the feasibility of SAR missions. However, these missions are made more feasible through a range of additional factors alongside visibility.

In the summer of 2018, I sat down with an advocacy and operational communications specialist (from hereon, Comms Specialist) and one of the key architects of MSF's search and rescue operations to discuss their experiences; from the inception of SAR as an idea, to an operational reality, and the particular border dynamics that made such operations possible. The discussion lasted many hours and was as much an act of critical self-reflection for the Comms Specialist as it was a research interview for me. In discussing the launch of MSF's first mission in

---

44   On the importance of vision, visibility and visualisation in search and rescue and border control, see H Dijstelbloem, R van Reekum and W Schinkel, 'Surveillance at Sea: The Transactional Politics of Border Control in the Aegean', *Security Dialogue* 48(3), 2017, 224–40; K Follis, 'Vision and Transterritory: The Borders of Europe', *Science, Technology, and Human Values* 42(6), 2017, 1003–30; C Heller and L Pezzani, 'Ebbing and Flowing: The EU's Shifting Practices of (Non-) Assistance and Bordering in a Time of Crisis', *Near Futures Online* 1, 2016, nearfuturesonline.org; P Musarò, 'Mare Nostrum: The Visual Politics of a Military-Humanitarian Operation in the Mediterranean Sea', *Media, Culture & Society* 39(1), 2017, 11–28; J Rijpma and M Vermeulen, 'EUROSUR: Saving Lives or Building Borders?'; M Tazzioli, 'Eurosur, Humanitarian Visibility and (Nearly) Real-Time Mapping in the Mediterranean', *ACME: An International Journal for Critical Geographers* 15(3), 2016, 561–79; R van Reekum and W Schinkel, 'Drawing Lines, Enacting Migration: Visual Prostheses of Bordering Europe', *Public Culture* 29(1), 2017, 27–51. On the role of visibility in offshore detention, see A Mountz, 'In/visibility and the Securitization of Migration Shaping Publics through Border Enforcement on Islands', *Cultural Politics* 11(2), 2015, 184–200.

conjunction with the Migrant Offshore Aid Station (MOAS), an event that incidentally first introduced me to the Comms Specialist, they said the following about luck and spectacular politics: 'we were very lucky, perhaps lucky is not the word, but the whole thing [SAR] got a lot of visibility because the launch date came two weeks after some horrible events, [when] one or two boats capsized and a lot of people drowned.'[45] Visibility and spectacle were repeated refrains throughout our three-hour conversation, covering a range of ways that visibility mattered in SAR. We discussed how the visibility of deaths at sea engendered a need to act – 'Who can object to a rescue of a drowning human being? That was so powerful and of course it was core MSF, saving lives.'[46] We also discussed what Kevin Rozario, a scholar of humanitarianism and popular culture, would call the power of the delicious horror of particular, spectacular tragedies,[47] such as the 'one or two boats' that sank a few weeks prior to the launch of MSF's first SAR operation in the spring of 2015.

The recording of deaths (itself related to visibility and the ability to know) is central to the mobilisation of compassion. In 2014, the year prior to MSF launching SAR operations, 3,283 people drowned in the Mediterranean according to the IOM's Missing Migrants Project.[48] Knowledge about deaths in the Mediterranean were, according to the Comms Specialist, 'already a central issue in our consciousness in Europe' making it 'very clear that the [MSF] operation was going to be rescue.'[49] However, while counting and recording deaths is a necessary part of acknowledging the need and subsequent possibility for intervention – after all how can you help, if you do not know you need to? – the counting of deaths is not enough to stir compassion alone.

The work of humanitarians is not only about relieving the suffering of others in the moment. According to Rozario, it has historically been a

---

45   Interview with key architect of MSF's SAR operation.

46   Ibid.

47   K Rozario, ' "Delicious Horrors": Mass Culture, The Red Cross, and the Appeal of Modern American Humanitarianism,' *American Quarterly* 55(3), 2003, 417–55.

48   '23,481 Missing Migrants Recorded in Mediterranean (Since 2014)' Missing Migrants Project, missingmigrants.iom.int.

49   Interview with key architect of MSF's SAR operation, Amsterdam, 10 July 2018.

task of making suffering (and relief work) 'interesting', 'exciting', and 'entertaining'. Suffering had to be graphic; it had to be stirring. Modern compassion, it seems has been enabled not only by revulsion against cruelty, and by desires to help those less fortunate, but also, in disconcerting ways, by the (covert) pleasures afforded by representations of suffering.[50]

In arguing for a consideration of the exciting and entertaining role of suffering in humanitarianism, Rozario draws on Friedrich Nietzsche's insistence in *The Genealogy of Morals* that 'any history of humanitarian sentiment [has] to take the deliciousness of horror into consideration when it [traces] the birth of conscience and compassion'.[51] This idea has been echoed by historian Karen Halttunen, who has argued that suffering is 'not merely a seamy sideline' but instead an 'integral aspect' of humanitarian sensibility.[52] But Rozario argues that our interest in delicious horrors is not enough on its own to engender compassion or to elicit humanitarian action; the medium of communication plays a key role in how the public have been turned into consumers of suffering and humanitarians into the traders of thrills.[53] In the case of MSF's SAR operation, that medium of communication was a combination of the established mainstream media and Twitter. 'We wanted to do it very high profile . . . The set up was – and we never did anything like this on any other operation before or after – I am still amazed that we managed to get it through [the organisation]. Every trip was going to have one or two journalists on board, there was going to be the @MSF_Sea account, which remains the most successful Twitter account we ever had and we were going to do it all live. "We are rescuing now!" "We rescued this many people today!" And we made it a bit tongue in cheek . . . Everyone wanted to get on board that boat, everyone wanted to, it was a media sensation. It was like, what is more interesting for a journalist than to go to the source of what the refugee crisis is? So, you know, you saw what it was like, there were cameras all over the boat . . . We were showing much more than in other places, other operations, we were talking much

50   Rozario, ' "Delicious Horrors" ', 421.
51   Ibid., 424.
52   K Halttunen, 'Humanitarianism and the Pornography of Pain in Anglo-American Culture', *The American Historical Review* 100(2), 1995.
53   Rozario, ' "Delicious Horrors" ', 429.

more about the people we were helping, putting more testimonies, and it was always on the edge: should we be showing this?'[54]

Visible suffering in the case of shipwrecks and deaths at sea worked to compel MSF into action. But visible suffering was also a key part of SAR operations that the Comms Specialist insisted could not be allowed to exist in silence. SAR was not only rescue missions operating at sea, but a publicity campaign designed to amplify the visibility of suffering. According to the Comms Specialist, 'when [MSF] started the operation, some politician in Brussels told me that what Europe cannot afford is the Lampedusa tragedies. But slow-burning deaths, a few here, a few there, that they can afford because of a lack of visibility'.[55] Thus MSF's job became one of making deaths at sea visible and keeping them visible. They were helped by the spectacular and 'delicious horror', the thrilling element of drowning and 'something incredibly sexy in terms of communications', and the 'incredible footage'[56] of the boats and the rescues – for which Twitter proved a powerful tool.

But publicising horror to elicit compassion was not the only communicative concern, and horror was not the only theme that MSF wanted to make visible through their advocacy. There was an additional and important need to build a narrative of intervention beyond one responding to death. So, while it might have been 'very clear that the operation was going to be rescue, it was not clear what we were going to say about that rescue'. According to people within MSF, 'it was doing a disservice to the whole issue to go in there and paint the situation as: "look, these people happen to be here, we have no option or analysis of what is going on, we are just rescuing them and then glossing over the lack of safe and legal routes"'.[57] Additionally, not 'glossing over' the why of rescue was important because 'if you don't explain what you're doing, how you are doing it, and what the problem is, somebody else is going to explain it for you'. This meant that the visibility of SAR along with social and mainstream media was used to 'install the narrative of a lack of safe and legal routes and to reinforce that notion, so this is why MSF will tell you we are rescuing people but we will also tell you these people are there

---

54 Interview with key architect of MSF's SAR operation.
55 Ibid.
56 Ibid.
57 Ibid.

Médecins Avec Frontières

because they have no other way'.[58] Therefore MSF's use of SAR and its communicative strategies of making things visible, or témoignage, were about the fostering of public support around the need for SAR and, just as importantly, the violence of unequal mobility.

Humanitarianism, since the emergence of non-governmental humanitarian organisations, has been concerned with the public as the bearers of compassion to be mined for much-needed funds and volunteer work. As a result, the public is one of the prime targets of advocacy campaigns.[59] However, the public was not only the bearer of compassion, the provider of funds, or even the source of volunteer humanitarian labour that keeps many humanitarian operations afloat; the public was also the source of political pressure necessary to bring about safe and legal routes. For the Comms Specialist, a key architect of the SAR missions, the public and their role in calling for political change was a key driver: 'I came into this as an activist . . . My agenda personally was this [SAR] as a means to that. Rescue is an end in itself of course, but as a means to activism around the lack of safe and legal routes. So the publicity aspect is what I pushed. I was like, look, you cannot do this in silence. You cannot do this without the publicity, that's Mare Nostrum [the Italian naval SAR operation] . . . I had to install the narrative of safe and legal routes and to reinforce that notion. So this is why we'll tell you we are rescuing people but we will also tell you these people are there because they have no other way. And for as long as the choices are made to continue with these kind of policies, and this kind of border control, this is reinforcing the mobility market that is managed by the smugglers because governments have created these conditions.'[60] Therefore, SAR was also about the ability to rally support around the need to reform unequal mobility, to pull deaths at sea and any response out of the realm of crisis, which is concerned with responding to 'bad things', and into the deliberative, democratic sphere. The organisation was careful, however, to remain on the side of fostering a public capable of generating political pressure for change, rather than to engage in outright calls for specific changes: 'Our aim was clear: we wanted SAR to be used

---

58 Ibid.

59 Work on the public has recently called for the pluralising of the term to publics, in recognition of the existence of a plurality of publics. See, for example, F Cody, 'Publics and Politics', *Annual Review of Anthropology* 40, 2011, 37–52.

60 Interview with key architect of MSF's SAR operation.

politically to become an example that would add to the pressure to manage borders differently, to have a different set-up. We were *not* going to prescribe what that set-up should be, we couldn't even agree internally what a different set-up would be, from open borders, more resettlement, more migrant visas – there was a whole spectrum of solutions that were put forward. There was no internal agreement about what the solution was, or *even* that there was a need for one; there was only an agreement that it was a complex issue and one we were not going to go into because it would have made the whole operation vulnerable to attacks. Instead, our strength was in saying "look, these people need rescue because there are a lack of safe and legal routes" and let's not say more about what those safe and legal routes should be.[61]

The extent to which MSF and its use of visibility and mainstream and social media was successful in fostering a public is clear from the mobilisation of the #safepassage campaign on Twitter that generated tens of thousands of tweets. Alongside this viral campaign, there have been a number of protest marches and other public events calling attention to deaths at sea and the need for safe and legal routes.

'We had this period where we were "heroes of the sea", painting SAR as a fantastic thing, and really seemingly creating an opening that said, this cannot be happening, governments need to be doing something different'.[62] However, this period of fostering a positive humanitarian public around the need for both search and rescue and safe and legal routes was joined by an altogether more exclusionary public against SAR, advocating for the creation of ever-harder, more violent borders. Therefore, talk of a pro-SAR public is inaccurate. Instead, we must talk about the emergence of pro- and anti-SAR publics with divergent views around whether lives should be saved. In the emergence of these publics, the role of visibility cannot be underestimated. Throughout my three-hour conversation with the Comms Specialist, the role of the organisation in fostering an increase in European racism, heralding the election of Matteo Salvini in Italy, and possibly contributing to the UK vote to

---

61   Ibid. Italics mine. The discussion of the differing approaches within the organisation to what safe and legal routes or #safepassage would look like is borne out by a number of internal MSF documents that I have had the privilege of being privy to; for example, 'Framing MSF's Response to Contemporary Migration: Fights to Pick, Blind Spots, How to Go about It', May 2017.

62   Interview with a key architect of MSF's SAR operation.

Médecins Avec Frontières   121

#safepassage protest Museumplein Amsterdam 26 February
2016. This was one of many #safepassage protests held around
the world on the same day. © Polly Pallister-Wilkins

leave the EU, was a repeated lament. 'It is without doubt that SAR has
been used politically, by everyone! By all sides in the most twisted
ways . . . Everyone used the visibility of [SAR] and gave it their own
interpretation and their own interpretation of what the problem was . . .
I do wonder whether the high visibility of the crisis that MSF contributed to is a good or bad thing? Probably neither. It was good that it
promoted the debate but bad for the appetites of the right-wing public
and the lobby in Brussels who want to fortify the border and all the
campaigns around that.'[63] Therefore, different publics have emerged.
One of these is repulsed by the delicious horrors of drowning – this is a

---

63   Ibid.

liberal, cosmopolitan, bourgeois public, that, as anthropologists of humanitarianism Peter Redfield and Liisa Maalki have remarked, finds an expression for its universalist worldview and distaste for suffering in humanitarian action.[64] This is the usual constituency for humanitarian appeals. The other is a public that is not moved to compassion but has been 'deadened' by the spectacle of suffering, as cultural theorist Susan Sontag would put it.[65] This public cannot be stirred to compassion by the spectacles of suffering made visible by MSF. This public is built around exclusivity and racism and is moved – by the delicious horrors of deaths at sea – to call for greater levels of mobility injustice.

Feasibility, and the Political Possibilities of Humanitarian Intervention

That SAR's success and visibility has had repercussions beyond the immediacy of humanitarian crisis is possible to witness only with the benefit of hindsight. Even if some MSF members warned of such eventualities in internal discussions, it was not a guaranteed outcome at the start of the operation, when the priority was saving lives and drawing attention to the apparatus of unequal mobility causing deaths at sea. But that search and rescue may have perversely contributed to a hardening of European borders through the mobilisation of a reactionary public and growing support for the far right is not the only way in which SAR bolsters the existence of border control or the power of states over land and sea. Importantly, search and rescue at sea in the Mediterranean by non-state actors like MSF is only possible with the permission of sovereign state authorities.

SAR missions in the Central Mediterranean take place in international and Libyan waters with the need to save lives as justification. However, such missions in international waters cannot operate free from all control. These missions are still enabled through a number of intersecting practices controlled by states, from surveillance monitoring of the seascape, instructions from the coastguard as the maritime

---

64 Redfield, *Life in Crisis*; LH Maalki, *The Need to Help: The Domestic Arts of International Humanitarianism*, Durham, NC: Duke University Press, 2015.

65 S Sontag, *On Photography*, New York: Farrar, Straus and Giroux, 1977.

Médecins Avec Frontières   123

authority, and the permission to disembark those rescued. In the case of the Central Mediterranean, these functions fall under the umbrella of the Italian Maritime Rescue Coordination Centre (MRCC) in Rome.

MSF can only undertake SAR operations in the Central Mediterranean with the cooperation and permission of the Italian authorities. As events in mid–late 2018 show – when the final MSF vessel, the *Aquarius*, which had been run jointly with SOS Mediterranée, another humanitarian SAR organisation, ceased operations due to lack of permission and restrictions placed on its activities – actions at sea, like those on land, are contingent on the political largesse of states. This should come as no surprise to those familiar with humanitarian operations, in which the ideals of a universal humanitarian attitude of 'go anywhere and do anything', under the banner of saving lives, is always tempered by political realities on the ground shaping what is and what is not feasible.

The role of feasibility in structuring and enabling MSF's SAR operations is complex. Firstly, the sea as a space of intervention offered greater levels of feasibility in terms of access for intervention. Secondly, however, that feasibility was conditioned by the practices of the MRCC being able to monitor the seascape, locate boats, coordinate rescues, and facilitate the disembarkation of rescued people. Thirdly, SAR operations enabled greater levels of témoignage or bearing witness to the suffering caused by violent borders. According to the Comms Specialist, this last point concerning 'accessibility for NGOs and journalists at a critical moment of people being at risk'[66] was the main driver of a decision to operate SAR at sea. However, the Comms Specialist's role was one of advocacy and communication and therefore such considerations structured their daily concerns. The sea gave 'incredible footage' but also 'the conditions were not there to do it [intervention] somewhere else'.[67] The conditions that are being spoken of are threefold: one, the possibility to intervene at sea under the Safety of Life at Sea Directive (SOLAS); two, the existence of a (state-run) maritime rescue infrastructure; and three, the relative safety and ease with which interventions at sea could take place.

The interception of vessels at sea is made legally possible by the SOLAS Directive, and this underpins MSF's SAR operations in international waters. However, before one can intervene to rescue at-risk

---

66   Interview with a key architect of MSF's SAR operation.
67   Ibid.

vessels, the rescuers need to know vessels are at risk. Here the surveillance and maritime monitoring capacity of the MRCC and EUROSUR (European Border Surveillance System) are crucial in making at-risk vessels visible to possible rescuers.[68] According to Rogier van Reekum, making at-risk vessels visible appears to produce stable, simplified evidence of what are complex, unstable moments. This capturing of fleeting moments, critical security studies scholar Julien Jeandesboz argues, helps to stabilise, mobilise and extend interventions at sea.[69] The surveillance infrastructure that is capable of stabilising and mapping what political geographer Martina Tazzioli calls (nearly) real-time events[70] makes possible and puts into practice the wider SAR coordination efforts of the MRCC. Once vessels are detected and located, the MRCC contacts what van Reekum has called 'response-able vessels',[71] such as coastguard vessels, commercial vessels, or humanitarian SAR vessels like those run by MSF. The MRCC then instructs these vessels to carry out rescue operations, informing them of where at-risk vessels can be located and approximating how many people are on board. Following this the MRCC directs the rescuing vessel to the port of disembarkation.

The Mediterranean Sea is, therefore, a space where intervention is made feasible. Additionally, boats are contained vehicles that can be captured in time and space, making intervention easier. Meanwhile, as these vessels are declared at risk (by the MRCC), intervention and saving lives becomes a humanitarian necessity. Contrast this with MSF's early explorations into carrying out operations to assist life seekers as they crossed the Sahara: 'There are parts of the Sahara where there are corpses and we have footage but we couldn't do anything. I mean setting up an operation there is much more complicated – it is a matter of accessibility. At sea we had feasibility with the MRCC, we

---

68   For more on EUROSUR and visibility, see J Jeandesboz, 'European Border Policing: EUROSUR, Knowledge, Calculation', *Global Crime* 18(3), 2017, 256–85; Rijpma and Vermeulen, 'EUROSUR'; R van Reekum, 'The Mediterranean: Migration Corridor, Border Spectacle, Ethical Landscape', *Mediterranean Politics* 21(2), 2016, 336–41; M Tazzioli, 'Eurosur, Humanitarian Visibility and (Nearly) Real-Time Mapping in the Mediterranean', *ACME: An International Journal for Critical Geographers* 15(3), 2016, 561–79.

69   Jeandesboz, 'European Border Policing'; van Reekum, 'The Mediterranean'.

70   Tazzioli, 'Eurosur, Humanitarian Visibility and (Nearly) Real-Time Mapping in the Mediterranean'.

71   van Reekum, 'The Mediterranean'.

had the possibility to find the ships. It's not the same as finding trucks in the Sahara . . . Trucks don't want to be stopped', and not only that but 'there are armed guys who have to deliver a cargo'. What this means is that 'you cannot just land there [in the Sahara] with your MSF T-shirt on and say, "hi, I'm MSF"'.[72] Therefore the particular processes of transit shape the feasibility or infeasibility of intervention to alleviate the risks of unsafe journeys. 'To some extent the sea was the end of the road. Those people were not in transit like in the Sahara anymore . . . in the Sahara things are much more dangerous, the people don't want to be stopped or uncovered, so the space to do it at sea was different, the space was there . . . [In the Sahara] these people are still managed and controlled by the people smuggling them. They are being transported; there is someone in charge. At sea it was different, it was possible'.[73]

At sea, 'the space was there' for intervention, and, importantly, those making the crossing were no longer under the control of smugglers. Life seekers were piloting the boats themselves, meaning that it was also safer for humanitarians to intervene. The mobility of people on the move at particular times and in particular spaces conditions how humanitarians can intervene. Like the buses and bus stop on Lesvos, what humanitarian work is possible is shaped by the specificities of SAR and the specificities of the SAR ship itself. 'These are not hospital ships, but first and foremost rescue vessels designed to save and accommodate as many lives as possible'.[74] The specificities of the sea, and the sea journey, present particular challenges for humanitarian medical work. According to one MSF doctor working on the *Aquarius*: 'Our biggest challenge is rapidly triaging the patients we get. We can get up to 700 patients in a matter of hours. They come on in groups of 18 and we have seconds to minutes to triage them. These people are dehydrated, seasick, often malnourished with open wounds, fuel burns and other traumas, so getting through them, picking out the sickest of the sick and helping them while trying not to miss anything important is really difficult and really stressful, but we do a pretty good job of it'.[75] Meanwhile, many of

---

72 Interview with key architect of MSF's SAR operation.
73 Ibid.
74 Pallister-Wilkins, 'Médecins Avec Frontières'.
75 Interview with MSF doctor, 31 October 2016.

the problems faced on the SAR ships cannot be addressed in the short period of time between rescue and disembarkation, as another MSF medic told me: 'Sometimes our patients don't need intensive medical intervention and we can't provide it on the ship in the brief time that we have with them. Sometimes the best that we can do is just to hold someone's hand and to make that human connection, to let them know that in that moment they are safe.'[76] This last sentiment of letting people know they are safe in the absence of other possibilities echoes the former international president of MSF James Orbinski's idea concerning preventing suffering alone.[77]

In being there to hold people's hands, or preventing life seekers from suffering alone, MSF simultaneously invokes and puts into practice a universal humanism and is reliant on the sovereign power of states to do so. These practices speak to the academic literature discussing humanitarianism's transversal nature concerning the coterminous presence of deterritorialisation and reterritorialisation at the heart of humanitarian practice.[78] Humanitarianism claims to transcend borders and the limits of space and state power. However, through its work, it (re)produces separation between victims and saviours as well as feasible spaces of intervention and non-intervention, in addition to particular spatial logics and the reaffirmation of state power. Through relying on the MRCC in Rome for expertise and guidance as well as permission to act, MSF helps to construct the MRCC as the sovereign actor responsible for determining who can act at sea and where. Through following the instructions of the MRCC on disembarkation, MSF becomes part of the wider border regime aimed at capturing rescued migrants. MSF is not free to disembark those it rescues at a port of its choosing. Instead, it becomes an active agent in the humanitarian border control nexus, helping to bring life seekers under sovereign control.

---

76   Interview with MSF doctor, 20 May 2017.

77   J Orbinski, *An Imperfect Offering: Humanitarian Action for the Twenty-First Century*, New York: Walker Publishing Company, 2008.

78   See, for example, F Debrix, 'Deterritorialised Territories, Borderless Borders: The New Geography of International Medical Assistance', *Third World Quarterly* 19(5), 1998, 827–46. The world of universal humanitarianism is a smooth space, while the world humanitarianism constructs through its operations is a striated space between victim and saviour.

Médecins Avec Frontières 127

However, there are limits to MSF's engagement with the border control regime. On Lesvos, the implementation of the EU-Turkey Statement saw MSF refuse to 'deliver' life seekers to the Moria Hotspot to be subjected to possible deportation, while previously being comfortable in assisting processes of registration. At sea, MSF has refused to engage in rescue efforts in coordination with the Libyan coastguard or to return those who were rescued to Libya, as they were instructed to do by the MRCC. Yet, through SAR efforts, MSF has been an active agent in shifting the European border into the Mediterranean's international waters.[79] At the same time, MSF's SAR operations were only enabled through close cooperation with the sovereign authorities responsible for making danger at sea visible and responses feasible. There is, therefore, ambivalence to such life-saving interventions, and a limit to the political possibilities that they can enact. MSF undertook SAR operations with the express purpose of bearing witness to and making visible the death and suffering caused by violent borders and unequal mobility. But such SAR operations were dependent on the sovereign power of states, and, while the high visibility of MSF's operations may have had an impact on the increasing support for European far right political parties, MSF also worked directly with sovereign state powers to reproduce the very same violent borders and unequal mobility.

Humanitarian Solutions to Political Problems?

Out here on Aquarius, we are merely slapping bandages on wounds that have been bleeding for many years but are now beginning to hemorrhage. We need to stop treating the symptoms and look at the cause. Let's stop trying to prevent people from coming to Europe by building legal and physical fences and walls. Let's end the practice of giving vast sums of money to 'border forces' in countries with terrible human rights records. Simply stemming the flow of people in lands where they are out of the sight of European eyes does not stop the

---

79 For more on this, see P Pallister-Wilkins, 'Humanitarian Borderwork', in Cengiz Günay and Nina Witjes eds, *Border Politics: Defining Spaces of Governance and Forms of Transgressions*, New York: Springer, 2017.

problem – it just hides it. NGOs cannot continue to pluck people out of the seas indefinitely.[80]

This analysis from Sarah Giles, a doctor on a number of MSF missions aboard the *Aquarius*, builds on the former head of UNHCR and current UN secretary-general Antonio Guterres's claim that 'there is no humanitarian solution to this tragic humanitarian crisis'[81] by suggesting that the Aquarius was not really responding to a humanitarian crisis at all. Here, Giles and Guterres agree with the former UNHCR head Sadako Ogata's similar claim.[82] Tom Scott-Smith uses Ogata's now well-known claim to open a special issue of *Refugee Survey Quarterly* in which MSF members explore the complexities and operational challenges of assisting people on the move. As Scott-Smith – like Sarah Giles above – says, death and suffering caused by unequal mobility are 'inescapably political, forcing aid agencies to come to terms with their limitations, able only to attend to the immediate manifestations of a deep-seated, systemic crisis'.[83] For Scott-Smith, therefore, 'it is difficult, if not impossible, to take effective humanitarian action in response to migration without also taking a political stand'.[84] This manifests itself for humanitarian organisations like MSF 'not [in] whether to be political, but what kind of politics to promote'.[85] With search and rescue, MSF aimed to highlight the politics behind deaths at sea but was wary of prescribing practical solutions beyond calling for safe and legal routes.[86] This leads Scott-Smith to argue that 'the key issue in contemporary humanitarianism ... is not that humanitarian solutions are insufficient. It is that humanitarian problems are insufficient'.[87] Here, framing an issue as a

---

80   Sarah Giles, 'Again', *Blogs from Doctors Without Borders*, 20 December 2016 blogs.msf.org.

81   L Doucet, 'Migrant Crisis: Why Is it Erupting Now?', *BBC News Online*, 13 September 2015, bbc.co.uk.

82   S Ogata, 'The Turbulent Decade: Confronting the Refugee Crisis of the 1990s', World Chronicle, Programme No. 970, interview by MA Williams, 14 March 2005, unmultimedia.org.

83   T Scott-Smith, 'Humanitarian Dilemmas in a Mobile World', *Refugee Survey Quarterly* 35(2), 2016, 2.

84   Ibid.

85   Ibid., 2.

86   Interview with key architect of MSF's SAR operation.

87   Scott-Smith, 'Humanitarian Dilemmas in a Mobile World', 3.

distinctly humanitarian one results in limiting the possible responses available.

MSF recognises that it is unequal mobility that causes risks to life and deaths at borders and during people's journeys. Their advocacy and communications are aimed at highlighting 'the cause' while their operations are treating 'the symptoms'. However, as a medical humanitarian organisation, their operations are limited to addressing the humanitarian problems caused by political policies and practices. So, while MSF's advocacy and communication efforts might be addressed at highlighting the deadly effects of a lack of safe and legal routes, everyday operations are tailored to providing limited assistance according to need.[88] Need, defined as medical need and vulnerability, becomes a way of categorising and dividing people on the move according to embodied symptoms, history of illness, or perceived categories of vulnerability that run along vectors such as gender and age. In this schema, young, physically healthy men are considered least vulnerable and least in need, while single, elderly women with an acute medical need are classified as most at risk. This is a form of humanitarian borderwork separating people according to a number of external pre-determined characteristics, which, while intended to help alleviate suffering, also affects people's ability to seek and find safety during their journeys.[89]

This gets to the heart of humanitarianism's limited potential. It is what leads its critics, such as Eyal Weizman, to discuss humanitarian action as a lesser evil, the least bad response among other bad responses. Such critics argue that humanitarianism is less a utopian ideal promoting a universal humanity free from suffering and death but instead a pragmatic, conservative (with a small c) response that operates within the pre-existing liberal order.[90] Most people I have encountered in MSF would agree with these criticisms. For my interlocutors in the organisation, humanitarianism is always contingent, and yet this, according to some in the organisation, can also be its strength.

There are those within the organisation who see the pragmatism of MSF and wider humanitarian efforts as a strength, and as a potentially

88 Interview with MSF displacement specialist, Brussels, 14 November 2016.

89 See Pallister-Wilkins, 'Médecins Sans Frontières and the Practice of Universalist Humanitarianism'.

90 E Weizman, *The Least of All Possible Evils: Humanitarian Violence from Arendt to Gaza*, London: Verso, 2012.

radical politics that refuses to presume to know the solution to crises caused by political failures. For these, the refusal to step outside of medical practice and expertise in addressing suffering is quietly radical – it is a politics that does not assume to know the answer or to take on the responsibility of fixing structural causes.[91] As such, it is an attempt to move away from humanitarianism's colonial connotation as a tool of white saviours.

In thinking about this in relation to unequal mobility and violent borders, and the idea of MSF staying in its lane to offer medical relief rather than a revolutionary political solution, the question is: What could a medical humanitarian organisation such as MSF do to restructure unequal mobility regimes? The organisation has addressed this question practically, through a range of interventions and operations that recognise the risks caused by exclusion from safe and legal forms of travel that include the provision of transportation itself; the creation of temporary 'pop-up' spaces offering limited services that respond to the particular dynamics of the migration-border assemblage; and search and rescue at sea. However, MSF has also attempted to use these actions, in particular SAR, to encourage civil society to advocate for larger political change. Therefore, while it might not be MSF's role to prescribe political solutions, the organisation does use its humanitarian work and its commitment to bearing witness as a form of political action capable of advocating for, and in certain instances facilitating, change.

These changes are not necessarily committed to an emancipatory politics premised on an inclusive universal humanity. Instead, they have been concerned with more exclusive border policies and a continuation of, for example, externalised border controls in countries such as Libya, highlighting the limited power and possibility for change that an organisation like MSF can achieve. Even with €1.53 billion in funds raised in 2017, 67 percent of which was spent on programmes and only 3 percent on awareness raising, MSF is not a sovereign power capable of overhauling unequal mobility regimes.[92] Even if MSF claims ingérence as the right to intervene beyond or in spite of borders, and even if MSF works with other humanitarian actors to reproduce borders based on categories of suffering and distinguishing between victims and saviours – what

---

91   Repeated conversations with MSF members, 2015–18.
92   See MSF, *Reports and Finance*, 2017, msf.org/reports-and-finances.

Didier Fassin has called the hierarchies of humanity that make up a politics of life[93] – the organisation's work is pragmatic and contingent, and reliant on the largesse of state actors. Nevertheless, in a political climate in which advocating for the basic humanity of life seekers is increasingly a radical politics, the work of MSF does offer an alternative politics and inspires other forms of humanitarian action. These other forms of action include more grassroots initiatives intended to save lives and foster a common humanity in response to the inequalities, deaths and suffering produced by violent borders.

---

93   Fassin, 'Humanitarianism as a Politics of Life'.

5

Grassroots™ Humanitarianism

We're on month nine of this now, month nine, and these people still can't do anything. OK they've laid on a couple of buses which is fantastic in and of itself. But these organisations . . . I used to have respect for these organisations because of what they do, but it's bullshit, it's absolute bullshit, because they don't feed people, most of them don't give out blankets, most of them don't give clothes, most of the people who are working for them are volunteers, you know they don't pay them wages.[1]

I was very uncomfortable that solidarity networks were subsumed into humanitarian service provision. And it blunted our focus and our discourse in critiquing policy. A lot of it was crowdfunding for temporary structures that we knew would be bulldozed in Calais, or working in hot-soup kitchens, and those were very basic, practical, and immediate needs and we had to respond to them in the vacuum of the state and the oftentimes deliberate negation of any duty of care.[2]

Grassroots humanitarianism is, and often explicitly markets itself as, a response to what 'grassroots' actors see as failures by state actors and

---

1 Interview with volunteer rescuer, Lesvos, 22 October 2015.
2 Interview with long-term activist, active across Europe and the Middle East, via Skype, 25 October 2018.

traditional NGOs alike, while simultaneously filling important gaps in the provision of relief and aid to life seekers and challenging border violence. The response of volunteer and grassroots actors to violent borders highlights the diversity of aims, practices and politics of humanitarian borderwork. The variety of ways those involved choose to refer to their activities – humanitarianism; aid provision; helping; volunteering; on-the-ground presence; stepping in; stepping-up; being human; activism; solidarity; and accompanying – shows the complexity of the people and practices that fall under the umbrella of what I call 'grassroots humanitarianism'. The decision to call it grassroots humanitarianism is not without tension; the term does not sit all that well with me, as the practices that fall under such a label extend from anarchist-inspired collective actions to entrepreneurial hyper-capitalist forms of extraction and brand building that involve the hyper-privileged 1 percent. 'Grassroots' here is co-opted as a brand marker and commoditised for the purposes of fundraising and 'doing things differently'. Therefore, the term 'grassroots' should not be read as encompassing a truly bottom-up attempt at caregiving, rather it is a catch-all term intended to contrast such practices to those of states and traditional professional humanitarian organisations.

Grassroots humanitarianism, with its focus on the provision of basic needs – recognising that some involved reject the label humanitarian altogether – has a longer history than some of the more organised and visible efforts of recent years would suggest. Grassroots humanitarians have been active in and around Calais since the closure of the Sangatte centre in 2002,[3] while in the US, No More Deaths/No Más Muertes was founded in 2004 to aid those crossing the Sonoran Desert on the US-Mexico border.[4] The individuals and groups that make up such activity are diverse temporally, spatially and politically. They respond to individual events and particular tragedies. At other times, they respond to particular issues such as border closures, or coalesce around a politics opposed to violent borders and unequal mobility. The politics of these volunteer humanitarians stretch from anarchist solidarity actions to liberal and traditional charity-inspired

---

3   For more on Sangatte, see D Fassin, 'Compassion and Repression: The Moral Economy of Immigration Policies in France', *Cultural Anthropology* 20(3), 2005, 362–87.

4   For more on No More Deaths/No Más Muertes, see forms.nomoredeaths.org/en.

efforts, revealing both the possibilities and limitations of grassroots humanitarianism.

People engage in grassroots humanitarianism because, in the words of one Scandinavian volunteer who had travelled to Greece in 2015, they 'feel useless sat at home doing nothing' and that they 'have to do something'[5] when faced with human suffering. This is reminiscent of Liisa Maalki's work with those who volunteer for the Finnish Red Cross, in which the need to help is prompted by a need to be active in the world.[6] Alternatively, in the words of a tourist-turned-volunteer who happened to get caught up in 'an unfolding humanitarian crisis' while on their two-week summer holiday, they 'just sort of made it up as they went along' because 'well, you just would, wouldn't you, when you see people in need – it's what makes us human'.[7] Meanwhile, others engage in providing basic needs to life seekers in places like Calais after many years of engagement with politically informed No Borders activism.[8] All of this highlights what one grassroots humanitarian active in organising volunteers and donations in Greece since 2015 referred to as 'the power of regular people'; even when those 'regular people' are actually celebrities or the mobility privileged. And even when their actions were often less than regular or simple – as this grassroots volunteer said while gesturing to a mountain of donations being sorted neatly into a complex logistics system of colour-coded boxes: 'All of this, all of these donations are because of the power of volunteers. People just getting together and collecting stuff.'[9]

However, humanitarianism is a flexible practice that 'can be harnessed for various ends, adapted and appropriated'[10] for a number of other activities, from individual self-improvement and the marketing and expansion of brands to Christian evangelism. The idea that the actions discussed here are all the work of 'regular people' is uncomfortable.

---

5   Interview with a new grassroots humanitarian, Molyvos, Lesvos, 21 October 2015.

6   LH Maalki, *The Need to Help: The Domestic Arts of International Humanitarianism*, Durham, NC: Duke University Press, 2015.

7   Interview with a tourist-turned-volunteer, Athens, 11 October 2015.

8   Repeated conversations with No Borders activists and regular Calais visitors, 2007–present.

9   Interview with long-term grassroots organiser, Lesvos, 22 October 2015.

10   K Storey, *Settler Anxiety at the Outposts of Empire: Colonial Relations, Humanitarian Discourses, and the Imperial Press*, Vancouver: UBC Press, 2016.

Many of those involved and their actions are not 'regular' in an everyday sense. However, the appeal to ordinariness distances such work from the humanitarian borderwork of states and professional humanitarians.[11] These volunteer efforts in many instances reaffirm differentiations and hierarchies between the included and empowered citizens of the Global North and the excluded, disempowered others. At the same time, they make use of and are enabled by exclusionary border control infrastructures and work to reproduce them in turn. Working where the Chicana poet Gloria Anzaldúa says, 'the third world grates against the first world and bleeds',[12] these volunteer activities, while attending to the bleeding, all too often ignore or leave the grater untouched.

The Privileges of the Ordinary

Infrastructures of differential mobility make grassroots humanitarianism possible. 'Mobilities are organised in and through mobility regimes and uneven infrastructure spaces that simultaneously presuppose and reproduce immobile "others".[13] If much borderwork is focused on immobile others – or at least those that state policies aim to make immobile – humanitarian responses make the most of mobility privileges. These privileges speak to what sociologist of mobility Mimi Sheller refers to as the 'always unequal' nature of mobility 'striated by gender, race, ethnicity, class, caste, colour, nationality, age, sexuality, and differential abilities'.[14] Grassroots humanitarianism – like the more established, 'traditional' actors – relies on the relatively free movement of privileged people from the Global North, making use of visa and passport privileges and using planes, ferries, cars and other transport infrastructures accessible to them to travel to spaces of crisis wherein they make use of hotels and other tourist facilities. Additionally, privileged forms of mobility are used to ship and move supplies and donations.

---

11 With thanks to Elisa Pascucci for pushing me to think more about 'regular' in this context.

12 G Anzaldua, *Borderlands/La Frontera: The New Mestizo*, San Francisco: Aunt Lute Books, 1987, 25.

13 M Sheller, *Mobility Justice: The Politics of Movement in an Age of Extremes*, London: Verso, 2018, 95.

14 Ibid.

One volunteer who set up a small NGO in Denmark was able to use their privilege and their existing connections to persuade Maersk to ship 200 tonnes of donated supplies from Copenhagen to Greece free of charge, whereupon they oversaw its distribution. Grassroots humanitarianism is enabled through its relation to, and its embedding in, wider privileged infrastructures of mobility and tourism.

There is an emerging body of work in the social sciences and humanities drawing attention to the constitutive role of tourism and crisis. Sheller has written about the intertwining of infrastructures of tourism and humanitarian responses in the Caribbean. International Relations scholar Debbie Lisle has called attention to the historical and central role of tourism and international networks from nineteenth-century imperial expansion up until the present, looking, for example, at the important role of the holiday company Thomas Cook in consolidating British power throughout the Empire. Political geographers Sara Fregonese and Adam Ramadan have drawn attention to the ways in which hotels are strategic infrastructures mediating geopolitical processes including responses to crises. Elisa Pascucci has unpacked the symbiotic relationship between humanitarian assistance, tourist and mobility infrastructures and subsequent journalistic reportage and academic research.[15]

Inequality in mobility access was starkly visible when, during a period of research leave, I travelled to Greece to gather much of the data that forms the basis of this book. Waiting at the gate to board an early evening flight from Athens to Lesvos, I was surrounded by people from across Europe, North America and Australia, heading to the island to 'be useful', to 'help' and to 'exercise a commitment to others'. Our journey could not have been easier: the flight cost me €55 and included boiled sweets for take-off. Upon landing in Lesvos forty minutes later, I picked up my hire car and drove to my hotel. Meanwhile, life seekers were arriving on the island in small boats, having made the 10km

---

15 M Sheller, 'The Islanding Effect: Post-Disaster Mobility Systems and Humanitarian Logistics in Haiti', *Cultural Geographies* 20(2), 2012, 185–204; D Lisle, *Holidays in the Danger Zone: Entanglements of War and Tourism*, Minneapolis: University of Minnesota Press, 2016; S Fregonese and A Ramadan, 'Hotel Geopolitics: A Research Agenda', *Geopolitics* 20(4), 2015, 793–813; E Pascucci, 'The Humanitarian Infrastructure and the Question of Over-Research: Reflections on Fieldwork in the Refugee Crisis in the Middle East and North Africa', *Area* 49(2), 2017, 249–55.

crossing from Turkey at a cost of €1,000 or more, before being escorted across the island by bus and having to register with the Greek and EU authorities. While I was settling under my duvet in my hotel room with its en-suite bathroom, life seekers were lucky to find a space in one of the IKEA Better Shelters or the large marquees that made up their basic sleeping accommodation. My presence on the island, my ability to do research, and the existence on the island of hundreds of grassroots humanitarians, there to act as volunteer rescuers, medics, basic needs providers, and so on, were enabled by the infrastructures of mobility and tourism.

Lesvos is a tourist island with an airport connecting the island not only to the rest of Greece, but to many other parts of Europe, and hundreds of hotels and guesthouses offering a range of accommodation. Fregonese and Ramadan suggest that hotels are 'flexible material infrastructures that can mediate geopolitical processes'.[16] In Lesvos, hotels were flexible in their reorientation towards accommodating grassroots humanitarians and in doing so played an important role in Lesvos' place in the humanitarian borderwork assemblage. Lesvos was a popular place of arrival due to both its geographical location in the Aegean and the presence of attendant infrastructures that were able to support humanitarian work, which at least made arrival more visible.

Lesvos was not the only Aegean island of arrival. I do not want to claim a causal relationship between the presence of hospitality infrastructures that can easily be turned from tourist attractions into humanitarian ones. Such a claim bolsters the argument made by some anti-migrant policymakers, keen to maintain the global colour line, that the provision of assistance acts as a 'pull factor'. However, the size of Lesvos' 'flexible material infrastructures', capable of 'mediating geopolitical processes', such as arrival and transit and the attendant provision of humanitarian assistance, certainly played a role in Lesvos emerging as a focal point in the global archipelago of border sites and spaces. Without such infrastructures of mobility and hospitality, grassroots humanitarianism on the island would not have been possible at the levels that were reached. But the presence of humanitarian activity is also related to what is made visible. As Lauren Berlant argues, 'infrastructures are the things that pattern social life' and within this we can include the media, as both

---

16   Fregonese and Ramadan, 'Hotel Geopolitics', 793.

a 'patterner of social life' but also something that is 'patterned' by other infrastructures.[17]

In the introduction, I referred to my encounter with Lesvos as a 'humanitarianesque carnival'. This carnival not only included a diverse number of grassroots volunteers from across the world, but it was fostered by an attendant media presence that worked to increase the amount of volunteers with every 'delicious horror' reported. The media played a central role in increasing the visibility of what was happening on Lesvos, and amplifying the calls of local people engaged in assisting arriving life seekers: 'We've always had refugees coming across, all the sixteen years I've been here but mainly they were men . . . Then last year [2014] we noticed more and more coming and there were women and children . . . and then February this year I was walking the beach and found a baby life jacket and that's what got to me. And I watched them sitting by the side of the road and then having to walk 65km and on wet days people were soaking wet and cold and so we decided we had to do something to help. That's how it all started. For the first five months there was just my family . . . trying our best . . . and we started shouting, we need help, we need help. And then in June [2015], a French reporter came and he put out something, not big, but something, then the *Daily Mail* put out an article . . . then it just sort of blew up from there. Towards the end of June, we started getting people coming to help us.'[18]

By the autumn of 2015, the number of people going to Lesvos and the attendant media presence had reached such a high level that one morning, I recorded as many people with large telephoto lenses snapping shots of arriving dinghies as I did grassroots humanitarian volunteers waiting to assist those arriving with dry clothes and thermal blankets. One 2015 volunteer reminisced with humour and horror (in 2018) about what they referred to as the 'refugee chasers' and the 'desperation among some of the volunteers and the media to be in the spotlight and be heroes'. These were people who were 'feeding off the horror'.[19] This carnival of testosterone-fuelled adventure-seeking and a desire to be where the action was, coupled with an expectant media reporting on

---

17   L Berlant, 'The Commons: Infrastructure for Troubling Times', *Environment and Planning D: Society and Space* 34(3), 2016, 393–419.

18   Interview with volunteer rescuer, Lesvos, 22 October 2015.

19   Interview with long-term humanitarian organiser, via Skype, 9 December 2018.

Journalists try and photograph a woman having a panic
attack, Lesvos, November 2015. © Polly Pallister-Wilkins

such antics to a global public keen to consume such exciting 'feel good'
stories, led this volunteer to leave Lesvos for their own psychological
well-being. Social anthropologist Evthymios Papataxiarchis not only
works on the island but has a long research relationship with the north
shore particularly. In his reflections, he suggests, 'from a volunteer point
of view, being on the front line and offering these services has a special
value. It is a mark of distinction. It makes all the difference,' and turns
the 'front line', as he calls it, into something of an obsession.[20] However,
such activities were all enabled and mediated through the leveraging of
mobility priviliges by those able – and importantly made able – to help
and report through such privileges.

The central role of mobility and hospitality infrastructures in making
Lesvos a key node in the network of humanitarian sites across Europe
and elsewhere, led to an outpouring of assistance and generosity, and to
grassroots humanitarians filling in the gaps left by a lack of assistance
from the state or larger NGOs. However, in response to the presence of

---

20   E Papataxiarchis, 'Being "There": At the Front Line of the "European Refugee
Crisis", Part 1', *Anthropology Today* 32(2), 2016, 5.

so many people, one local volunteer exclaimed: 'They're not necessary, why don't they go to a refugee reception centre in the Netherlands and help there?'[21] This was indeed a good question, and one that I think can be, in part, answered by a combination of the attendant media presence on the island – generating a spectacle that made the idea of volunteering an attractive and exciting prospect – and the ease with which people with privileged mobility could travel to Lesvos.

The Entrepreneurial Lightness of Being

The intersection of privileged mobility regimes, tourist infrastructures and economies is best epitomised by travel companies, such as Sunweb, offering special 'holiday deals' at reduced rates to those going to Lesvos to help, and online booking platforms, such as Booking.com, partnering with humanitarian groups like Movement On The Ground. Here, profit-seeking companies both facilitate the ability of grassroots humanitarians to travel to 'save distant strangers' and take advantage of the existence of crises and the subsequent need for a response. The centrality of entrepreneurial economies and, in many instances, online platforms in the creation and consolidation of grassroots humanitarian activity in response to the 'refugee crisis' is a central feature across many border spaces, linking the local to the global through physical tourist infrastructures and online networks.

Occupying a liminal role as a social anthropologist, Evthymios Papataxiarchis is able to narrate the dynamics of grassroots humanitarian action while being based at the University of the Aegean in Mytilene, where his own graduates have gone on to have careers working in the humanitarian industry that has come to shape Lesvos. In reflecting on the entrepreneurial dynamics of some 'foreign freelance "volunteers" who seem to place humanitarian action on the ground in the service of an e-career', he suggests:

> These e-volunteers pursue their careers with words, photos and all kinds of signifiers, before a global audience on the internet. Their strategy is largely performative: their actions are meant to be placed

---

21   Interview with local volunteer, Lesvos, 24 October 2015.

on a visual register that becomes available to everyone, primarily through social media, thus attracting large audiences of 'followers' and the necessary resources to keep on travelling. Some are activists of repute; others are just agile travellers. A few among the most successful of them are surfing the globe in the quest for natural disasters, the field of distinction par excellence for a volunteer. In its turn, their presence on the front line, together with other disaster specialists, places Skala and Lesbos on the global map of the great disaster sites of the 21st century alongside the Indian Ocean tsunami (2004), Hurricane Katrina (2005) or the Haiti earthquake (2010).[22]

The role of humanitarian action in the reproduction of capitalism is a key concern of many scholars of humanitarian intervention. For instance, Mark Duffield, Katharyne Mitchell and Simon Reid-Henry have all explored the ways the provision of aid reproduces and in some instances expands (neo)liberal markets through saving lives.[23] Humanitarianism not only brings the market in its wake but allows unjust economic systems to continue by offering an 'insurance of last resort'.[24] In these practices, market-based ideas about efficiency are seen as central to the effective provision of relief through the (re)imposition of a (neo)liberal order. Humanitarian crises provide opportunities for the use of experimental techniques and technologies, such as collaborative mapping, aimed at creating marketable and marketised humanitarian service users. Meanwhile, compassionate sentiments underpinning humanitarian action are increasingly blurred and blended with supposedly more 'rational' or unsentimental economic logics in late capitalism.[25] Monika

---

22   Papataxiarchis, ' "Being There" ', 9.

23   M Duffield, 'The Liberal Way of Development and the Development–Security Impasse: Exploring the Global Life-Chance Divide', *Security Dialogue* 41(1), 2010; K Mitchell, 'Ungoverned Space: Global Security and the Geopolitics of Broken Windows', *Political Geography* 29, 2010, 289–97; SM Reid-Henry, 'Humanitarianism as Liberal Diagnostic: Humanitarian Reason and the Political Rationalities of the Liberal Will-to-Care', *Transactions of the Institute of British Geographers* 39(3), 2014.

24   Duffield, 'The Liberal Way of Development and the Development-Security Impasse', 14, and Reid-Henry, 'Humanitarianism as Liberal Diagnostic', 427.

25   K Lindskov Jacobsen and KB Sandvik, 'UNHCR and the Pursuit of International Protection: Accountability through Technology?' *Third Wold Quarterly* 39(8), 2018, 1508–24; M Mostafanezhad, 'Celebrity Humanitarianism and the Popular Geopolitics of Hope along the Thai-Burma Border', 70.

Krause has argued that the humanitarian sector's focus as a whole is on the production of projects that can be sold to key donors with the result that projects and beneficiaries become commodities in a humanitarian industry.[26] Here the presence of Booking.com, as a partner of the aforementioned Movement On The Ground, alongside other corporate partners including the global consultancy firm Accenture and web-based platform Bynder – a 'brand' platform that provides the opportunity 'to collaborate globally, produce, review and approve new marketing collateral, and circulate company content at the click of a button' – is particularly illustrative.[27]

Like Movement On The Ground, many grassroots humanitarian volunteers from Lesvos to Calais engage in entrepreneurial activities more akin to Silicon Valley startups-cum-multinational megacorporations. These groups are reliant on small-is-beautiful, adapt-or-die methods coupled with a 'just-in-time' Amazon Prime approach to the efficient and effective delivery of assistance. This small-is-beautiful approach, like the Silicon Valley corporations they emulate, utilise the latest social media technologies and online marketplaces like Amazon for both fundraising and the sourcing and delivery of aid. In addition, they demonstrate a distrust of both state-level approaches to aid and the operations of more traditional international humanitarian organisations.

What has become clear through my ongoing engagement with these groups, both on and offline, is that they are humanitarian entrepreneurs often armed with only smartphones, social media platforms, PayPal accounts, and an affective desire to help. There have been critiques of humanitarian action that suggest that for some involved, humanitarian work is as much about building people's own personal brands as it is a commitment to helping. Media and communication studies scholar Lilie Chouliaraki, for example, criticised celebrity humanitarian Angelina Jolie's humanitarian assistance as being part of building 'Brangelina'.[28] Such entrepreneurial brand-building efforts were present among some of the volunteers I encountered, including, in one particularly striking case, a young US citizen who admitted travelling to Lesvos

---

26 M Krause, *The Good Project: Humanitarian Relief NGOs and the Fragmentation of Reason*, Chicago: The University of Chicago Press, 2014.

27 See 'Sponsors & Partners' at movementontheground.com.

28 L Chouliaraki, 'The Theatricality of Humanitarianism: A Critique of Celebrity Advocacy', *Communication and Critical/Cultural Studies* 9(1), 2012, 1–21.

because he wanted to be on a Most Influential People list by the time he was thirty.

However, for the most part, volunteer humanitarians are deeply and sincerely committed to making the world a better place and believe that their logistical lightness of being and mastery of affective networks can more readily identify needs, mobilise compassion in the shape of both monetary and material donations and deliver relief. It is argued by many of my interlocutors in this volunteer humanitarian sector that this light-touch, just-in-time approach is better suited to the 'fluidity of situations' caused by mobility and the increasingly pop-up nature of relief. However, this 'light-touch' approach is also a marketing tool of grassroots™ humanitarianism hiding the considerable effort in labour and material costs of setting up and maintaining a start-up enterprise.[29] This speaks to what Tom Scott-Smith calls 'humanitarian neophilia', a 'distinctive approach to aid, which combines an optimistic faith in the possibilities of technology with a commitment to the expansion of markets' and what Katharyne Mitchell calls a 'type of depoliticized global "care citizenship"' whereby 'neoliberal citizenship is underpinned by a waning faith in governments and a growing confidence in individual enterprise, people power, and the efficiency of market systems and logics'.[30]

Alongside this focus on the efficiency of the market, neoliberal humanitarian entrepreneurs couple a belief in radical transparency with a belief in the rationality and apolitical nature of 'facts' and quantitative data measurements. When combined with compassion and 'New Left' forms of activism that are distrustful of state-based, institutionalised responses to political problem-solving, what results are new forms of humanitarian activity that, Mitchell suggests, privilege 'social relationships that foreground individualising forms of care and duty at a global or post-national scale, but operate above and beyond a state-based rhetoric of interventionism'.[31] Meanwhile, Scott-Smith argues that new

---

29   Again, I am thankful to Elisa Pascucci for pushing me to think more about what lightness conceals here.

30   T Scott-Smith, 'Humanitarian Neophilia: The "Innovation Turn" and Its Implications', *Third World Quarterly* 37(12), 2016, 2230; K Mitchell, 'Celebrity Humanitarianism, Transnational Emotion and the Rise of Neoliberal Citizenship', *Global Networks* 16(3), 2016, 290.

31   K Mitchell, ' "Factavism": A New Configuration of Humanitarian Reason', *Geopolitics* 22(1), 2016, 114.

Grassroots™ Humanitarianism

entrepreneurial forms of humanitarianism speak to 'Californian Ideology', combining elements of both the New Right and the New Left that are focused on 'individual rebellion, radical individualism and a utopian technological determinism'.[32] In this formulation, counter-cultural ideas from the 1960s concerned with celebrating marginalised communities and unsettling and abandoning older forms of authority mix with a radical individualism driven by the opportunities and expansion of capitalism into new markets. In the California Ideology, these values were and continue to be brought together by information technology and the internet's emancipatory potential.

Katharyne Mitchell's work in online forms of humanitarian action explores how the internet enables citizens to express themselves and create diverse new political alliances across and beyond state politics. The internet provides new – market(able) – opportunities for the expansion of both capitalism and humanitarian action.[33] The internet, and the social media platforms and networks it has enabled, facilitates and creates a virtual space for people to come together around affective ideals of care. In addition, online spaces enable non-professional humanitarians to organise humanitarian interventions in a number of ways, including through the identification of needs and the collection of resources. Online spaces also allow for easier monitoring of the apparent effectiveness of such interventions, in celebration of neoliberal transparency. Mitchell argues that transnational migration activism and concomitant humanitarian responses make considerable use of these emergent and multi-scalar – what she calls geosocial – discourses and networks.[34] Political scientist Nicholas Micinski argues that platforms such as Facebook and group messenger services like WhatsApp have been central in more horizontal coordinating efforts and decision-making in emergency responses on the Greek islands.[35] Anthropologist of humanitarianism Katerina Rozakou has called such efforts 'solidarity

---

32   Scott-Smith, 'Humanitarian Neophilia'.

33   K Mitchell, 'Celebrity Humanitarianism' and ' "Factavism" '.

34   K Mitchell and KP Kallio, 'Spaces of the Geosocial: Exploring Transnational Topologies', *Geopolitics* 22(1), 2017, 1–14; K Mitchell and M Sparke, 'Hotspot Geopolitics versus Geosocial Solidarity: Contending Constructions of Safe Space for Migrants in Europe', *Environment and Planning D: Society and Space* 38(6), 2020, 1046–66.

35   NR Micinski, 'Everyday Coordination in EU Migration Management: Civil Society Responses in Greece', *International Studies Perspectives* 20(2), 2019, 129–48.

'#humanitarianism' in recognition of the way social media was, borrowing from Thomas L Haskell, 'a key recipe' as a 'source of information and the means of funding through crowds-funding – that enabled "independent volunteers" to reach Greece.'[36] The importance of such technologies has been reiterated time and again by the volunteer humanitarians I have come to know. These platforms, in turn, have considerable ability to speed up the identification of needs and the targeting of assistance. I had to remove myself from the Lesvos WhatsApp group for volunteers, as my phone buzzed constantly with so many new messages and information that it became overwhelming to deal with while I was thousands of kilometres away, working on other things.

Facebook is literally awash with hundreds of groups with tens of thousands of members set up both to amplify the needs of life seekers and those wanting to help and to coordinate activities across not only Europe and throughout the United States and Canada, but globally. Their presence online means that these groups are simultaneously local and global in scope. Calais Action, for example, might be an ostensibly UK-based group, but just among those members that are visible to me (as I am Facebook friends with them), there are people in the United States, Ireland, Greece, the Netherlands and Italy, as well as the UK. Meanwhile, Facebook's community-building algorithm links groups such as Calais Action to similar groups working to strengthen and build a network of grassroots groups across geosocial space. These online groups and platforms make it possible for someone sitting at home in Vancouver to respond to an urgent Facebook call for nappies on Lesvos using online delivery services like Amazon. Additionally, online platforms such as PayPal, Kickstarter and GoFundMe enable individuals and groups to fund their efforts more directly through peer-to-peer donations from individuals anywhere in the world. These various platforms and services are designed to be interoperable and to work together and in doing so foster the geosocial. Moreover, they are fast becoming a central feature of humanitarian provision, collapsing space and time between giver, aid provider and receiver like never before, and appearing to enable the overcoming of borders and the creation of an online, transversal, borderless world.

---

36 K Rozakou, 'Solidarity #Humanitarianism: The Blurred Boundaries of Humanitarianism in Greece', *Etnofoor* 29(2), 2017, 99–104.

Grassroots™ Humanitarianism

However, like other forms of humanitarian advocacy and fundraising, they require the imagery and narrative of crisis and despair, often extracted without consent. Life seekers are not just the recipients of aid that is increasingly sourced and delivered using profit-driven companies. Life seekers have become a commodity in themselves, driving this economy of affective aid. Anja K Franck has written about the centrality of photographs and selfie-taking as a core activity of humanitarian volunteers.[37] Here, the quickly snapped image of the life seeker becomes a way for entrepreneurial volunteers, plugged into social networks like Instagram and Twitter and ready with the appropriate hashtags (Rozakou's 'solidarity #humanitarianism'), to swiftly and simply convey an affective message and sense of place across distance. Differing from some of the traditional uses of imagery in humanitarianism intended to generate compassion, a selfie of the volunteer and the life seeker together becomes a way of centring the volunteer in the story. The selfie appears to place the volunteer squarely in the middle of the crisis and works to strengthen their presence as essential and necessary. When these selfies become tied to fundraising efforts, funds are raised on behalf of the usually nameless life seeker – whose often only connection with the volunteer is this fleeting moment, digitally converted to pixels on a smartphone, transcending time and space – and for the volunteer. This says nothing of the hierarchies between racialised bodies and compassionate white saviours fostered and reproduced through such images and so succinctly satirised by websites such as 'Barbie Savior' and 'Humanitarians of Tinder'.[38] In all these instances, the bodies of life seekers become commodities used to generate much-needed money – such practices have a long history in humanitarian fundraising efforts – and assist in the self-improvement and brand building of humanitarian entrepreneurs, who use such images to generate particular narratives of themselves as caregivers that extend beyond the immediate humanitarian context.

An illustrative example is Charlie MacGregor, one of the founders – along with Dutch actor Johnny de Mol – of Movement On The Ground.

---

37 AK Franck, 'The Lesvos Refugee Crisis as Disaster Capitalism', *Peace Review: A Journal of Social Justice* 30(2), 2018.

38 For more on this, see N Toomey, 'Humanitarians of Tinder: Constructing Whiteness and Consuming the Other', *Critical Ethnic Studies* 3(2), 2017, 151–72.

MacGregor is an Amsterdam-based entrepreneur specialising in providing student accommodation in European cities with severe housing shortages, such as Amsterdam. His social media is full of Franck's 'refugee selfies', used to narrate his personal journey from entrepreneurial businessman to entrepreneurial humanitarian offering innovative, fast-moving relief efforts on Lesvos. MacGregor uses his work with Movement On The Ground as an active form of brand-boosting and marketing for his The Student Hotel chain. In this marketing, international students associate The Student Hotel brand with a globally conscious and caring approach to life seekers and therefore see their accommodation choice as being not only ethical but signalling a similar cosmopolitan worldview. Yet The Student Hotel has hosted events by the climate change denying, white supremacist, misogynist, neo-fascist and anti-science Dutch political party Forum voor Democratie, which has campaigned against the presence of refugees in the Netherlands and against the moderate reforms proposed under the UN-led Global Compacts for Migration and Refugees.[39] This apparent contradiction shows the performative limits of such 'humanitarian' efforts while speaking to the long-standing colonial tradition of doing humanitarianism at a distance, a long way from home.

The Frontiers of Fame

Geosocial discourses and networks concerned with entrepreneurial activity and affective production often come together most succinctly with celebrity humanitarianism. It is recognised by a wide variety of humanitarian organisations that celebrities play a useful role in drawing attention to humanitarian crises.[40] However, that is not to say such involvement is without its problems, as the 2017 and 2019 controversies

---

39   Forum voor Democratie, 'FVD stelt 100 kamervragen aan Mark Harbers (VVD) over de omstreden Marrakesh Immigratiepact', 2018, fvd.nl (in Dutch). Interestingly, Forum voor Democratie present the Global Compact on Migration (GCM) as an 'immigration pact', which misrepresents the contents and aims of the GCM for purposes of populist, anti-migrant sentiment.

40   For an exploration of the dynamics and drivers of celebrity humanitarianism, see D Brockington, 'The Production and Construction of Celebrity Advocacy in International Development', *Third World Quarterly* 35(1), 2014, 88–108.

in the UK about Comic Relief show.[41] These controversies revolved around Comic Relief (re)producing a white colonial gaze in its portrayal of 'Africa', its places, and people through the involvement of actors such as Eddie Redmayne and Tom Hardy, and the singer Ed Sheeran. This white colonial gaze was criticised in 2019 by the British MP for Tottenham, David Lammy, when Comic Relief, after promising to reform its approach in 2017, instead created yet another white saviour-centring report by the broadcaster Stacey Dooley. Lammy argued that Comic Relief should 'establish an image of African people as equals to be respected rather than helpless victims to be pitied. So rather than Western celebrities acting as our tour guides to Band Aid Africa, why not let those who live there speak about the continent they know?'[42] Critiques like Lammy's have an established history in academic work on celebrity humanitarianism. For example, Mitchell has focused on the work of Bono as promoting a particular brand of neoliberal humanitarianism and development aid that portrays Bono as a messianic figure. Chouliaraki has examined Angelina Jolie's humanitarianism as a form of brand-boosting for Jolie as the archetypal global citizen that we should all aspire to be. Political geographer Mary Mostafanezhad has focused on Jolie and Madonna and the ways their work erases deep structural and racial inequalities between people and places. Meanwhile, Jo Littler has suggested Jolie's humanitarian work aims at shrinking distance and fostering an intimacy between herself and others while producing Jolie as the authoritative voice on refugees.[43]

Unsurprisingly, then, celebrities have played an important affective role in building the geosocial response to the violence faced by life seekers in border spaces. Utilising many of the same platforms as volunteers, celebrities, including Jude Law and Lily Allen in Calais, and celebrity artist Ai Weiwei, various *Game of Thrones* cast members and Susan

---

41 Comic Relief was founded in 1985 in the UK by filmmaker Richard Curtis and comedian Lenny Henry in response to the Ethiopian Famine.

42 D Lammy, 'Africa Deserves Better From Comic Relief', the *Guardian*, 24 March 2019, theguardian.com.

43 For more on celebrity humanitarianism, see Chouliaraki, 'The Theatricality of Humanitarianism'; J Littler, ' "I Feel Your Pain": Cosmopolitan Charity and the Public Fashioning of the Celebrity Soul', *Social Semiotics* 18(2), 2008, 237–51; K Mitchell, ' "Factavism" '; M Mostafanezhad, ' "Getting in Touch with your Inner Angelina": Celebrity Humanitarianism and the Cultural Politics of Gendered Generosity in Volunteer Tourism', *Third World Quarterly* 34(3), 2013, 485–99.

Sarandon in Lesvos, have brought attention to the risks faced by life seekers and boosted their own public images as humanitarians in the process. Such celebrity involvement, while highlighting certain issues, can, like celebrity itself, be more performative than politically effective and obscure more than it reveals. At the same time, the work of artists such as Ai Weiwei illustrates the extractive capacity and commodification of such humanitarian work that seeks to profit from the 'refugee crisis' in the contemporary art scene.[44]

Performing Rozakou's 'solidarity #humanitarianism', Susan Sarandon tweeted about her December 2015 visit to Lesvos, where she engaged with grassroots volunteers. These tweets worked to reproduce a simplistic narrative around risk and heroism relating to boat arrivals. They centred Sarandon as a messianic figure of succour and displayed a naivety around why life seekers were travelling in such a way. These tweets worked to conceal and normalise rather than uncover and protest unequal mobility regimes. Furthermore, Sarandon's tweets always included a picture of herself in a variety of contexts; in boats, on beaches and kissing refugee children. In one, Sarandon is seen leaning out of a rescue RIB (rigid inflatable boat) belonging to the Danish grassroots organisation Team Humanity, her hand outstretched to a dinghy full of life seekers. This photograph of Sarandon the rescuer was accompanied with the words: 'We wave. They wave. It's a great feeling to be an instrument of deliverance.'[45] In another, Sarandon is pictured standing on a beach waving at a boat of life seekers as they near the shore, supplemented with the words, 'I hope I can make it possible for them to have a voice so that we can understand.'[46] In another, she suggests, 'you have to ask yourself what kind of desperation would make getting on these boats seem like a good idea.'[47] In an interview with the *Guardian* newspaper, Sarandon was clear that her 'main goal was to humanise the issue and have them be real people, not politicise it'.[48] This work, lasting a week, would see her nominated for 2016's Nobel Peace Prize alongside two local Greeks.

44   With thanks to Elisa Pascucci for pushing this point.
45   The tweet can be found here: twitter.com/SusanSarandon/status/678685104772792321.
46   The tweet can be found here: twitter.com/SusanSarandon/status/678244585563377665.
47   The tweet can be found here: twitter.com/SusanSarandon/status/677940631910686721.
48   N Sayej, 'Susan Sarandon's Christmas with Refugees: "I Want to Humanise the Issue" ', the *Guardian*, 29 December 2015, theguardian.com.

Grassroots™ Humanitarianism   151

The artist Ai Weiwei set up an art studio on Lesvos in 2015, from which he produced a number of photographic pieces aimed at highlighting and drawing attention to the 'refugee crisis'. In many of the photographs, simplistic motifs of lifejackets are used to denote the peril of the sea crossing, or Ai himself is the main subject. In one particularly startling photograph, he lies face down on the beach in a re-enactment of the now infamous image of the dead body of Aylan Kurdi. However, Ai is in Greece, whereas Kurdi never made it that far.[49] The artist also produced a film about his encounters with the 'refugee crisis' across a number of European and non-European border spaces including Izmir, Lesvos and Idomeni. The film has a problematic title, 'Human Flow', that reproduces the idea that people's movement is some kind of unstoppable force of nature rather than a deeply, unequally infrastructured process, and, like many of the works from his Lesvos studio, continually places Ai at the centre of the story he is trying to tell. The film is filled with lingering shots of the artist as he: walks along roads or through ports, alone or accompanying life seekers; traverses fields, forests, transit and camp spaces; or sits pensively on Aegean beaches contemplating an empty sea. Through these artfully composed, lingering shots Ai seems to romanticise life seekers as nomadic citizens of the world, as opposed to people confronting deep, violent inequalities, who would no doubt rather be on a plane to Berlin (Ai's home) than have to hang out with Ai in a muddy field in northern Greece.

In one particularly gauche scene, Ai hands his passport to a life seeker he meets in Idomeni, suggesting they swap. While this is at least an acknowledgement of the role passports and other documentation play in structuring unequal mobility, the audience is supposed to see this as an act of immense daring and protest on the part of Ai. However, even if Ai was to give his passport to someone with less privileged mobility, he could simply replace it, especially given the resources at his disposal (both material and social). At the same time, his privilege remains unaffected and unequal mobility remains unchallenged. The idea presented in this scene suggests that if only these men swapped passports, somehow things would be different, and like the celebrity humanitarianism of Sarandon, it glosses over the politics and processes

---

49   M Tan, 'Ai Weiwei Poses as Drowned Infant Refugee in "Haunting" Photo', the *Guardian*, 1 February 2016, theguardian.com.

of difference underpinning both men's presence in Idomeni. The fact that this act was filmed is also just that, an act – a true passport swap meant to enable illicit travel would not take place in front of a film crew.

What is particularly interesting about the activities of Sarandon and Ai in the recent 'refugee crisis' is the way – unlike the cast of *Game of Thrones*, who have worked with the International Rescue Committee (IRC) – their interventions were unmediated by large, professional organisations. Instead, both Sarandon and Ai chose to eschew such 'traditional' celebrity encounters with humanitarian advocacy that most often sees celebrities working closely with organisations such as UNHCR, as in the case of Jolie and Cate Blanchett, or the IRC as in the case of Lena Headey, Maisie Williams and other members of the *Game of Thrones* cast. Sarandon's and Ai's presence, like that of Lily Allen and Jude Law in Calais, suggested a belief in the power of more bottom-up, on-the-ground work with volunteers and grassroots, solidarity humanitarians. Sarandon's choice to work with volunteer groups Team Humanity and Because We Carry, among others, and Ai's peripatetic encounters with the wide variety of grassroots groups and solidarity activists present in Lesvos and elsewhere in Greece hinted at a distrust in the large-scale efforts of established humanitarian organisations and an alternative way of doing relief. Even if groups such as Team Humanity quickly began to consolidate themselves with branding and more professional structures, they were, importantly, seen as offering an alternative, effective and faster way of reacting to life seekers' needs. These groups were attractive not just to the likes of Sarandon and Ai, but, as many of them appeared to grow organically from a combination of local people, tourists and those who were already plugged into nascent geosocial networks, they also appeared to offer 'better solutions to the problems of people on the move', as one interviewee put it to me.[50] Yet the presence of Sarandon and Ai in Lesvos, as well as Allen and Law in Calais, also worked to consolidate these places as humanitarian volunteer spaces, through the way their celebrity, in conjunction with geosocial networks and more traditional media, publicised their presence and

---

50   Interview with tourist turned humanitarian solidarity activist, Athens, 11 October 2015.

Grassroots™ Humanitarianism

amplified the 'crises' and their humanitarian nature alongside the potential for grassroots volunteering.[51]

While celebrity humanitarianism brings attention to a cause and to celebrities themselves, while often working to boost the celebrity's brand, not all the attention is positive. Lily Allen faced attacks by the UK tabloid press after a visit to Calais, where she tearfully apologised, on camera, to a thirteen-year-old Afghan, saying, '[I] apologise on behalf of my country. I'm sorry for what we put you through.'[52] While such a statement might have been clumsy and hinted at an arrogance that Allen could speak for and apologise on behalf of an entire nation, it did draw attention to the structural conditions stranding life seekers in Calais. Allen, unlike Sarandon, has not shied away from the politics of unequal mobility underpinning her desire to help. In a self-penned *Vice* article, Allen explained the apology as her attempt to convey the way the UK Home Office has ignored the Dubs Amendment that promised to resettle 3,000 unaccompanied refugee children in the UK, as well as the conditions in Calais, where 'people are in a holding pen. They have no idea what comes next. There is no life plan. There is nothing to work towards except for getting across the channel.'[53] In the same article, she went on to examine the ways migration and refugees have been politicised in UK public discourse. According to Allen, the UK has

> found a group of vulnerable people they can blame their own failures on, but we shouldn't lose sight of the fact that the problems in this country are the fault of a self-interested Conservative Party and people and companies who aren't paying their share of tax. They're the ones cheating the system, not a child trying to come here because they have been driven away from everywhere else.[54]

Allen's experiences highlight the frontiers of celebrity humanitarian engagement with unequal mobility and border suffering: step over the line from compassionate engagement and the performance of an

---

51   S Oneko, 'Ai Weiwei's New Project: Documenting Refugees in Lesbos', *Deutsche Welle*, 14 August 2015, dw.com; Sayej, 'Susan Sarandon's Christmas with Refugees'.

52   L Allen, 'Why the Press Want to Stop Celebrities Like Me Talking about the Migrant Crisis', *Vice*, 26 October 2016, vice.com.

53   Ibid.

54   Ibid.

affective desire to help into political critique, and celebrities risk provoking a backlash, becoming the subjects of attack and ultimately distracting from those they are trying to help. The message here is that humanitarianism that sticks within the boundaries of apolitical caregiving is allowed, but a politics capable of bringing about substantive change is not.

A Bag of Chocolate Milk and a Shoe . . .

Affective material networks connect disparate spaces. The Calais Jungle as a long-time place of suffering and neglect has, like Lesvos, gained a place in European consciousness for the role of volunteers in providing much-needed supplies.[55] Alongside more routine deliveries of aid, there have been large convoys from the UK aimed at bringing much-needed clothing, personal hygiene products, toys and food, and highlighting the immobility and immobilisation of those stuck by the UK and French border regimes. Meanwhile, other solidarity humanitarian efforts have been focused on breaking the immobility of life seekers stuck in places like Greece because of European border controls. The Dutch movement We Gaan Ze Halen, clunkily translated into English as Let's Bring Them Here, aims at getting people to use their own vehicles to join convoys from the Netherlands to Greece to collect and bring 1,000 people to the Netherlands in accordance with wider, yet stalled, EU relocation targets.

The movement of volunteers and the delivery of donations across Europe are now well established, making use of online spaces for organisation, various modes of transportation and traditional shipping methods. Grassroots solidarity groups have, over time, developed intricate logistics systems to identify key needs and handle donations. For example, people in Glasgow collect unwanted children's clothes to be shipped to Greece or Calais, fostering what scholar of colonialism Lisa Lowe would call 'intimacy across space' in contradistinction to exclusive forms of bordering.[56]

---

55   For more on Calais as a space of neglect, see T Davies, A Isakjee and S Dhesi, 'Violent Inaction: The Necropolitical Experience of Refugees in Europe', *Antipode* 49(5), 2017, 1263–84. For more on volunteer humanitarianism in Calais, see E Sandri, ' "Volunteer Humanitarianism": Volunteers and Humanitarian Aid in the Jungle Refugee Camp of Calais', *Journal of Ethnic and Migration Studies* 44(1), 2018, 65–80.

56   L Lowe, *The Intimacies of Four Continents*, Durham, NC: Duke University Press, 2015, 19.

Grassroots™ Humanitarianism

These donations and the systems that enable them generate 'close connections in relation to a global geography that one more often conceives in terms of vast spatial distance.'[57] These networks are not only affective and built around a shared will to care but they have a materiality that fosters and contends with the physical 'stuff' of donations as well as the electronic, virtual world of online monetary systems, such as PayPal. This materiality extends from the important facilitating work of the shipping container – that great logistical technology enabling and mediating global trade – to the box, and its contents: clothes, shoes, personal hygiene products, medicine and toys.[58]

Wheelie bins, Lesvos, October 2018. © Polly Pallister-Wilkins

These materials, donated or otherwise, connect spaces and places across distance and across issues not reducible to humanitarianism alone, as many of the items have purposes beyond humanitarianism. Clothes, pushchairs and personal hygiene products are all 'non-humanitarian' or

---

57 Ibid., 18.

58 For work on the shipping container, see C Chua, 'The Container: Stacking, Packing, and Moving the World', *The Funambulist* 6, Object Politics, 2016; D Cowen, *The Deadly Life of Logistics: Mapping Violence in Global Trade*, Minneapolis, MN: University of Minnesota Press, 2014, and L Khalili, *Sinews of War and Trade: Shipping and Capitalism in the Arabian Peninsula*, London: Verso, 2020. For work on the box in humanitarianism, see P Redfield, *Life in Crisis: The Ethical Journey of Doctors Without Borders*, Berkeley: University of California Press, 2013.

'normal' everyday products that are not immediately associated with humanitarian crises, unlike the logo-strewn tarpaulins and floor mats that often come to construct places of displacement. Humanitarian professionals argue that these objects are logoed to prevent them from being sold for cash. In economies of scarcity that exclude the displaced from regular markets and modes of consumption, items repurposed or transformed to address needs become commodities enabling life seekers to obtain other goods and access wider markets through exchange and reselling. On Lesvos, for instance, children's prams and pushchairs are a rare item of donation and are particularly prized as transporters of heavy items, not children. As a result, their 'market' value has led to a roaring black market in prams and pushchairs, according to one long-time grassroots humanitarian.[59] These goods then, like the Rochdale Borough Council wheelie bins 'recycled' by Care UK, connect faraway places along vectors of both humanitarianism and everyday life, while these donated goods also help to break down barriers to everyday market interactions.

Yet, while these donations shrink space and include diverse places and people in affective and intimate networks of exchange, they also highlight the unequal mobility at the heart of such performances. That recycled wheelie bins can travel from Rochdale to Mytilene in Lesvos while life seekers are warehoused on the island is particularly telling. Additionally, such donations are often paternalistic performances. Why was it necessary to send wheelie bins from Greater Manchester to the Aegean islands? Managing the safe disposal of waste during humanitarian crises is an important and often less sexy part of humanitarian management, and waste disposal solutions are a key part of daily operations in camp spaces. In some displacement crises, such solutions are desperately needed when there is no organised refuse collection and alternatives include burning, burying or dumping, with all the environmental hazards and damage that this can incur. However, Lesvos has a fully functioning refuse collection system and refuse collection infrastructure, including bins. At times, especially during 2015, the use of such general, municipal waste bins has been a point of contention among some local people who refused to allow life seekers to dispose of wet clothes and empty water bottles. This led humanitarian organisations,

59 Interview with long-term grassroots humanitarian, Kara Tepe, Lesvos, 15 October 2018.

including UNHCR and IRC, to provide additional large metal dumpsters replete with the requisite logos.

But donations, recycled or otherwise, are not always necessary. Donations often speak to a general aspect of humanitarian caregiving built on assumed power hierarchies between givers and receivers and between the assumed spaces and places of donation; in this case, the wealthy, resource-rich Global North and the resource-poor Global South. Simplistic hierarchies do not fit neatly into humanitarian contexts when it is better to locally source as many goods as possible, as a way of fostering rather than undermining local markets. The same is true of Greece. These Rochdale wheelie bins, for example, can be found in a warehouse space containing items donated from all over Europe, near the Kara Tepe camp just north of Mytilene, and next door to both a large Chinese shop selling a range of items targeted at life seekers and a Lidl supermarket. Interestingly, this Chinese shop, the second on the island, caters almost exclusively to the population of Kara Tepe and those from Moria who visit the area daily to access various humanitarian services from the array of organisations that have based themselves around old warehouses – both international ones, such as Médecins du Monde, and more grassroots organisations, such as One Happy Family. It is clear that the target market for this Chinese shop is the life seeker population of the island. This observation is based on their stock, which includes a range of scarfs suitable for hijabs, abayas in a variety of colours and styles, sleeping bags and other camping style equipment, and cheap suitcases that have been seen being carried by life seekers on the gang plank of the ferry in Mytilene harbour – if and when people are allowed to move to the mainland.

The warehouse with the wheelie bins belongs to a grassroots solidarity organisation that does not handle monetary donations directly for fear of being accused of corruption, meaning that material donations are more readily welcomed. Large shipping containers arrive periodically full of unwanted and recycled clothes, including football kits and memorabilia, such as scarves and hats from Arsenal and Tottenham Hotspur supporters' clubs, and organised in conjunction with other solidarity organisations located in the UK, the Netherlands, Poland, Denmark, Sweden and elsewhere. Alongside this, the warehouse receives regular visits from tourists wanting to do something or donate. In such instances, the tourists are summarily dispatched across the road to Lidl and return with boxes of toothpaste and shower gel. However, not all donations are as useful or needed. In discussing the logistics of donations with one of the organisers of the project, while they moved and restacked fifty large boxes of sanitary towels, they told me they tried as much as possible to source things locally on the island or within Greece, but so powerful were the desires of non-Greeks to help, and so desperate were the life seekers on the island, that they were happy to accept donations from anywhere with three caveats: they can clear Greek customs, are useful and are needed. To this end, the organisation keeps a permanently updated online list of items on their Facebook page to help those wanting to donate.[60] And even though there are clear instructions saying, 'please only send items from this list', I was regaled with a litany of unacceptable items that had been sent over the years, including numerous pairs of high heels, a bag of dirty underwear, and one bag, sent all the way from northern Europe, full of single small cartons of expired (by two years) chocolate milk and a solitary shoe.[61]

No White Saviour Bullshit Here

The delivery of a bag full of undrinkable chocolate milk and a lonely shoe, while funny, also generated a certain amount of anger in the long-term grassroots humanitarian to whom it was sent. It not only illustrates the unhelpfulness of some people's desire to help, but also shows the way humanitarian work comes to be experienced as a routine with set expectations and a script that those involved are expected to follow. The bag of undrinkable and possibly dangerous chocolate milk cartons and a useless single shoe is funny exactly because it failed so spectacularly to follow the assumed script. 'How could anyone think that was helpful?' I wrote in my notebook alongside the story. However, the assumed script of how people are supposed to practise humanitarianism is also a target

---

60   This list currently reads: underwear for all (only new please), bras, socks for all, sports shoes for all, sun hats & baseball caps, trousers for all, shorts for men and children, crocs & flip flops, T-shirts, towels, shampoo, soap, shower gel, toothpaste, toothbrushes, sun cream, moisturiser, diapers, baby wipes, strollers/push chairs (especially for young babies), baby beds/carry cots, items for newborns, and toys and games (especially soft toys).

61   Discussion with long-term grassroots organiser, Mytilene, 8 October 2018.

Grassroots™ Humanitarianism 159

of some border-space activities attempting to upset and unsettle traditional ways of working.

Much humanitarianism follows particular routines but 'when people become a routine, you have a problem'.[62] This idea of people becoming a routine was a topic brought up by a volunteer I interviewed during the 'height' of the arrivals in Lesvos in 2015. As they recounted their history of volunteering to me, time slowed down and expanded, and it seemed as if they were recounting a long history of such efforts. In fact, they were only discussing the previous two weeks since their arrival on the island. The fear that people would become a routine related to the relentless pace of humanitarian activity within a crisis situation that slowed and expanded time. It meant the volunteer had gone from being determined to help everyone as best as they could, allowing themselves to feel and experience the full emotions of what they were witnessing and a part of, to their daily tasks becoming a routine. Their 'naïve desire to do good', as they put it, slowly turned to a pragmatic view about what was actually possible and what was actually 'good'. The volunteer was worried that such pragmatism and seeing people as a routine – 'as numbers rather than people with lives and histories' – in such circumstances could lead to dehumanisation.

There are organisations attempting to challenge the routinisation and dehumanisation of not only humanitarian work but also of the experience of life seekers as they are stranded on the Aegean islands. One organisation (hereafter referred to as The Organisation)[63] that I have encountered seeks to, in their words, 'do what we can to make a difference and to empower and restore dignity to as many people as we can'. The focus here on people, as opposed to a particular category of people, life seekers or refugees, suggests a different politics in approaching relief efforts. Additionally, the focus on empowerment as opposed to passivity challenges the traditional top-down hierarchy of the humanitarian subject with the power to help on top, and the helpless recipient below. Empowerment, unsurprisingly, is a popular buzzword

---

62 Interview with volunteer humanitarian, Skala Sykamineas, Lesvos, 22 October 2015.

63 Due to increasing attacks, legal, political and physical attacks against humanitarian work in Greece, especially that from the grassroots, I have chosen not to name the organisation in question.

in the humanitarian industry today.[64] This is not without cause, as humanitarians across a range of sites, spaces and organisations have addressed the problematic subject positions of saviour and victim within humanitarian assistance and have recognised that refugees have agency. But, consequently, such empowerment efforts have been met with critiques that suggest these efforts impose a neoliberal humanitarianism on life seekers.[65] There are merits to both positions – the critique of humanitarianism as disempowering and its counter that empowerment masks structural relations and underlying inequalities – that highlight the political nature of much of this type of work. However, all forms of empowerment should not be assumed to be equal. The Organisation on Lesvos is a case in point. Set up as an attempt to, in the words of one of the founders, 'get over the white saviour bullshit', The Organisation is 'refugee-led' and comprises a distribution warehouse for basic items, including clothes and hygiene products, space for small enterprises, including a hairdresser and barber, and a tailor's studio, as well as a performing arts space and visual arts studio.[66]

A large sign outside the space announces that they are 'not an NGO' and that they are 'refugee-run'. The art studio has been set up to tackle the growing issues of poor mental health and well-being among those warehoused on Lesvos, providing lessons to new artists and a space for seasoned pros whose work has been commissioned and exhibited internationally. However, the space and the art produced is not just therapeutic. All the art that is made is for sale, with 85 percent of the proceeds

---

64 See A Betts and P Collier, *Refuge: Rethinking Refugee Policy in a Changing World*, London: Allen Lane, 2017; J. Crisp, *UNHCR, Refugee Livelihoods and Self-Reliance: A Brief History*, 2003, unhcr.org.

65 Refugee assistance has a long history of incorporating refugees into managing their own relief. The United Nations Relief Works Agency (UNRWA) predates the UNHCR and is focused, as its name suggests, on providing both relief and work for the Palestinian refugees that fall under its mandate; see S Hanafi, L Hilal and L Takkenberg eds, *UNRWA and Palestinian Refugees: From Relief and Works to Human Development*, 2014, Abingdon: Routledge. For more on refugee labour, see K Lenner and L Turner, 'Making Refugees Work? The Politics of Integrating Syrian Refugees into the Labor Market in Jordan', *Middle East Critique* 28(1), 2019, 65–95; E Pascucci, 'The Local Labour Building the International Community: Precarious Work within Humanitarian Spaces', *Environment and Planning A: Economy and Space* 51(3), 2019, 743–60.

66 Conversation with long-term local grassroots humanitarian, Mytilene, Lesvos, 8 October 2018.

Grassroots™ Humanitarianism 161

going to the artist and the remaining 15 percent going into the communal pot to buy canvases, brushes and paints, making the studio self-sufficient. The works are displayed on the walls of the studio space and online and can be purchased anywhere in the world, either as originals or reprints. The ability to sell their art is intended to provide life seekers with much-needed money to supplement the small amount of cash assistance they receive, if eligible, through the ESTIA (Emergency Support to Integration and Accommodation) programme of the UNHCR, funded by the EU's Asylum and Integration Fund.[67]

The distribution centre next door has rows of clothes racks, with clothes arranged by gender, type and size. The clothes are meticulously inventoried on the large computer in the corner, behind the counter that separates the 'customer' space from the storage space, which contains rows of clothes racks and is bordered on three sides by boxes piled floor to ceiling. At the end of each rack of clothes hang signs that read, 'This is not a supermarket', in English, French, Arabic and Farsi. A large electric urn sits next to the computer, always ready to provide hot water for cups of tea or coffee. People zip up and down the aisles picking out items for the 'customers' waiting on the other side of the partition, while the manager inputs data on the computer. Everyone who 'works' here is a refugee stuck on Lesvos. A range of languages are spoken with the customers, but all 'staff', as they refer to themselves, must speak English as a common language. This is the language that they have decided they will speak with each other at all times while they are 'at work'.

Each member of the team wears a laminated name tag, hung around their neck on a red cord, with their name in Latin script, the script of their native language and the name of The Organisation. People work in the distribution centre from early in the morning until late in the afternoon, either organising donations before and after the space is open or managing the thirty families that visit every day to collect items. At other times they prepare bundles of clothes and hygiene packs for use by other humanitarian organisations. The whole, apparently smooth, operation is

---

67 Cash assistance amounts per month range from €90 for an individual in catered accommodation to €550 for a family of seven members or more in self-catered accommodation. 'Greece Cash Assistance', UNHCR, 2018, data2.unhcr.org. For more on cash assistance, see M Tazzioli, 'Refugees' Subjectivities, Debit Cards and Data Circuits: Financial Humanitarianism in the Greek Migration Laboratory', *International Political Sociology* 13(4), 2019, 392–408.

Attempting to challenge routinisation and dehumanisation,
Lesvos, October 2018. © Polly Pallister-Wilkins

run through a complex system that makes use of the registration system and documents of the Moria hotspot. The limited resources are triaged and distributed by a system that supplies thirty next-day tickets a day to residents of Moria and Kara Tepe by staff who are also residents there. Each time someone receives a ticket, it is recorded on their A4-sized registration documents, which are often laminated and carried around like sacred relics, as they offer access to scarce resources. These registration documents then enable access to clothes, shoes and hygiene products. With their individual registration numbers, these documents are used to record who has received what and when on the Project's database. The Moria Hotspot, its registration system and its materialisation in registration documents mediate life seekers' access to the supplies offered by The Organisation. Here, a system of border control, designed to make life seekers visible and governable, has been reappropriated for the provision of humanitarian assistance.[68]

---

68   D Bulley, 'Inside the Tent: Community and Government in Refugee Camps', *Security Dialogue* 45(1), 2014.

The border and its architecture create the conditions of precarity under which life seekers on Lesvos live and also the very conditions for and of their assistance. This suggests that escape from such border controls through humanitarianism is impossible, as the border structures the very possibility and practices of humanitarianism in this context. Therefore, The Organisation's attempts at less hierarchical forms of humanitarian assistance based on the empowerment of life seekers rather than top-down, paternalistic, white saviour forms of charity are tempered when such practices take place in response to border violence and make use of border systems. In this instance, a radical politics of empowerment and the transcendence of racialised hierarchies of humanitarianism are not only limited, but also through systems of care reproduce the power of sovereign systems of registration, inclusion and exclusion on which unequal mobility rests.

Mapping Border Spaces, Making Mobility

Grassroots volunteers and solidarity activists play a central role in building and mapping border spaces for the purposes of rescue and assistance. Maurice Stierl, an international relations scholar, has reflected on his own engagement with the Watch The Med Alarm Phone, an activist collective that aims to pressure responseable actors into rescue, while watching, tracking and recording border violence and deaths at sea. In this reflection, Stierl argues that the collective has fought against the idea of the sea as an ungovernable and 'unaccountable space of human loss', while also advocating for freedom of movement.[69] The Alarm Phone is, according to Stierl, drawing on the work of Peter Nyers,

> made up of various trans-border and trans-categorical alliances, transcends activist and migrant signifiers, and is a (constitutive) part of 'mobile commons', 'the space-time of the social life of migrants', worlds of mobile connections and knowledges that often emerge through and are maintained by novel technologies.[70]

---

69   M Stierl, 'A Sea of Struggle – Activist Border Interventions in the Mediterranean Sea', *Citizenship Studies* 20(5), 2016, 574.

70   Ibid., 562. See also P Nyers, 'Migrant Citizenships and Autonomous Mobilities', *Migration, Mobility and Displacement* 1(1), 2015, 23–39.

In the actions of the Watch The Med Alarm Phone and other similar ventures, migrant mobility is acknowledged, worked with, and fostered through technological interventions working to make border spaces visible. The Watch The Med collective works to make unsafe and unequal mobility across the Mediterranean visible to rescuers and to a wider public. Many humanitarian volunteer groups and collectives have worked to map rescue, both so that it can be made visible politically and possible practically. This virtual mapping makes use of online technologies and platforms to record boats in distress on a pan-European scale.

On a more local level, volunteer rescuers have developed mapping tools to help with the often messy and chaotic nature of on-the-ground/sea rescue realities, providing key information to volunteers often unfamiliar with the local terrain. In certain instances, the creation of maps with consistent labelling for previously unnamed beaches helped to structure coordination efforts between groups of eager volunteers. These attempts at mapping also recognise, channel and structure migrant mobility, while making border spaces visible (and possible) as spaces of intervention. These maps foreclose the possibility of some lines of flight and insist on others while foregrounding border control infrastructures, such as the Hotspots. Maps are therefore a central tool structuring unequal mobility in, across and beyond border spaces.

Volunteer map, Lesvos, October 2015. © Polly Pallister-Wilkins

There is a rich tradition of critical cartographers drawing our attention to the ways maps – where we map, what we map and how we map – help to produce the world in specific ways and impact how we interact with it. Jeremy Crampton and John Krygier suggest that a 'map is a specific set of power-knowledge claims'.[71] Sociologist of science and technology Jess Bier argues that maps create the 'very constitution, naturalisation, and domination of specific kinds of knowledge over others'.[72] Following this logic, maps are not only representative of, or handy guides to, the routes and journeys we can take as we move about. Maps also actively intervene in shaping our journeys, making certain routes seem more attractive than others through what is represented on the map, and sometimes giving us actual routes to follow in the case of online mapping apps. Mapping as a tool of humanitarian borderwork by volunteer activists and solidarity collectives works in a similar, if often more low-key, way. As maps can never represent the whole, choices are made around what to show and what to leave out, shaping life seekers' journeys in particular. 'Mapping', political geographer John Pickles suggests, 'even as it is claimed to represent the world, produces it', while Crampton asserts that 'maps make space as much as they record space'.[73] With this in mind, I argue that the maps developed as a part of humanitarian borderwork make mobility as much as they record it.

Maps developed and drawn by volunteers in Lesvos during 2015 showed only those routes life seekers had to take on the presumed next stages of their journey. Mobility, while assisted, was still limited within the confines of a particular journey subjectively produced by volunteers in concert with their understanding of the governing mechanisms and mobility regimes that life seekers must be subjected to. Here, the need to 'help' life seekers on their journeys played a role in the volunteers' conceptions of what a life seeker's journey should look like. Rather than allowing people on the move the freedom to determine their own journeys through border spaces, volunteers opened certain routes and

---

71 JW Crampton and J Krygier, 'An Introduction to Critical Cartography', *ACME* 4(1), 2005, 12.

72 J Bier, *Mapping Israel, Mapping Palestine: How Occupied Landscapes Shape Scientific Knowledge*, Boston: The MIT Press, 2017, 4.

73 J Pickles ed., *A History of Spaces: Cartographic Reason, Mapping, and the Geo-Coded World*, New York: Routledge, 2004, 93; JW Crampton, *Mapping: A Critical Introduction to Cartography and GIS*, Malden, MA: Wiley-Blackwell, 2010, 48.

foreclosed others, driven by a desire to direct life seekers to basic needs and to border governance sites, such as the Hotspots, through making maps. A typical journey depicted on these often hand-drawn maps went something like this: beach – aid station – bus route – registration centre – port – ferry. Therefore, these maps not only represented the journeys of life seekers as perceived by volunteers, but as infrastructures of mobility, they actively came to pattern mobility in particular ways.[74] For example, no map I encountered ever showed Mytilene Airport even though migrants with airline-suitable ID (like passports) were able to fly domestic within Greece to Athens or Thessaloniki for a price often lower than the ferry. When only certain routes, corridors, passages and lines of flight are shown on a map – based on the subjectivities of the volunteers making them – they are naturally the only ones used by life seekers. Volunteer maps are thus not only a form of humanitarian borderwork, coming to construct space in particular ways through making visible certain places and practices, but also infrastructures of mobility, shifting and shaping the trajectories of migrants and playing a role in creating and upholding unequal mobility regimes.

Criminalising Humanitarianism

If solidarity humanitarianism works to produce spaces of intervention and structure mobility in ways that appear to consolidate the humanitarian border, in other ways the practices of solidarity humanitarians are deeply contested by sovereign authorities. The ability for grassroots humanitarians to operate is conditioned by powerful state and transnational actors keen to assert their sovereignty over mobility and who has the right to intervene. This limits the ability for a transversal global citizenship to emerge around universal ideals of freedom and justice for all based on principles of solidarity and a radical commitment to human rights.

The late-summer 2018 arrests of solidarity activists working with the Emergency Response Centre International (ERCI) in Greece caused consternation among the non-state humanitarian community. These arrests came amid other attempts around Europe and the Mediterranean

---

74   Berlant, 'The Commons'.

to prevent the assistance and rescue of life seekers by non-state actors. The Italian government has pursued efforts to prevent the disembarkation of search and rescue vessels in Italian ports, while at the end of August 2018, Gibraltar decided to strip SOS Méditerranée's vessel, the *Aquarius*, of its flag.[75] In addition, there have been repeated attempts by authorities to clamp down on solidarity activities, including the arrest of activists from Tous Migrants working in the Alps between the Italian town of Bardonecchia and the French city of Briançon, and in the better-known border space of Calais.[76] Beyond Europe, US Border Patrol continue to disrupt the activities of solidarity activists working in the US-Mexico borderland through slashing the life-saving water bottles left for life seekers, as Fabio Cantú acknowledged in his auto-ethnographic account of his time as a Border Patrol agent.[77] Meanwhile, activists from No More Deaths claim cases of repeated 'intimidation, harassment, and surveillance'.[78] Scott Warren, a geographer and activist with No More Deaths, was prosecuted by US authorities for assisting 'illegal migrants' after being intercepted by US Border patrol agents with two border crossers he had encountered while leaving water in the desert. He was found not guilty at retrial after the jury in Arizona failed to reach a verdict in his first trial. All of these actions have cast a shadow over the last few years of humanitarian attempts to place the lives of migrants and the risks they face at the border front and centre.

That said, attempts to prevent solidarity and rescue activities by non-state actors are not new. Consider the 2004 *Cap Anamur* case, when the captain and first officer of the *Cap Anamur* vessel belonging to the German NGO of the same name were arrested and charged with aiding and abetting illegal immigration. Indeed, *Cap Anamur* remains a large presence in the minds of those engaged in SAR activities and acts as a central point of departure for more recent efforts keen to avoid a similar fate.[79] Political geographer and border studies scholar Paolo Cuttitta has

---

75   SOS Méditerranée, 'SOS MEDITERRANEE Urges EU Leaders to Guarantee Safe Port of Disembarkation for People Rescued at Sea', 23 June 2018, sosmediterranee.com.

76   Clara Hernanz, 'When Helping a Refugee Gets You Threatened with a Prison Sentence', *Vice*, 8 June 2018, vice.com.

77   F Cantú, *The Line Becomes the River*, London: Penguin Random House, 2018.

78   No More Deaths, 'Part 2, Interference with Humanitarian Aid: Death and Disappearance on the US-Mexico Border', 2018, thedisappearedreport.org.

79   H del Valle, 'Search and Rescue in the Mediterranean Sea: Negotiating Political Differences', *Refugee Survey Quarterly* 35(2), 2016, 22–40.

argued that the *Cap Anamur* case even encouraged early European attempts at outsourcing – also known as externalising – migration control to North Africa, under the rubric of saving lives.[80] Taking Cuttitta's argument as a jumping-off point, can we see similar logics at work in recent criminalisation attempts?

I argue that criminalisation attempts by state authorities are attempts to reassert control. They are an easy and politically effective yet unethical way to conflate solidarity and rescue efforts with smuggling. Alongside this, they create a confusing operational and legal terrain for solidarity activities. In Europe, member states and the EU have worked hard to bring the forces of compassion and the solidarity actions of citizens under control. When confronted with a groundswell of solidarity actions aimed at rescue and humanitarian assistance, state actors have attempted to introduce systems of order in which their sovereignty over migrant lives and their ability to have the final say over who is mobile and who receives assistance remain uncontested. In many instances, such as in Lesvos in 2015, solidarity activists were quicker to aid life seekers than state or EU actors, and as a result we are witnessing the slow re-imposition of control over life by state and supra-state authorities in Lesvos and other places of – borrowing from the EU's own jargon – 'high migratory pressure'. In many instances, these attempts at control have worked through co-opting the forces of solidarity to create a hodgepodge assemblage of state and non-state actors engaged in humanitarian borderwork.

As EU member states and the EU as a whole have built up the capacity to respond to 'migratory pressure' amid rising xenophobia and anti-migrant sentiment, activities that could be understood as contesting or overtly challenging the control of sovereign authorities have begun to come under attack more acutely. Within this environment, member states and the EU have worked hard to consolidate unequal mobility regimes, while often claiming to be mitigating the electoral risks of the racist far right by preventing arrivals of life seekers. These mechanisms, such as the EUTF and the EU-Turkey Statement, form an important foundation for the emergence of a humanitarian-criminalisation nexus. The EU-Turkey Statement aims to deter arrivals under the rubric of

---

80 P Cuttitta, 'Delocalization, Humanitarianism and Human Rights: The Mediterranean Border Between Exclusion and Inclusion', *Antipode* 50(3), 2017.

saving lives by tackling people smuggling, with the people smuggler looming large as the bogeyman endangering life seekers and undermining Europe's borders. This is a lazy understanding of the illicit smuggling economy facilitated by hyper-restrictive European border controls.[81] But it is an affective formulation helping to mobilise particular policing responses to govern 'bad things' and 'bad guys', and rearticulating migration and its control as a law-and-order problem, casting life seekers as victims in need of rescue by 'legitimate', state authorities. Alongside this, there have been attempts to cast non-state SAR efforts and other solidarity work as 'pull factors', with rescue efforts in the central Mediterranean being dubbed a 'ferry service' by certain Dutch security officials.[82] In Lesvos, local solidarity efforts have been repeatedly accused of being a pull factor.[83] Meanwhile, other reactionary forces have attacked the naivety of pro-migrant solidarity work and that of more mainstream humanitarian efforts. These attempts to delegitimise solidarity work are motivated by state authorities wanting to reassert their ultimate sovereign control over the border and life itself. States feel they have lost some of their control to both solidarity activists and people smugglers, and so the conflation of solidarity with smuggling becomes an easy and effective tool.

There are, of course, very clear legal differences between solidarity and smuggling. However, following anthropologist of migration Nicolas De Genova, if the border is a spectacle and part of a performance of sovereign power,[84] then accusations of smuggling are less about finding proof and more about the work the accusation itself does. Many of these accusations do not result in convictions, but is conviction really the point of these attempts at criminalisation, when the accusation and charge themselves have the effect of making solidarity efforts more and

---

81 R Andersson, *Illegality, Inc.: Clandestine Migration and the Business of Bordering Europe*, Berkeley: University of California Press, 2014.

82 These comments were made at a Dutch Association for Migration Research held at the Ministry of Justice and Security, 27 May 2016. Similar arguments have been made by Italian officials, such as the former deputy prime minister and current minister of foreign affairs, Luigi Di Maio, from the M5S party when he referred to SAR boats operated by NGOs as 'sea taxis'.

83 Interviews with local humanitarians, Lesvos, 22 October 2015 and 15 October 2018.

84 NP De Genova, 'Spectacles of Migrant "Illegality": The Scene of Exclusion, the Obscene of Inclusion', *Ethnic and Racial Studies* 36(7), 2013, 1180–98.

more difficult? For instance, at the end of August 2018, the Spanish SAR NGO Proactiva Open Arms announced they would end rescue missions in the Central Mediterranean due to the criminalisation efforts of states. Earlier that year they had had their ship impounded (and then released) by the Italian authorities after they refused to hand over rescued migrants to Libyan authorities.[85] Proactiva Open Arms have not been convicted of any charges, but the previous accusations and fear of future accusations have been enough to see them alter their activities to focus on other parts of the Mediterranean and the Aegean.

Perhaps the most famous attempted case of criminalisation is that of Carola Rackete, the captain of the *Sea-Watch 3* vessel who defied the June 2019 ban on SAR vessels entering Italian ports instituted as an act of racist posturing by then–interior minister Matteo Salvini. On 29 June, with 53 rescued people on board, Rackete docked in Lampedusa and was promptly arrested. Sea-Watch is a predominantly German organisation but sailed under a Dutch flag. Following the actions of *Sea-Watch 3*, the party of Dutch prime minister Mark Rutte, the People's Party for Freedom and Democracy, with support from the Christian Democratic Appeal party in the coalition government, accused Rackete and her crew of running a ferry service and human trafficking in a now repetitive refrain from the Dutch right wing. In response to Rackete's actions and subsequent arrest, the German magazine *Der Spiegel* featured Rackete as their July 2019 cover story with the headline 'Captain Europe'. Rackete was cleared of all charges and was later awarded, along with her *Sea-Watch 3* co-captain Pia Klempe, who was facing criminalisation attempts of her own, the Parisian Grand Vermeil Medal for 'solidarity and respect for human lives'. Both women refused the honour, claiming it was hypocritical considering Paris' treatment of life seekers. However, this did not stop Rackete from continuing to be hailed as a hero and the 'Notre 'de L'Europe' by some in Paris.

For all its attempts to unsettle and upset existing orders, solidarity work and humanitarian assistance more generally can only safely, and therefore effectively, operate within an environment of clear legal boundaries. Increasingly, many humanitarian organisations claim that the humanitarian space, defined as the possibility for action, is

---

85   Human Rights Watch, 'Italy: Migrant Rescue Ship Impounded', 19 March 2018, hrw.org.

shrinking amid global attempts to limit non-state, independent human-itarian efforts in a variety of ways, from the deliberate targeting of aid workers in conflict zones, to unsettling and shrinking the (legal) terrain in which humanitarian work occurs. Confusion around what is legal and what is not is one way in which such disruption to, and shrinking of, the humanitarian space takes place. Importantly, however, confusion rather than complete prohibition avoids the political problems an outright attack on humanitarian endeavours would cause. Such an attack would contest the idea of a liberal order in the Global North, its exceptionalism and its self-mythologising as a place of welcome and sanctuary.

No Borders?

To what extent do grassroots humanitarian efforts perform a politics capable of challenging violent borders and the dangers of unequal mobility? Katerina Rozakou has been clear that Greece has its own political dynamics when it comes to humanitarian work. Her work has drawn attention to the tensions between more 'professional' forms of humanitarian action and more grassroots, solidarity efforts. She argues that events of recent years have exacerbated what she sees as a 'previ-ously clearly delineated distinction between solidarity and humanitarianism'.[86] Meanwhile, social anthropologist Heath Cabot, in her work on solidarity clinics in Greece that have arisen in response to neoliberal austerity measures, argued that 'solidarity has an ambivalent life as both a potentially liberatory response to and a direct product of austerity'.[87] Grassroots humanitarianism encompasses a wider political spectrum than the solidarity efforts studied by Cabot. Her 'solidarians' have a 'political profile that most often lies somewhere on the Left'.[88] Grassroots volunteers, while often focusing 'less on explicit political mobilisation and more on addressing basic, often urgent, human needs',[89] range from Christian evangelists to liberals and anarchists.

---

86 Rozakou, 'Solidarity #Humanitarianism', 99.

87 H Cabot, "'Contagious' Solidarity: Reconfiguring Care and Citizenship in Greece's Social Clinics', *Social Anthropology* 24(2), 2016, 162.

88 Ibid., 154.

89 Ibid.

These divergent motivations and politics unsurprisingly generate different relationships to violent borders and unequal mobility. So, while some might be clear that 'you can't get into this [responding to the needs of life seekers] without the politics',[90] others, like Susan Sarandon, are concerned with 'keeping the politics out of it'.

Importantly, while it is possible to trace trends and themes, grassroots humanitarianism, solidarity/#solidarity humanitarianism, or volunteer humanitarianism do not follow identical logics across different times and spaces. In Greece, there has been a wide variety of political positions and ideologies underpinning the grassroots humanitarian work experienced there. Meanwhile, in other contexts, such as Calais, the dynamics have been both similar and different. In her work on volunteer humanitarianism in Calais, social anthropologist Elisa Sandri argues that much of the volunteer work has been 'anti-government' by 'creating strong activist networks as a reaction to the void left by institutions' and refusing to 'collaborate with governments to provide humanitarian assistance', while avoiding 'becoming complicit in border regime practices'.[91] Sandri argues that this last point makes the volunteer humanitarianism seen in Calais different from that seen in Greece, where, in many instances, 'solidarity efforts, as well as being subsumed into humanitarian responses',[92] also become subsumed into state border responses. The sociologist Sevasti Trubeta has discussed this subsuming as 'post-bureaucratic humanitarianism' in work that has examined how certain solidarity efforts in Lesvos, such as the running of an open reception centre for life seekers – the well-known PIKPA – was placed directly under the auspices of the Greek Coastguard.[93]

However, while Sandri is keen to stress the lack of collaboration with state border authorities by volunteer humanitarians in Calais, she shows in other instances the apolitical nature of this volunteering. Some volunteers 'were not initially mobilised by particular political ideals and provided humanitarian aid to refugees without an explicit political

---

90   Interview with long-term humanitarian organiser, 9 December 2018.

91   Sandri, '"Volunteer Humanitarianism"'.

92   Interview with long-term activist, active across Europe and the Middle East, 25 October 2018.

93   S Trubeta, ' "Rights" in the Grey Area: Undocumented Border Crossers on Lesvos', *Race & Class* 56(4), 2015, 56–72.

narrative'.[94] These volunteers suggested 'that originally they were moved by feelings of compassion and hospitality and explained their role as humanitarian rather than political', while 'many . . . had never taken part in political activism and before going to the Jungle were not interested in politics'.[95] However, this 'differed from other organisations in Calais, such as CMS [Calais Migrant Solidarity], whose focus is on border contestation and solidarity activism'.[96] Furthermore, this stark divide between non-political or apolitical approaches to humanitarian aid delivery and more politically active relief efforts belies the potential for such humanitarian work to politicise those who engage in it. In many of the discussions I have had with grassroots volunteers, they have undergone a journey from being humanitarian providers of basic needs to political activists aware of the political structures of the border and mobility in both the lives of those they are trying to help and in their own ability to help.

Grassroots humanitarianism, therefore, might, for the most part, appear to take place along a political spectrum from liberal to anarchist, with apolitical caregiving at the liberal end and a commitment to non-state, no-border politics at the anarchist end. Yet there are others engaged in relief work that fall outside of this spectrum. Alongside young entrepreneurial humanitarian tech-bros, neo-philanthropists, volunteers with a long history of charity organising, and solidarity activists well versed in a range of alternative, left initiatives, there are Christian evangelists keen to attain recruits to the message of Jesus Christ. These evangelists, while engaging in the provision of basic needs, approach aid provision from a fundamentally different normative position.

Humanitarianism, despite its long-established entanglement with different forms of white supremacist Christian charity and older forms of pastoralism, is – as it is understood and practised by mainstream humanitarian actors – secular. This is not to say that faith does not play a role in an individual's motivations for relieving suffering. For example, Henry Dunant, the founder of what became the International Committee of the Red Cross (ICRC), was driven by his

---

94   Sandri, '"Volunteer Humanitarianism"', 74.
95   Ibid.
96   Ibid., 75.

Protestant faith and mobilised the wider Geneva Protestant community to his cause in the founding of the ICRC.[97] However, the ICRC, often assumed to be the guardian of humanitarianism with its set of seven fundamental principles (humanity, impartiality, neutrality, independence, voluntary service, unity and universality), and other humanitarian organisations who accept these principles alongside the important 'do no harm' doctrine, do not see proselytising as part of humanitarian work. In fact, such activity would be counter to the universality and impartiality of humanitarianism, as it is generally understood, even if we acknowledge such universality's Eurocentric, white supremacist roots.[98]

For example, the evangelical organisation #HowWillTheyHear 'believe the single greatest need of all migrants and refugees is to hear the gospel of Jesus Christ'.[99] Relief is, therefore, a vehicle for Christian conversion. #HowWillTheyHear is part of a wide network of evangelical organisations active across Europe and North America. This network recruits and sends volunteers to undertake proselytising relief efforts in places like Lesvos, where they are welcomed into spaces like the Moria Hotspot to work with Eurorelief and carry out important tasks, such as assigning accommodation to newly arrived life seekers.[100] As an example, one Illinois-based evangelical church sent a number of 'missionaries' to Lesvos in the summer of 2018. Their online diaries reveal the motivations for their involvement, with one missionary being clear that 'we are not doing this work for refugees but we are doing this work for Christ'. Here their purpose is to 'teach them [refugees] to obey everything that Jesus has commanded', with the diary's author going on to say that 'we ourselves are refugees, seeking God for our refuge'. In other instances, the missionaries express surprise that those they encounter are 'just like us', while praying that what they call 'people of concern' will

97   M Barnett, *Empire of Humanity: A History of Humanitarianism*, Ithaca, NY: Cornell University Press, 2011.

98   On the white supremacy of universality, see AA Azoulay, 'Open Letter to Sylvia Wynter: Unlearning the Disappearance of Jews from Africa', *The Funambulist* 30, July–August 2020, 22–9.

99   See 'About Partners" at #HowWillTheyHear website: howwilltheyhear.net.

100   Eurorelief has a history of being active across Greece and the Balkans. See eurorelief.net. It has faced accusations of aid workers in Moria trying to convert Muslims to Christianity; see P Kingsley, 'Aid Workers Accused of Trying to Convert Muslim Refugees at Greek Camp', the *Guardian*, 2 August 2016, theguardian.com.

Grassroots™ Humanitarianism

ask questions to 'enable us to share how Jesus has given us the love to serve them'.[101]

In other instances, evangelist missionaries highlight how unsuited many volunteer humanitarians are for the realities of displacement. Reviews of online diaries not only highlight the centring of the volunteers themselves in their white saviour narrative of 'helping', but also show a deep paternalism and dangerous naivety as to the structural conditions in which they work. Take the diary entry of one evangelical volunteer working in Moria on food distribution – Moria is known for its lack of adequate food provision[102] – when faced with the reactions of those stuck in the Hotspot and subjected to the slow violence of poor nutrition:

In my fair-minded and fatherly mindset, I was thinking to myself, 'You're acting like children that have just been served brussels sprouts'. However, when dinner is the highlight of your boring day and you've been waiting for it in the hot sun for three or four hours, I can understand a little childishness. Most of the people that actually received the food only ate the bread and orange. The boxes were stacked like Legos all over the camp, unopened.[103]

The reference to childishness on the part of life seekers, subjected to the indignity of having to queue for meals for hours at a time, stripped of agency and exposed to a regime that repeatedly fails to provide nutritious meals highlights a continuing and problematic aspect of some grassroots humanitarianism. Such attitudes are by no means limited to the work of evangelicals; often, when I have asked activists and volunteers about the hardest aspects of providing relief in border spaces, they refer to the attitudes and behaviours of other volunteers as being paternalistic and degrading towards those they are trying to help. In one particularly shocking incident, an experienced activist who was working as a cultural mediator and what they called an 'accompanier',

---

101   All quotes from the Lesvos Mission Team Reflections, from the Calvary Memorial, can be viewed here: calvarymemorial.com/article/lesvos-mission-team-reflections.

102   Dutch Council for Refugees (and Partners), 'The Implementation of the Hotspots in Greece and Italy: A Study', 2016, 24, ecre.org.

103   Found on the Greater Europe Mission website on a blog post titled 'Lines', 2016, gemedot.com/lines/.

due to their language skills, recounted how they were witness to an elderly man being brought to tears after he was denied a second sandwich for his wife who was recovering from heat stroke under the shade of a nearby tarpaulin. These volunteers apparently accused the man of being greedy and a liar, trying to steal 'more than his share' when he asked for a second sandwich. This incident had stuck with the experienced activist for the way it was, in their words, 'just so profoundly humiliating', and the ways in which this life seeker was reduced to, according to the accompanier, feeling like a burden.[104]

These dynamics of volunteering highlight both the limited politics of such work but also the forms of power they produce in turn. In his study of the 'front-line' in Lesvos, Papataxiarchis argues that 'being there, on the front line, differentiates everybody – even the activists whose egalitarian ethos despises hierarchies – according to the length of stay and the type of duties they perform', suggesting that such work fosters the creation of borders between the helpers themselves.[105] Meanwhile, in one volunteer's eyes and words, '[my] critique of volunteering is that it creates this subtle power dynamic of beneficiary and provider and replicates something that we all know is problematic in development work in the Global South . . . I didn't want to be the naysayer in that context but . . . there was no race analysis, no power analysis and you could see the impacts of that. Well, we all wore different hats out of necessity, but for those of us who came from more long-term political engagement with refugee solidarity and migrant justice and a more rights-based discourse, there was definitely an unease at times where we knew that, while we were expending so much collective energy in just trying to respond to humanitarian needs, that policies were solidifying and gaining a cohesion. [A cohesion] that we didn't have organisationally in trying to just challenge them.'[106] At other times, some grassroots humanitarians saw other volunteers as the biggest challenge. 'A lot of these young people, they weren't helpless, but they weren't helpful either. They caused more problems than they solved.'[107] When I pushed this particular grassroots humanitarian on whether they meant helpful practically

---

104   Interview with long-term activist, active across Europe and the Middle East, 25 October 2018.

105   Papataxiarchis, 'Being "There"', 6.

106   Interview with activist, 25 October 2018.

107   Interview with long-term humanitarian organiser, 9 December 2018.

or politically, they said both. They returned again to an oft-cited criticism of many of the grassroots humanitarians, which is voiced by others too, that many people got involved for the adventure or at least because it is seen as an exciting thing to do, offering as one young interviewee said to me, 'the opportunity to travel and build your CV while helping people'. This, the interviewee went on, causes a problem because 'if you don't also challenge the governments who are responsible for this, how will anything change?'[108]

Thus, this failure to be helpful relates to an inexperience in the delivery of humanitarian assistance, a lack of understanding about the specific contexts in which such assistance takes place, and the depoliticising aspects of distance. Humanitarianism has a long history of doing work at a distance to save distant strangers even while – as Lily Allen cogently pointed out about her work in Calais – there are inequalities and political injustices 'at home'. Grassroots humanitarianism works to produce distinct and separate spaces of relief and particular spaces of politics, meaning relief happens away from 'home', while politics (might or might not) happen at home. In the meantime, this relief and the grassroots humanitarians that provide it are aided by transport and tourist infrastructures that differentiate between privileged mobile subjects and those subjected to the violence and risks of unequal mobility. Heroic narratives of humanitarian risk taking, that anthropologist Adia Benton argues (re)produce racial hierarchies and white supremacy,[109] animate grassroots initiatives as much as organised institutionalised interventions. Violent borders and unequal mobility are transversal, meaning territorial and state- and citizen-based responses that see humanitarian work happen 'over there' and politics happen 'here' can only ever relieve symptoms rather than effect substantive change. So, what next for mobility justice?

108 Interview with long-term humanitarian volunteer active in the Aegean and Greek mainland, Athens, 7 October 2018.
109 A Benton, 'Risky Business: Race, Nonequivalence and the Humanitarian Politics of Life', *Visual Anthropology* 29(2), 2016, 187–293.

6

Decolonising Mobility and Humanitarianism?

For the master's tools will never dismantle the master's house. They may allow us temporarily to beat him at his own game, but they will never enable us to bring about genuine change. And this fact is only threatening to those . . . who still define the master's house as their only source of support.[1]

It is probably a cliché by now in certain radical, feminist circles to begin a critique with Audre Lorde's devastating appraisal of white supremacist, patriarchal power structures. However, I can think of no better place to start for mobility justice and humanitarian practice. Throughout this book, I have demonstrated the inadequacy, ambivalence and often complicity of humanitarian work in response to the violence of borders. Together with questioning mobility justice, I have questioned what happens to humanitarianism as it operates within, through and in response to (im)mobility regimes. I have shown that violent borders and mobility injustice unsettle, challenge and create new humanitarian ways of working, meaning that alongside questioning, 'What now?' for mobility justice, it is also necessary to question the future of humanitarianism. I return to questions posed at the outset: What is humanitarianism, and who is it for?

---

1 A Lorde, *Sister Outsider: Essays and Speeches*, Berkeley, CA: Crossing Points, 1984, 113.

Drawing on the discussion thus far, I argue that while humanitarian action might succeed in saving the lives of those migrants exposed to border violence, it simultaneously (re)produces and structures violence. For example, through what Jasbir K Puar calls 'processes of maiming' and 'debilitation that keep people alive but unequal',[2] as well as through attempts to address the structural causes of (some) mobility by development programmes and economic initiatives that aim at consolidating neoliberalism while keeping people 'unable to "make a life"'[3] in place. These processes, like humanitarianism itself, maintain white supremacist geographies based on Eurocentric, Enlightenment conceptions of what human life means and who gets to be considered fully human.[4]

I argue that we should think differently about mobility beyond critiques offered by activists and scholars who advocate for a world without mobility controls that privileges mobility above the right and possibility to stay in place. As Mimi Sheller importantly asserts, 'Who can "appropriate" the potential for mobility (including the right to stay still, as well as to move) matters.'[5] In recognition of the need to simultaneously think about both mobility and staying still, on equal terms, without privileging one or the other, I discuss what Indigenous, Pacific understandings of movement and place can offer. Through a focus on Indigenous knowledge, I interrogate non-dualist ways of thinking about mobility and the human, leading me to reflect on the promises and pitfalls of post-humanist ways of approaching life and what decolonial approaches open up. Finally, I wrap up by questioning where a decolonisation of mobility and post-humanist ways of thinking leaves humanitarian practice going forward. How can humanitarianism – as a practice oriented around the human subject and intimately shaped by its

---

2   JK Puar, *The Right to Maim: Debility, Capacity, Disability*, Durham NC: Duke University Press, 2018.

3   G Ramsay, 'Humanitarian Exploits: Ordinary Displacement and the Political Economy of the Global Refugee Regime', *Critique of Anthropology* 40(1), 2019, 1.

4   For a discussion of white supremacist understandings of the human, see SV Hartman, *Scenes of Subjection: Terror, Slavery, and Self-Making in Nineteenth Century America*, Oxford: Oxford University Press, 1997; TL King, *The Black Shoals: Offshore Formations of Black and Native* Studies, Durham, NC: Duke University Press, 2019; AG Weheliye, *Habeas Viscus: Racializing Assemblages, Biopolitics, And Black Feminist Theories of the Human*, Durham, NC: Duke University Press, 2014.

5   M Sheller, *Mobility Justice: The Politics of Movement in an Age of Extremes*, London: Verso, 2018, 16.

colonial past and its relationship to whiteness – function as an ethical commitment to others understood as equal, especially when faced with the challenge of anthropogenic climate change?

Humanitarian Borderwork and the Debilitation of Movement

In her work on the role of mobility in modern liberalism, political theorist Hagar Kotef argues that freedom of movement is foundational to modernity and constitutive of modern liberal states, as well as civil society and the individual. The modern liberal state in turn forms the basis of what Michael Barnett refers to as 'twentieth-century humanitarianism',[6] structured around a liberal understanding of human beings as mobile individuals and civil society as providing the space for humanitarian organisation. 'Twentieth-century humanitarianism' understands humanitarian action as emanating from civil society and thus humanitarian organisations and actions as separate from the state. However, humanitarianism is not only practised by non-state, independent actors, but also by state bureaucrats, police forces and military personnel, and has been used in both the past and present as the basis, justification and means for the creation of freedom for some at the expense of greater levels of control for others.

At the same time, humanitarian sentiments underpin, drive and structure extractive practices and exercises in neoliberal brand building. As has been made clear, humanitarianism and by extension humanitarian borderwork play a role in restoring and securing a particular type of liberal order, expanding neoliberal market logics, and therefore maintaining liberal politics more broadly.[7] But, as Kotef argues, and I have illustrated, this liberal model relies on limited mobility for many, whose mobility is restricted and structured by laws and infrastructures of control, designed to police potentially 'excessively mobile' subjects. This

---

6   M Barnett, *Empire of Humanity: A History of Humanitarianism*, Ithaca, NY: Cornell University Press, 2011.

7   For more on this, see P Pallister-Wilkins, 'Hotspots and the Geographies of Humanitarianism', *Environment and Planning D: Society and Space* 38(6), 2020; SM Reid-Henry, 'Humanitarianism as Liberal Diagnostic: Humanitarian Reason and the Political Rationalities of the Liberal Will-to-Care', *Transactions of the Institute of British Geographers* 39(3), 2014.

leads Kotef to suggest that both violence and liberal mobility regimes are two sides of the same coin.[8]

The foundational role of white man's mobility underpinning modernity and what it means to be (non)human has been the focus of works by Sylvia Wynter and Hortense Spillers. These Black feminist scholars have worked to uncover the European conquests of the African and American continents in 1441 and 1492, respectively, and the consequent making of race and the over-representation of the white man as the human subject.[9] In this making of what Wynter calls 'Man', mobility, the conquering of space, genocide, the Middle Passage, enslavement, plantation capitalism and land enclosures are fundamental processes in the modernist production of the human at the heart of universalist notions of humanitarianism – as well as the violence which humanitarianism, as a colonial tool of government, grew to appease. In this vein, Tiffany Lethabo King argues that the human

> as an exclusive category demands an outside and requires the death of Indigenous and Black people. For the human to continue to evolve as an unfettered form of self-actualising (and expanding) form of Whiteness, Black and Indigenous people must die or be transformed into lesser forms of humanity – and in some cases, become nonhuman altogether.[10]

Building on King, Black and Indigenous genocide are foundational for what we understand as humanitarianism that is concerned with saving distant strangers.

Humanitarian borderwork exists within this symbiotic relationship: relieving the violence that underpins liberal mobility regimes and responding to the death and suffering caused by border violence and unequal mobility while securing whiteness from its necessary other.

---

8 H Kotef, *Movement and the Ordering of Freedom: On Liberal Governances of Mobility*, Durham, NC: Duke University Press, 2015.

9 H Spillers, 'Mama's Baby, Papa's Maybe: An American Grammar Book', *Diacritics* 17(2), 1987, 65–81; S Wynter, '1492: A New World View', in V Lawrence Hyatt and R Nettleford eds, *Race, Discourse, and the Origin of the Americas: A New World View*, Washington, DC: Smithsonian Institution Press, 1996, 5–57; S Wynter, 'Unsettling the Coloniality of Being/Power/Truth/Freedom: Towards the Human, After Man, Its Overrepresentation – An Argument', *CR: The New Centennial Review* 3(3), 2003.

10 King, *The Black Shoals*, 20–21.

Decolonising Mobility and Humanitarianism?

Humanitarian borderwork responds by engaging in search and rescue missions at sea, and on land in deserts and mountains, but also through providing for basic needs: food, water, sanitation, shelter and medical services. As a result, humanitarian borderwork finds a middle ground between, on the one hand, migrant deaths caused by neglect and failures to act, as well as deaths caused by the specific targeting of migrants; and on the other, interventions that provide populations with the possibilities to make a full life. Here, and to borrow from Puar's work on maiming and debilitation, humanitarian borderwork aims at 'not letting migrants die'.[11]

Puar bases her argument on an exploration of the maiming practices of the Israeli Occupation Forces that seek to debilitate rather than kill occupied Palestinians in concert with humanitarian principles that set the limits of and structure possible violence in a liberal order. Humanitarian borderwork might, at first, appear to operate within an entirely different register and operational reality, focused as it is on border violence and not on the continuation of Israeli settler colonialism. And yet, search and rescue operations exist within a framework in which those prevented from accessing safe and legal routes are not allowed to die in order to uphold a Western liberal order and sense of self and mitigate opposition to violent border policies from compassionate publics. But, importantly, alongside this, the rescued, those not allowed to die, are not accorded full freedom either, echoing Khalili and Hajjar's argument that humanitarianism is about an ethical commitment towards others who are not quite regarded as equal.[12] In these instances, the act of saving lives actively restricts freedom, debilitating migrants' mobility. Debilitation is achieved through incarcerating migrants in the island prisons of Manus and Nauru while, as successive Australian governments have done, claiming to be saving lives by stopping boats; or by trapping migrants in a carceral system in the Aegean hotspots that aims to save lives through debilitating the mobility of those seen as suspect and troubling to a white order.[13]

---

11 Puar, *The Right to Maim*, 139.

12 L Khalili and L Hajjar, 'Torture, Drones, and Detention: A Conversation between Laleh Khalili and Lisa Hajjar', *Jadaliyya*, 2013, jadaliyya.com.

13 These efforts at debilitation have been called 'carceral humanitarianism' by Kelly Oliver. See K Oliver, *Carceral Humanitarianism: Logics of Refugee Detention*, Minneapolis, MT: University of Minnesota Press, 2017.

Puar's concept of debilitation echoes earlier humanitarian interventions in colonial spaces. We can uncover similarities across time and space between the ameliorative policies of George Arthur – intended to not let Black and Indigenous enslaved people or Van Diemen's Land Aborigines die as a result of the genocidal violence of slavery and settler colonialism – and humanitarian borderwork, with both utilising a range of spatial repertoires to care through mobility controls. Humanitarian borderwork, therefore, exists in response to violent borders and relieves the worst of their violence. But humanitarian borderwork enables the continuation of borders and is a way for whiteness to act and (re)produce itself in the world.

Alongside this, humanitarian borderwork actively works with and through the infrastructural underpinnings of unequal mobility. I have shown the countless ways humanitarian borderwork uses the very tools that underpin global, unequal mobility and violent borders. For example, search and rescue missions are only possible through utilising the surveillance capacities of states and operate only with the express permission of state authorities. Transportation provided to save lives, such as buses, brings migrants to registration points where their intimate details, family histories and biometrics are captured by state border control mechanisms. Distribution systems for important basic needs such as hygiene products and clothing rely on migrant and refugee registration systems. Meanwhile, maps designed to assist migrants on their journeys, and to direct them to humanitarian services, open certain routes and pre-emptively foreclose others. But what about alternatives to humanitarian borderwork that address structural causes or that foster different and more equitable mobilities?

Developmental Borderwork

There are some, working for organisations such as the UN Migration Agency (IOM), that advocate for addressing the poverty and underdevelopment they believe cause global migration today. In this approach, as detailed by Philippe M. Frowd, IOM argues for development-led intervention because of the need to save lives. This logic believes that preventing the 'root causes' of migration will reduce dangerous and risky journeys.[14] This developmental borderwork is supported by leading scholars in refugee studies such as Alexander Betts and economists like Paul Collier, who together propose 'special enterprise zones' where, according to one of their critics, historian Benjamin Thomas White, 'refugees can be set to work without being given free access to either the labour market or whatever legal protections the host states afford citizen workers'.[15] Proposals such as Betts's and Collier's do not challenge or counter the limits of humanitarian borderwork. Instead, according to international migration scholar Heaven Crawley, they are 'new wine in old bottles', continuing the liberal framing of saving lives as the foundation for the promotion of policies designed to maintain colonial orders, push neoliberal market logics and secure a particular global status quo.[16] In addition, such proposals rest on white supremacist fears of backwardness, continuing the belief that underdevelopment leads to unrest and excessive mobility that can be combatted through particular modes of intervention.

Meanwhile, Georgina Ramsay has explored how refugee policies are increasingly aimed at transforming refugees from economic burdens to economic benefit.[17] These policies make use of the criticisms arguing that humanitarian intervention turns refugees and displaced populations into the passive recipients of aid. The policies take advantage of refugees' agency in making a life in spite of debilitation to promote particular neoliberal solutions.[18] Attempts to incorporate refugees into local economies do not resolve the core issue of displacement; instead, they shift refugee protection from a 'humanitarian imperative to an economic incentive', transforming refugees from aid recipients into

---

14 PM Frowd, 'Developmental Borderwork and the International Organization for Migration', *Journal of Ethnic and Migration Studies* 44(10), 2017.

15 BT White, '*Refuge* and History: A Critical Reading of a Polemic', *Migration and Society: Advances in Research* 2(1), 2019, 113.

16 H Crawley, 'Why Jobs in Special Economic Zones Won't Solve the Problems Facing the World's Refugees', *The Conversation*, April 2017, theconversation.com; see also H Crawley, 'Migration: Refugee Economics', *Nature* 544, 2017, 26–7.

17 Ramsay, 'Humanitarian Exploits', 3–27.

18 For more on how refugees resist efforts to debilitate them through the poor provision of assistance, see L Newhouse, 'More than Mere Survival: Violence, Humanitarian Governance, and Practical Material Politics in a Kenyan Refugee Camp', *Environment and Planning A: Economy and Space* 47(11), 2015.

'highly exploitable workers' who are 'unable to "make a life"'.[19] And, yet, seeing these economic incorporation projects as an extension of humanitarianism reproduces 'the exceptionality of refugee experiences' and conceals how refugees and the displaced are 'implicated within and indicative of new forms of global capitalism'.[20]

These attempts to address and govern mobility and migrants through development assistance and economic reforms speak to and yet disturb Hagar Kotef's argument that, within modern liberal states, if you move too much you are suspect, but move too little and you are 'primitive'. As policymakers recognise the structural limitations of humanitarian approaches and turn their attention to 'the root causes of migration', this dichotomy between mobility as modernity and stasis as primitive is unsettled, bringing to the fore the racialised hierarchies underpinning whose mobility is celebrated and whose is seen as dangerous.

In these economic interventions, there is little focus on making the immobile 'primitive' modern and more mobile. The primitives' racialisation marks their mobility as suspect and a challenge to white supremacy. Hence, attention is instead directed to the rudimentary or underdeveloped aspects of their countries' political economy as a 'root cause' of people going in search of a better life. In this developmental borderwork approach, primitive subjects become the target of neoliberal market schemes, such as export processing zones in refugee camps or self-reliance schemes in migrant settlements, with the purpose of keeping those deemed less equal – most often people of colour – in place and immobile. Here, political economy is commandeered for mobility control. Underdevelopment resulting from global capitalism, founded on colonial extraction, dispossession and genocide, is used against its victims to maintain the global colour line. It is a game that migrants or potential future migrants – who, as Anne McNevin argues, use migration to address insecurity – cannot win, as the goalposts of governance continually shift to capture and restrict those who are not allowed the freedom to move.[21]

---

19   Ramsay, 'Humanitarian Exploits', 3.
20   Ibid.
21   A McNevin, 'Learning to Live with Irregular Migration: Towards a More Ambitious Debate in the Politics of "the Problem"', *Citizenship Studies* 21(3), 2017, 255–74.

Autonomy of Migration and Mobility Justice

Therefore, humanitarian borderwork and its sibling, developmental borderwork, produce debilitated migrant subjects, alongside precarious neoliberal subjects, capturing and using migrant agency and foreclosing possibilities for resistance. Such practices stand in stark contrast to those scholars and activists who argue for freedom of movement as a form of political resistance. This approach, known as the autonomy of migration, argues that freedom of movement is a political act challenging global wealth inequalities and the territorial state.[22] Autonomy of migration advocates argue that irregularised mobility – that is, mobility made irregular by state policies of control and containment – is a form of resistance that sidesteps or overcomes being governed by the spatial repertories of states.

For those with a normative commitment to freedom of movement for all as a fundamental right and the desire to see an end to unequal mobility, the autonomy of migration approach is attractive. Many would think it a logical conclusion for this book. I have spent many pages outlining how border deaths rest on a lack of access to safe and legal routes, or #safepassage. It would seem logical that the enactment of freedom of movement for all is what I would advocate in a commitment to mobility justice. However, feminist scholars of security and migration, such as Heather L Johnson, have developed a critique of the reification of mobility within the autonomy of migration approach, arguing that the types of irregular migration it sees as resistance are highly gendered, privileging masculine and ableist access to movement. The mobility-as-resistance celebrated in the autonomy of migration approach is not only gendered, but it also often overlooks how intersections of race and bodily capacity impact people's ability to resist through movement. Furthermore, it often ignores how these relations are historically constructed and tied to the production of racial hierarchies and white men's conquering journeys, and it reproduces white supremacist ideas of modernity as being linked to mobility.[23] As such,

---

22   A Monsutti, 'Mobility as a Political Act', *Ethnic and Racial Studies* 41(3), 2018, 448–55.

23   Sheller, *Mobility Justice*, 45–67. See also Spillers, 'Mama's Baby, Papa's Maybe'; Wynter, '1492: A New World View'; and Wynter, 'Unsettling the Coloniality of Being/ Power/Truth/Freedom'.

it also rests on what sociologist Gurminder K Bhambra calls 'methodological whiteness',[24] taking the experiences of how white men practise mobility in the world as the norm through which mobility-as-resistance can be undertaken.[25]

The mobility-as-resistance argued for by autonomy of migration advocates precludes and silences those who find themselves 'still here', such as the female life seekers Johnson has researched who are stuck on the Aegean islands, debilitated by border controls. In the accounts of these women, their immobility is understood as a failure – they are, perhaps, Kotef's 'primitive' subjects.[26] But this overshadows the violent systems of capture and containment they are subjected to. Furthermore, even while states make migrants immobile, they also, as Martina Tazzioli has argued, use the 'excessive mobility' of (some) migrants as a way of governing mobility and abrogating responsibility for those migrants within their borders. In what Tazzioli calls 'governing through mobility', states deliberately create hostile environments to 'encourage' migrants to move on somewhere else.[27]

Therefore, within the autonomy of migration framework, the differential mobility capacities and experiences of migrants, alongside their subsequent needs, are often overshadowed – in an approach that centres modernist mobility above the right to 'stillness', as Johnson calls it.[28] The autonomy of migration approach ignores the reality that not everyone can exercise resistance through mobility in the same way. Additionally, as Johnson makes clear, perhaps people do not want to seek security from war, systemic violence, human rights abuses or poverty through (forced) mobility. In privileging mobility, autonomy of migration hides or elides the very real structural – yet often differentially experienced – violence many people face. By suggesting that mobility is the answer or political challenge to a world of inequality,

---

24 GK Bhambra, 'Brexit, Trump, and "Methodological Whiteness": On the Misrecognition of Race and Class', *The British Journal of Sociology* 68(1), 2017, 219–32.

25 See also Sheller, *Mobility Justice*.

26 HL Johnson, 'Stillness: Thinking through Critical Migration Studies and Challenging Citizenship', paper presented at the conference of the International Studies Association, San Francisco, April 2018.

27 M Tazzioli, 'Governing Migrant Mobility through Mobility: Containment and Dispersal at the Internal Frontiers of Europe', *Environment and Planning C: Politics and Space* 38(1), 2019, 3–19.

28 Johnson, 'Stillness'.

Decolonising Mobility and Humanitarianism?

such an approach works to (re)produce large parts of the world, most often understood as the Global South, as incapable of change. As such, autonomy of migration does not offer the radical break in how we think of and conceive of (im)mobility as first appears; instead, mobility remains a mark of modernity as determined by colonial and conquering powers. Mobility remains the central issue, privileged and perpetuating the dichotomy between the modern mobile subject, historically produced as white, and the 'primitive savage'.

In contrast to this, scholars working within a mobility justice framework advocate for different ways of approaching mobility in the present and future by understanding and being sensitive to mobilities' historical role in creating racialised subjects – through the transatlantic slave trade, plantation capitalism, and later abolition, forced sedentarisation of Indigenous communities and (settler) colonialism. Tamara Vukov argues that mobility justice should include 'the building of a world in which safe, accessible, and just forms of movement and dwelling are open and available to all'. Vukov therefore incorporates not just safe and legal routes but, similar to Johnson, also raises the issue of dwelling, or staying in place. Being able to dwell is all the more important considering that mobility sits at the heart of colonial conquest, genocidal dispossession, and the transportation of millions of Black Africans across the Atlantic as well as the destruction of Indigenous ways of living in the lands conquered and settled by white people. However, dwelling, or staying in place, should not be understood in the same terms as developmental borderwork policies that use neoliberal interventions to keep people in place. Dwelling, here, is about the right and freedom to dwell, to stay in place on your own terms, as opposed to being kept in place through colonial modernist projects, as a part of containment, or being forced to move through the imposition of unjust systems of capitalism, environmental degradation, war and violence.

Therefore, mobility justice must also include equal access to housing and rights to remain in place, including equitable residency and citizenship policies alongside recognition of rights to and redistribution of land and reparations. In fact, when such equitable policies are actively denied, then forced onward mobility becomes a tool through which states and their societies avoid having to confront issues of mobility justice and the systemic inequalities on which they rest. This leads Vukov to demand 'an end to the many micro and macro forms of forced mobility and displacement (from colonial and war-based displacements to deportation and evictions due to gentrification)'. Alongside this, she calls for 'the dismantling of imposed forms of immobility, including detention, incarceration, the legacy of colonial confinement (such as reservations) and separation walls and barriers'.[29]

Decolonising Mobility

In their discussion of the global colour line, Lake and Reynolds end their investigation with early anti-colonial appeals to ideals of universal humanity as a counter to white supremacist settler colonialism and the hegemony of 'white men's countries'.[30] These appeals to universalism augmented a shift to self-determination and a recalibration of the global colour line around the less explicitly racialised concept of national identity and, no less paternalistic, ideas of underdevelopment. The recognition of racialised others' right to self-determination works as a form of 'redemption, containment and closure'[31] of past colonial injustices, and hides the continued importance of colonial hauntings in the present. Furthermore, recognition reproduces and reifies the state system as the only means through which injustices can be addressed and overcome. This consolidates the move discussed by Lake and Reynolds in which the global colour line of white settler colonialism was replaced by nation-states, allowing for differential inclusions and exclusions based on national identities and citizenship.

As a result of the inadequacy of this recognition and the continued imperial duress of racialised mobility inequalities, some mobility scholars are turning to different ways of thinking about mobility in concert with Indigenous scholars and activists and attempting to decolonise how we understand mobility today beyond the binary of mobility and

---

29   T Vukov, 'Strange Moves: Speculations and Propositions on Mobility Justice', in L Montegary and MA White eds, *Mobile Desires: The Politics and Erotics of Mobility Justice*, 2015, Basingstoke: Palgrave Macmillan; see also Sheller, *Mobility Justice*, 67.

30   M Lake and H Reynolds, *Drawing the Global Colour Line: White Men's Countries and the International Challenge of Racial Equality*, Cambridge: Cambridge University Press, 2008, 335–56.

31   K Nisancioglu, 'Racial Sovereignty', *European Journal of International Relations* 26(1), 2019, 45.

stasis. Like the feminist-inspired work of Johnson and Vukov, these attempts at decolonisation are asking for movement and dwelling to be seen on equal terms and occurring simultaneously, regardless of the particular people or histories involved.

In these calls, movement would be accepted as a central part of human life, without being either demonised or celebrated depending on who moves. Alongside this, movement would no longer be considered evidence of modernity. It would be decoupled from its relationship to primitive/civilised hierarchies, neither actively facilitated for some nor violently policed for others. Policymakers from the Global North would no longer attempt to address inequalities and systemic poverty through governing movement and the powerful would stop assuming how their type of mobility is the norm. In addition, the privileged would recognise how they have used mobility and its infrastructures to enrich themselves while impoverishing others and destroying alternative ways of life in colonial spaces.[32]

Some of the most urgent work challenging Western understandings of mobility come from Pacific scholars and activists as they confront the effects of climate change on their communities. These ways of thinking concern both 'routes and roots', in which moving and dwelling are simultaneously central ways of being and making a life in the world.[33] One of these ways of thinking is *banua, which 'suggests an unfolding, emergent and yet holistic system across space and time; a complex network of mobilities and immobilities connecting people, ancestors, stars, canoes and other vessels, ocean, islands and continents'.[34] Within this system, the self is considered to be still while the cosmos and the oceans move around you. The self is therefore always in place and can never be lost or displaced.

Thus, some contemporary mobility scholars are attempting to take Indigenous knowledges out of the realm of 'specialised and localised

---

32   For more on this, see, W Rodney, *How Europe Underdeveloped Africa*, Washington DC: Howard University Press, 1982, and L Khalili, *Sinews of War and Trade: Shipping and Capitalism in the Arabian Peninsula*, London: Verso, 2020.

33   See J Clifford, *Routes: Travel and Translation in the Late Twentieth Century*, Cambridge, MA: Harvard University Press, 1997; K Teaiwa, 'Moving People, Moving Islands in Oceania', *Paradigm Shift* 3, 2018, 69. [Asterisks preceding words such as *banua are used by linguists to denote an unattested form that is proposed as a hypothetical reconstruction, in this case of a Proto-Austronesian word.]

34   S Suliman, C Farbotko, H Ransan-Cooper, KE McNamara, F Thornton, C McMichael and T Kitara, 'Indigenous (Im)Mobilities in the Anthropocene', *Mobilities* 14(3), 2019, 301.

forms of expertise'[35] and to think about what they mean for the pursuit of mobility justice in the past, present and future, and beyond the local. But these knowledges are also important for thinking about humanitarian practices in a present and future when anthropogenic climate change impacts peoples' abilities to make a life, and when Indigenous peoples are too often considered objects to be either rescued or made resilient, rather than the architects of different ways of being in the world.[36] Within understandings of mobility and dwelling such as *banua*, with its 'relational cosmology that allows for dynamic configurations of terrestriality and fluidity, of kinesis and stasis', moving because one is forced to – by continuing colonial systems of extraction and government, or by rising sea levels caused by anthropogenic climate change – is a continued form of domination and dispossession.[37]

As social anthropologist and historian Katerina Teaiwa reminds us, to prevent forced migration, 'institutions such as the World Bank have called upon Australia and New Zealand to plan for and allow open access migration from those countries most urgently threatened [by climate change]'. Mobility is once again seen as the solution. However, 'at the same time Pacific countries have pushed back against discourses of victimhood and vulnerability'[38] and have refused the mobility solution, arguing that it spells the end for Pacific cultures – ways of life and living that are intimately 'rooted and routed' to oceans and islands. Meanwhile, the limits of humanitarianism are interwoven into Pacific critiques of proposed climate change solutions. These critiques play with ideas of visibility and emergency as well as drowning and rescue, to argue that humanitarianism 'will not let die' while critically asking if saving people alone, and not also cultures and ways of life, is enough.[39] A popular resistance slogan across the Pacific is, 'We're not drowning,

---

35 Ibid., 6.

36 Ibid.; L Carter, 'Criss-Crossing Highways: Pacific Travelling and Dwelling in Times of Global Warming', *Journal of New Zealand and Pacific Studies* 2(1), 2014, 57–64. For more on climate change and migration, see A Baldwin and G Bettini eds, *Life Adrift: Climate Change, Migration, Critique*, London: Rowman and Littlefield, 2017.

37 Suliman et al., 'Indigenous (Im)Mobilities in the Anthropocene', 15.

38 Teaiwa, 'Moving People, Moving Islands in Oceania', 67.

39 Suliman et al., 'Indigenous (Im)Mobilities in the Anthropocene', 13, wherein they discuss the performance artwork of Latai Taumopeau, who performs a traditional Tongan dance inside a clear tank while the tank fills with water until she is completely submerged. L Taumopeau, *Liveworks: Repatriate Part I*, 2018.

we're fighting';[40] a slogan suggestive of an insurgent cosmopolitanism not rooted in a European tradition but routed through Pacific mobilities across time and space.

Post-humanist Possibilities

Dualist thought runs through Western modes of thinking. I acknowledge that an unintended dualism runs throughout this book between the human and the nonhuman. In contrast, efforts to decolonise mobility as offered by Pacific climate activists hint at different ways of configuring the place and role of humans in a wider non-dualist cosmology that consider nonhuman elements and actors: land, water, weather, fish, animals, birds, sky and stars. Meanwhile, Black feminist thinkers, such as Spillers and Wynter challenge dominant white supremacist ideas about who is human, whose humanity matters, and who is expelled from humanity.

The human stands at the centre of humanitarian thought and practice. Efforts to think about humanity differently contain both emancipatory and potentially decolonial promise as well as possible political pitfalls. Tiffany Lethabo King, building on Donna Haraway, has argued that fixed boundaries are a colonial deception predicated on European Enlightenment and the emergence of the natural sciences that distinguished between 'human (culture) and nonhuman biomatter (nature)', with these 'human and nonhuman organisms . . . imagined as inert objects rather than interrelated, dynamic, ever-changing systems'.[41] As Pacific climate change activists make clear, dualist thinking about human and nonhuman is not only unsatisfactory for understanding historical relations to place and mobility in Pacific Island cultures, but also insufficient for facing current and future challenges, such as climate change.

In reorienting the relationship between human and nonhuman worlds and to give space to the agency of nonhuman actors – what is

---

40 Teaiwa, 'Moving People, Moving Islands in Oceania'; Suliman et al., 'Indigenous (Im)Mobilities in the Anthropocene', 5.

41 TL King, 'Racial Ecologies: Black Landscapes in Flux', in L Nishine and KD Hester Williams eds, *Racial Ecologies*, Seattle: University of Washington Press, 2018, 67. See also D Haraway, *Simians, Cyborgs, and Women: The Reinvention of Nature*, London: Routledge, 1991, 65–75.

known as post-humanism or the ontological turn in dominant Western thinking – Métis anthropologist Zoe Todd discusses Sila, a concept that denotes both climate and what Inuk author Rachel Qitsualik discusses as 'the breath that circulates into and out of every living thing'.[42] Different conceptions of life encompassed in concepts such as Sila work to decentre the human. They challenge the dualism of Western, and by extension humanitarianism's, understanding of human life as separate from and needing to conquer nature. The decentring makes space for other actors and life forms within a conception of the living. Post-humanism, according to feminist geographer Juanita Sundberg, therefore offers 'powerful tools to identify and critique dualist constructions of nature and culture that work to uphold Eurocentric knowledge and the colonial present'.[43]

We see post-humanist approaches to human and nonhuman relations at work in the 2016–17 Dakota Access Pipeline (#NoDAPL) protests, where Standing Rock Sioux, together with other tribes from across the Great Sioux Nation and further afield, as well as non-Indigenous activists, set up protest camps to protect the Missouri River basin from harm caused by the oil pipeline. These water protectors made intimate links between water, land, animals, ancestors and community, couching their resistance in the idea that harm to one is harm to all. Similar arguments have been made by the Wet'suwet'en resisting the Coastal GasLink pipeline on unceded, colonised land, with Wet'suwet'en resistance seen by the Canadian government as the 'ideological and physical focal point of Aboriginal resistance to resource extraction projects'.[44]

Other instances of nonhuman agency stemming from Indigenous culture are found in Aotearoa (New Zealand), where ecosystems are being granted legal personhood following Māori demands that the government respect Te Tiriti o Waitangi, the treaty signed between

42 Z Todd, 'An Indigenous Feminist's Take on the Ontological Turn: "Ontology Is Just Another Word for Colonialism" ', *Journal of Historical Sociology* 29(1), 2016, 4–22; R Qitsualik, 'Word and Will — Part Two: Words and the Substance of Life', *Nunatsiaq News*, 12 November 1998.

43 J Sundberg, 'Decolonising Posthumanist Geographies', *Cultural Geographies* 21(1), 2014, 33.

44 A Brown and A Bracken, 'No Surrender: After Police Defend a Gas Pipeline over Indigenous Land Rights, Protestors Shut Down Railways across Canada', *The Intercept*, 23 February 2020, theintercept.com.

Māori Rangatira and the British Crown in 1840. Under these decisions, ecological systems in their entirety are acknowledged as living entities and as part of iwi whānau (tribe's extended family). These include Te Urewera, a sparsely populated mountainous area of thick forest on the east coast of Te Ika-a-Māui (the North Island), Taranaki Maunga, a volcano in the west of Te Ika-a-Māui, and Te Apa Tupua (the Whanganui River) that runs from the slopes of Tonagriro to the Tasman Sea in the west of Te Ika-a-Māui. The granting of legal personhood to Te Apa Tupua recognised it as 'an indivisible and living whole from the mountains to the sea, incorporating the Whanganui River and all of its physical and metaphysical elements'.[45]

Yet, at the same time, post-humanism, when it remains rooted in other Western knowledge systems, too often reproduces the very dualism it has the potential to overcome.[46] For example, dualism can be seen in the term 'anthropogenic climate change', presenting a separation between a universalised human world (anthro) and the climate, while simultaneously erasing the role of carbon capitalism in such change – placing responsibility onto a universal human rather than amplifying differential responsibilities and effects of climate change. It is important to recognise that climate has always been changing. Thus, there is a political need to mark carbon capitalist climate change as the result and responsibility of specific socio-economic and political processes with specific geographies located in the military-industrial and consumerist Global North.

Attempts to move beyond dualism and to decentre the human in the Anthropocene talk about humans as 'species-humans', in a post-humanist move that positions humans as only one species impacted under climate change. But as Sundberg cautions in relation to universalising tendencies, we need to consider what is captured or not captured in this species-human move. As Claire Colebrook makes clear, climate change is the responsibility of the 'hyper-consuming' portion of humanity that has maintained its sovereign existence at the expense of others and 'congratulates itself for exercising compassion towards the refugees and migrants', while 'it is now this same humanity that is imagining itself as

---

45 EA Roy, 'New Zealand River Granted Same Legal Rights as Human Being', the *Guardian*, 16 March 2017, theguardian.com.

46 Ibid.

a species facing the condition of being an exile in its own once-sovereign space'.[47] For Colebrook, talk of humanity in universal terms invisiblises and excuses the 'indulgent strategy' of liberal humanism that talks of 'we' and is unable to conceive of other modes of existence.[48] This 'we' that Colebrook speaks of is a privileged, white 'we' who under climate change face exile and forms of violence that have been wrought on Black and Indigenous people through conquest and colonisation.

Alexander G Weheliye argues that

> many invocations of posthumanism ... reinscribe the humanist subject (Man) as the personification of the human by insisting that this is the category to be overcome, rarely considering cultural and political formations outside the world of Man that might offer alternative versions of humanity. Posthumanism and animal studies isomorphically yoke humanity to the limited possessive individualism of Man, because these discourses also presume that we have now entered a stage in human development where all subjects have been granted equal access to western humanity and that this is, indeed, what we all have to overcome.[49]

With this in mind, we need to recognise the dualism of human and climate within predominant ways of thinking about the Anthropocene and to foreground concepts such as Sila, in which human/climate separation is ontologically impossible.

Therefore, attempts to challenge climate change continue privileging Western knowledge systems, such as Western scientific methods, over other ways of knowing, 'earth-writings', and cosmologies and experiences of living with but not attempting to conquer climate, such as those seen in the #NoDAPL protests and the granting of legal personhood to Aotearoan ecologies. As in humanitarian practice, Western knowledge systems are elevated above those of Indigenous communities, from Pacific climate activists to Inuit women activists, such as Rosemarie Kuptana and Sheila Watt-Cloutier (Sheila, incidentally, was dropped

---

47   C Colebrook, 'Transcendental Migration: Taking Refuge from Climate Change', in A Baldwin and G Bettini eds, *Life Adrift : Climate Change, Migration, Critique*, London: Rowman Littlefield, 2017, 125.

48   Ibid., 123.

49   Weheliye, *Habeas Viscus*, 9–10.

from the 2007 Nobel Prize nomination that ultimately went to her fellow nominees Al Gore and the IPCC). Such white supremacy and racist erasure can be seen in recent calls by activist groups such as Extinction Rebellion to focus on the science. But whose science? The failure to ask such important questions and to take seriously other ways of knowing, alongside a failure to understand histories of anti-Blackness, Indigenous erasure and racist policing, have led to charges of white supremacy being levelled at Extinction Rebellion, as it reproduces a particular view of the world steeped in white privilege.

Decolonising Humanitarianism

In the summer of 2020, the Black Lives Matter (BLM) movement collided with humanitarianism. Following the murder of George Floyd at the hands of the US police and the global reanimation of BLM after its emergence in 2013, humanitarian organisations have begun to seriously question their relationships to race. Save the Children declared, 'The harm that has been caused – and continues to be caused – by racism in our organisation is . . . an affront to our values'.[50] The President of MSF, Christos Christou, along with Kenyan board member Samuel Bumicho, acknowledged that the organisation had 'failed people of colour, both staff and patients'.[51] And while a thousand MSF staff labelled the organisation 'institutionally racist',[52] there were others in the organisation who claimed that 'All Lives Matter' and that it was not the work of MSF to resolve the 'historical social and racial tensions shattering the American society'.[53]

Claiming that calls for valuing Black lives in the face of violent and systemic racism is an American problem alone shows an astounding ignorance of not only colonial histories of race and racism but also of humanitarianism's intimate role in such histories. It is what Eve Tuck

---

50   B Parker, 'Médecins Sans Frontières Needs a "Radical Change" on Racism: MSF President', *The New Humanitarian*, 24 June 2020, thenewhumanitarian.org.

51   Ibid.

52   K McVeigh, 'Médecins Sans Frontières is "Institutionally Racist", Say 1,000 Insiders', the *Guardian*, 10 July 2020, theguardian.com.

53   Parker, 'Médecins Sans Frontières Needs a "Radical Change" on Racism'.

and K Wayne Yang call a 'move to innocence'[54] that, according to another MSF staff member, reflects a naive ' "we're all part of the human race" crap that avoided serious debate about the "structural racism" within the organisation'. Another staffer stated: 'I am appalled that a white man in France is deciding [what MSF's position should be] . . . but I am not surprised.' Yet another declared: 'What better time to start dismantling colonial thinking/structures and showing solidarity to our staff and patients that bear the brunt of racism than now?'[55]

Save the Children's claim that racism is an affront to their values is a move to innocence. It performs both sympathy with racisms' victims and organisational suffering by claiming racism goes against their values.[56] Save the Children's claim attempts a separation between humanitarianism as a normative ideal and the origins of such ideals. It speaks to humanitarianism as an institutional practice with internal dynamics separate from its external operations and appears to claim that racism is an internal problem alone. Furthermore, the appeal to values is a negation of how those values came into being through colonial conquest. It fails to address Sylvia Wynter's argument that:

> All our present struggles with respect to race, class, gender, sexual orientation, ethnicity, struggles over the environment, global warming, severe climate change, the sharply unequal distribution of the earth resources . . . these are all differing facets of the central ethnoclass Man vs. Human struggle.[57]

In this Man vs. Human struggle, Wynter suggests that the human as a truly universal category has never existed. The modern human is built on the creation and subjugation of nonhuman, Black others and the elevation of a white self. Humanitarianism is therefore a way of elevating whiteness built on anti-Blackness. It is *Der Spiegel* calling Carola Rackete 'Captain Europe' for her work in rescuing Black life seekers in the

---

54   E Tuck and KW Yang, 'Decolonization Is Not a Metaphor', *Decolonization: Indigeneity, Education & Society* 1(1), 2012, 1–40.

55   Parker, 'Médecins Sans Frontières Needs a "Radical Change" on Racism'.

56   See Tuck and Yang, 'Decolonization Is Not a Metaphor', 16, wherein they talk about both performing sympathy and suffering among (settler) colonisers as moves to innocence.

57   Wynter, 'Unsettling the Coloniality of Being/Power/Truth/Freedom', 260–1.

Mediterranean. Decolonising work would recognise the (re)production of a heroic and innocent Europe in the proclamation of Captain Europe and hold up a mirror to such claims.

Following Wynter, anti-racist struggles are a way of bringing a truly universal human subject into being.[58] This thinking is echoed in the Black Lives Matter claim that all lives do not matter until Black lives matter. Therefore, decolonising modernist understandings of the human as (white) man is central to a decolonised humanitarianism. Following Wynter and BLM, if humanitarians want to consider themselves acting for a truly universal humanity, then anti-racism and dismantling colonial hierarchies of race is humanitarian work. Attempts to tackle internal racism within humanitarian organisations alone amid appeals to humanitarianism's current, yet demonstrably false, universal values do little to unsettle white supremacy or reorder the world.

Meanwhile, moves to dismantle 'colonial thinking/structures and show solidarity to staff and patients that bear the brunt of racism'[59] appear to be moving along a path to decolonising humanitarianism. But are they? Tuck and Yang argue that decolonisation is not a metaphor. Writing from a settler colonial context, they suggest that decolonisation work aimed at unsettling Eurocentric thinking treats decolonisation as a metaphor for other types of work. This means it cannot be ' "easily grafted on to pre-existing discourses/frameworks, even if they are critical, even if they are anti-racist, even if they are justice frameworks'.[60] For Tuck and Yang, decolonisation requires repatriation of the land stolen and the lives destroyed by settler colonialism.

Their focus on the material aspects of settler colonialism roots Tuck and Yang's critique of much decolonising work in the specificities of settler colonial contexts that are not always relevant for humanitarian practice. However, they provide salient critiques of relevance to humanitarian impulses alongside highlighting limitations for decolonisation. Decolonisation, to Tuck and Yang, is not a 'philanthropic process of "helping" the at-risk and alleviating suffering'[61] – echoing the limits of a humanitarian frame outlined by Pacific climate activists. Nor is it

---

58   Wynter, '1492: A New World View', 41.
59   Parker, 'Médecins Sans Frontières Needs a "Radical Change" on Racism'.
60   Tuck and Yang, 'Decolonization Is Not a Metaphor', 3.
61   Ibid., 21.

'converting Indigenous politics to a Western doctrine of liberation.'[62] Consequently, decolonisation does not offer a framework for 'generic struggle against oppressive conditions and outcomes.'[63]

Any moves to decolonise humanitarianism (and mobility for that matter) can also be 'moves to innocence – diversions, distractions, which relieve the settler of feelings of guilt or responsibility, and conceal the need to give up land or power or privilege.'[64] Humanitarianism as a diverse practice cannot be conflated with settler colonialism, even while it is historically imbricated in settler colonial practices. Nevertheless, Tuck and Yang's assertion that decolonisation requires giving up power and privilege is important for any decolonial project – humanitarian or otherwise.

Decolonisation cannot be just another form of social justice, or it risks being a way for humanitarians, who are 'disturbed by their own status, to try and escape or contain the unbearable searchlight of complicity, of having harmed others'[65] through humanitarian work. Therefore, it is important that decolonisation is not simply an exercise in 'harm reduction' for humanitarianism alone. Decolonisation efforts must avoid becoming a way for humanitarianism, and by extension white supremacy, to secure itself. According to Tuck and Yang, such efforts at harm reduction are only going to become more acute in the face of escalating environmental crises.[66] However, decolonisation is just a metaphor if it lacks a programme of concrete changes that are anti-racist and challenge power and privilege.

Humanitarian Futures

Attempts emanating from the Global North to move beyond the need to save lives threatened by unequal mobility, such as developmental borderwork and economic incorporation and incentivisation projects, not only reproduce existing structures of control but introduce new forms of oppression, inequalities and forms of mobility injustice. Radical and transformative alternatives to liberal systems of government cannot

---

62 Ibid.
63 Ibid.
64 Ibid., 21.
65 Ibid., 9.
66 Ibid., 21.

Decolonising Mobility and Humanitarianism? 201

come in the form of liberal solutions. And yet radical reorientations such as post-humanism and decolonisation also threaten to retrench existing white supremacist hierarchies and foster white innocence as much as they might simultaneously overturn others, such as those between humans and the natural world. To return to the quote from Audre Lorde at the start of this chapter, 'the master's tools will never dismantle the master's house',[67] meaning the need for different ways of conceiving of and existing in the world remain.

Humanitarianism, therefore, faces a dilemma as it confronts a white supremacist future in which mobility for the few continues to be valorised and secured on the one hand – as evidenced by the European Commission talking about 'Protecting Our European Way of Life' and the electoral successes of politicians such as Donald Trump, Boris Johnson and Jair Bolsonaro on ethnonationalist exclusionary platforms – and denied to the majority on the other along vectors of white privilege and unequal wealth distribution. When global inequalities, militarism and war continue to deny people the ability to make a life, and carbon capitalist climate change threatens that ability even further, what is next for humanitarianism?

Does humanitarianism continue to be used to constrain, contain, disable, debilitate and 'not let die' those impacted by global inequalities, militarism, war and anthropogenic climate change? Will humanitarianism continue to be the handmaiden of a security-driven, militarised response aiding the wealthy Global North's attempts to seal itself off from the effects of displacement and people on the move? Will it continue existing hierarchies of humanity and create new ones in the process? Or can humanitarianism, which is currently practised as a false universalist and totalising project built around modernist conceptions of 'Man', be brought into conversation with different cosmopolitanisms and different ways of conceiving of the world? Can humanitarianism ever be compatible with radical solidarity attempts rooted in ideas of connectedness across difference? Or can we envisage humanitarianism engaging in anti-racist work that enables Black lives to matter and through that bring into being a universal humanity?

It is beyond the scope of this book to answer these questions. They need to be answered in concert with others. It is not my place or my

---

67   Lorde, *Sister Outsider: Essays and Speeches.*

202   Humanitarian Borders

desire to build worlds or futures. And I take caution from Tuck and Yang
in asking questions, being careful not to 'hybridise decolonial thought
with Western critical traditions' that serve to maintain my white
supremacy and my identity as a critical scholar.[68] Nevertheless, these
questions need to be asked of scholars and humanitarian practitioners.
More importantly, they need to be asked in consultation with the
subjects of white saviourism and those impacted by mobility injustice.
We need to think about what possibilities there are for caring for each
other while pursuing justice in the future and in the face of new challenges, while being conscious of who is elevated and who is silenced
with talks of 'we'. All the while, it must be recognised that thinking about
new futures is not enough, and that decolonising the mind – as Frantz
Fanon made clear – is the first but not the only step.[69]

The question remains, however: What and whose politics will form
the basis of a future humanitarianism? In thinking about this, we need
to consider what is offered by decolonial and post-humanist approaches
that reorient our thinking about our planet, life and its relationship to
movement. At the same time, we must be sensitive to who is excluded
from discussions, and whose visions for planetary futures are exalted
and whose are denied. We must guard against policies designed to
cement the status quo, elide responsibility, and foster innocence. We
need to think about and acknowledge whose and what lives matter, not
only to decolonise humanitarianism but also to reconfigure how we care
and what we care for under carbon capitalist climate change. As carbon
capitalist climate change threatens the very things that make life, can
humanitarianism reorient itself to consider saving other subjects beyond
the human subject of traditional practice? And can this be done without
reproducing white supremacy?

As post-humanism opens up our thinking to include nonhuman
subjects in socio-political processes, does humanitarianism need to
reorient itself to consider caring for other life forms too? And can it do
so without reproducing what Sylvia Wynter identifies as the overdeter-
mined (white) Man,[70] alongside universalising categories that foreclose

68   Tuck and Yang, 'Decolonization Is Not a Metaphor', 16.
69   F Fanon, *The Wretched of the Earth*, London: Penguin, 1963.
70   For more on this see P Pallister-Wilkins, 'HuManitarianism: Race and the
overrepresentation of 'Man'', *Transactions of the Institute of British Geographers*, 2022,
https://doi.org/10.1111/tran.12531.

other ways of being and knowing? How can *banua, with its relational cosmology allowing for dynamic configurations of terrestriality and fluidity and movement and stasis, transform our relationship between subjects previously understood as separate: humans, nature, climate and (im)mobility? Or how can Sila, for example, as expressed as 'the breath that circulates into and out of every living thing', open up humanitarianism to nonhuman subjects and reorient its focus on caring for and saving other life forms and ecologies as well?

It would be easy to end with a dismissal of humanitarianism as a modernist humanist venture. Indeed, would that really be so bad? There are legitimate concerns that if one pursues what I have outlined, humanitarianism is beyond saving and should not be saved. That a humanitarian future is one without humanitarianism. Olivia Umurerwa Rutazibwa asks whether humanitarianism as a Eurocentric modernist venture should be mourned.[71] In the face of continued border violence amid rampant global inequality, the continuation of humanitarianism is a necessary lesser evil until we see an end to mobility injustice and the global colour line. Without an end to violent borders, humanitarian borderwork will remain a solution that (re)produces inequalities.

But humanitarianism – or something like it – can move beyond narratives and practices of survival that debilitate, and begin working for life and dignity for all on equal terms. Therefore, going forward, I want to think and encourage others to think with me about the possibilities offered by decolonising humanitarianism and to consider the 'pluriverse'. All of this is in the hope of reorienting humanitarian practice as an ethical commitment to others, rooted in often quietly radical acts of 'doing' without assuming to know the 'right' solutions, and as a way of acting in the world beyond its historical roots as a tool of whiteness.

---

71   OU Rutazibwa, 'What's There to Mourn? Decolonial Reflections on (the End of) Liberal Humanitarianism', *Journal of Humanitarian Affairs* 1(1), 2019, 66–7.

Index

Abbott, Tony, 11, 84
Aegean 73, 74, 78, 83-4, 89, 96, 101, 103, 138, 141, 151, 156, 159, 170, 183, 188
Ai Weiwei 149-51
Alps 50, 38, 167,
Amelioration 38, 41
Ameliorative 8, 40-1, 184
Amnesty International 63-4
Anti-Blackness 197-8
Apartheid (global) 29, 52
Asylum (seekers) 5, 10, 27, 32-4, 42, 52, 66-7, 74, 82, 85, 87, 109, 113, 161
Athens 12, 49, 95-6, 104, 137, 166
Australia 10-12, 24-5, 29, 30, 32-3, 36, 43, 48, 54, 75, 84, 92, 137, 183, 192

Barnado's 35, 75
Biometrics 28, 75, 82,
Black Lives Matter (BLM) 197, 199
Border fence 58, 95, 96
Border police 13, 37, 54, 55-8, 60-1, 72, 77-9, 96-8 (Border Security Teams) 71-2, 75-6, 78-80 (Greek) 12, 58, 60 (Guardia di Finanzia) 37 (Koninklijke Marechaussee) 35, 71 (Macedonian) 96-8 (Police Aux Frontières) 38 (Turkish) 78, 88
British Empire 25, 42
Bureaucracy 20, 22, 25, 39, 172
Bus 2, 30, 35, 37-8, 92, 98, 104-12, 114, 125, 133, 138, 166, 184

Calais 5, 16, 133-5, 143, 146, 149, 152-4, 167, 172-3, 177
Canada 25, 29, 30, 146
Cap Anamur 9, 10, 167-8
Care and control 15, 45-6, 60, 62, 70, 76-8, 80, 83-4, 88
Carriers liability 30-2
Celebrity humanitarianism 5, 143, 148-54, 177
Chios 72, 75, 79
Christian evangelism 135, 171, 173-4

Christmas Island 32

Climate change 148, 181, 191-3, 195-6, 198, 201-2

Colonial 8, 20-3, 25, 38, 40-5, 47, 51-2, 92-3, 130, 148-9, 181-2, 184-6, 189-94, 197-200

Colonialism 14, 20-1, 24, 38, 40, 42, 47, 51, 154, 183-4, 189-90, 199-200

Covid-19 114

Criminalisation 166-70

Customs and Border Patrol (CBP) 35, 69-70, 96

Death and deaths 3-4, 6, 11, 15, 20-1, 29, 36-7, 45, 54-6, 66, 69-70, 78, 84, 95, 103-4, 116, 118-20, 122, 128-9, 131, 163, 182-3, 187

Decolonisation 180, 190, 199-201

Decolonising 190, 197, 199, 202-3

Debilitation 16, 180-1, 183-5

Detention 35, 60, 75, 89, 92, 190

Distant strangers 8, 11, 38-9, 76, 141, 177, 182

Do no harm 17, 174

Ethics 15-6, 39, 48, 61, 87, 92-3, 110-2, 148, 181, 183, 203

Eurocentrism 8, 76, 93, 174, 180, 194, 199, 203

EUTF 67-9, 168

EU-Turkey 'Deal' 54, 74, 83, 85-8, 112, 127, 168

Evros 1-4, 15, 58-9, 79

Facebook 11, 145-6, 158

Ferry 30, 32, 34, 136, 157, 166, 169-70

Frontex (European Border and Coast Guard Agency) 15, 55-6, 58, 64, 68, 72, 80

Hautes-Alpes 37-8, 50

Hellenic Coast Guard 73

Hostile Environment 34

Hotspot 74, 79-81, 83, 87, 107, 112-3, 127, 162, 174-5

Humanitarian branding 134, 143, 147-9, 153, 181

Humanitarian entrepreneurialism 39, 134, 141, 143, 145, 147-8, 173

Humanitarian logistics 39, 74, 94, 102, 105, 135, 154, 158

Humanitarian mapping 142, 163-166

Humanitarian markets and marketing 133, 135, 142-5, 148

Idomeni 95-101, 110, 151-2

Infrastructure 9, 15, 24-5, 94-5, 103-8, 110-2, 136-41, 164, 166, 177, 181, 191

International Committee of the Red Cross (ICRC) 44, 173-4

International Rescue Committee (IRC) 103, 152

Immigration and Customs Enforcement (ICE) 35

Ingérence 93-4, 130

Integrated Border Management 70, 72, 74

International Maritime Organisation 33

International Organisation for Migration, UN Migration Agency (IOM) 89, 184

Jolie, Angelina, 143, 149, 152

Kara Tepe 157, 162
Kurdi, Aylan 151

Legality 11, 20, 27-9, 33-4, 36, 46,
    77-8, 115, 118-20, 127-30, 168-71,
    183, 185, 187, 189, 194-6
Lesser evil 55-9, 129, 203
Lesvos 12-3, 16, 32, 72, 75, 79-80,
    103-5, 107-11, 113-4, 125, 127,
    137-41, 143, 146, 148, 150-2,
    154-6, 159-65, 168-9, 172, 174, 176
Libya 10, 67-8, 85, 89-90, 127, 130
Light-touch humanitarianism 96, 144

Mantamados 107-13
Manus 10, 13, 33-4, 48, 92, 183
Mare Nostrum 4, 63-5, 68, 119
Maritime Rescue and Coordination
    Centre (MRCC) 123-4, 126-7
Materiality 6, 20, 28, 101-3, 108, 138,
    144, 151, 154-5, 157, 199
Médecins du Monde 4, 157
Médecins Sans Frontières (MSF) 4, 5,
    9, 12-3, 19, 48, 92-3
Mediterranean 3-4, 6, 9-12, 20, 32,
    36, 56, 63-7, 70, 89-90, 92, 114,
    116, 122-4, 164, 166, 169-70, 199
Migrant Offshore Aid Station
    (MOAS) 4, 12, 116
Missing Migrants Project 36, 116
Moria 79-83, 107, 109, 112-3, 127,
    157, 162, 174-5
Movement On The Ground 141, 143,
    147-8
MV *Tampa* 32-4

Nauru 10, 13, 33, 48, 92, 183
Navy (Australian) 33 (British) 51
    (Dutch) 71-2 (Italian) 4, 66 (US)
    51

Netherlands 35, 70-1, 89, 141, 146,
    148, 154, 157
No More Deaths 134, 167
Nonhuman 23, 182, 193-4, 198,
    202-3

Online networks 141, 143, 145-6,
    154-5, 158, 164-5
Operation Sovereign Borders 10, 20,
    34, 48
Orestiada 1-2, 58, 77

Pacific Solution 10, 33, 48
Passports 14, 20, 25-7, 29-30, 56, 151,
    166
Plantation capitalism 14, 20, 22, 182,
    189
Polykastro 98-101
Posthumanism 194-6, 201-2
Proactiva Open Arms 4, 170

Race 19, 22, 25, 28, 136, 176, 182,
    187, 197-9
Racism 43, 120, 122, 197-9
Racist 17, 22-5, 29, 40, 44, 62, 168,
    170, 197, 199, 200
Refugee Convention 32, 51, 87

Safe and legal routes 11, 19-20, 28-9,
    36, 46, 77-8, 115, 118-20, 128-30,
    183, 187, 189
Safe Passage (#safepassage) 11, 115,
    120-1, 187
Safety of Life at Sea Directive
    (SOLAS) 64, 123
Sahara 124-5,
Salvini, Matteo, 120, 170
Sarandon, Susan 150, 172
Save the Children 4, 197
Schengen 29-32

Search and Rescue (SAR) 4, 12, 64-5,
    73, 79, 89-90, 114-20, 122-7, 130,
    167, 169-70
Sea Watch 3, 170
Smugglers, smuggling 2, 4, 29, 33, 37,
    55-7, 60-2, 67, 69, 71-2, 82, 84-6,
    119, 125, 168-9
Solidarity 4, 49, 133-4, 145, 147, 150,
    152, 154, 157, 163, 165-73, 176,
    198-9, 201
SOS Méditerranée 123, 167
Spectacle 103, 116, 122, 141, 169
Surveillance 1, 28, 30, 66, 73, 80, 122,
    124, 167, 184

Technology (border) 1, 28, 70
    (humanitarian) 92, 97, 102, 110,
    142, 144 (online) 141-147, 155
Thessaloniki 95, 98, 166
Tourism 137-8
Trains 3, 4, 30, 37
Transatlantic Slavery 14, 20, 22-3, 40,
    51, 189
Transit 13, 30, 38, 67, 83, 88, 92, 96,

98-9, 101, 108, 114, 125, 138, 151
Turkey 1-2, 10, 32, 54, 59, 68, 84-90,
    103, 138,
Twitter 11, 13, 92, 117-8, 120, 147

UNHCR 9-10, 50-1, 67, 89, 99, 128,
    152, 157, 161,

Ventimiglia 36-7
Visas 6-7, 27, 29-30, 32, 34, 75, 77,
    136
Vulnerability 15, 83, 87, 129, 192

Watch The Med 163-4
WASH 80, 97
White Australia Policy 24, 29
White innocence 201
White men's countries 25, 43, 190
White men's mobility 25
White supremacy 14, 24-6, 39, 41, 43,
    52, 177, 186, 197, 199-200, 202
Whiteness 14, 20, 21, 38, 44, 46,
    181-2, 184, 188, 198, 203